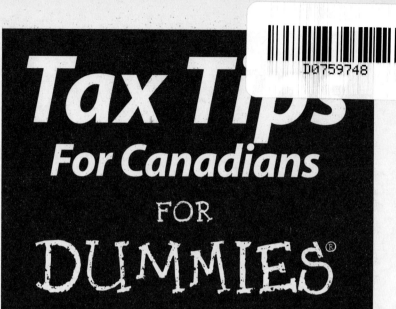

Tax Tips
For Canadians

FOR

DUMMIES®

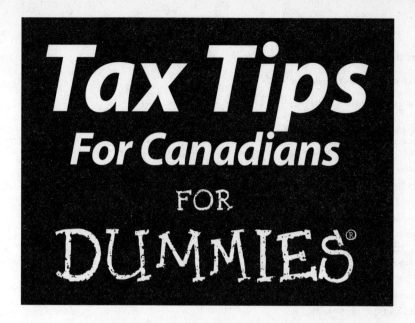

Tax Tips
For Canadians
FOR DUMMIES®

by Christie Henderson, CA, CFP, TEP
Brian Quinlan, CA, CFP, TEP
Suzanne Schultz, CA, CFP
Leigh Vyn, CA, CFP

John Wiley & Sons Canada, Ltd

Tax Tips For Canadians For Dummies®

Published by
John Wiley & Sons Canada, Ltd
22 Worcester Road
Etobicoke, ON M9W 1L1
www.wiley.ca

National Library of Canada Cataloguing in Publication

Tax tips for Canadians for dummies / Christie Henderson ... [et al.]. – 2004 ed.

Previously publ. under title: Taxes for Canadians for dummies.

Includes index.

ISBN 0-470-83416-1

1. Income tax–Law and legislation–Canada–Popular works. 2. Tax returns–Canada–Popular works.
3. Tax planning–Canada–Popular works. I. Henderson, Christie II. Title: Taxes for Canadians for dummies.

KE5682.T39 2003   343.7105'2   C2003-905905-7

Printed in Canada

1 2 3 4 5 TRI 07 06 05 04 03

Distributed in Canada by John Wiley & Sons Canada, Ltd.

For general information on John Wiley & Sons Canada, Ltd., including all books published by
Wiley Publishing, Inc., please call our warehouse, Tel 1-800-567-4797. For reseller information, including discounts and premium sales, please call our sales department, Tel 416-646-7992. For press review
copies, author interviews, or other publicity information, please contact our marketing department,
Tel: 416-646-4584, Fax 416-236-4448.

For authorization to photocopy items for corporate, personal, or educational use, please contact Cancopy,
The Canadian Copyright Licensing Agency, One Yonge Street, Suite 1900, Toronto, ON, M5E 1E5
Tel 416-868-1620 Fax 416-868-1621; www.cancopy.com.

About the Authors

Christie Henderson, CA, CFP, TEP is a partner with Henderson Partners LLP specializing in tax and financial planning. Christie qualified for the CharteredAccountant designation with Ernst & Young, Toronto. Christie is a Certified Financial Planner, a Trust and Estate Practitioner and has completed the CICA's in-depth Tax Course, the Canadian Securities Course and the Canadian Investment Funds Course. Christie's clientele consists largely of entrepreneurial owner-managers, executives, and their families. She provides comprehensive financial planning, including retirement planning, investment planning, insurance needs, estate planning, stock option planning, and business succession planning. Christie makes appearances on various Canadian radio and television programs and contributes articles to business publications. Christie would like to thank her husband, Kirk, and their two young sons, Charlie and Finlay, for being just plain wonderful!

Brian Quinlan, CA, CFP, TEP, is a partner with Campbell Lawless Professional Corporation in Toronto. He works with individuals and owner-managed businesses to maximize cash by minimizing tax! Brian is a contributing editor at *Canadian MoneySaver Magazine* and has also been a guest on TVOntario's *Money Talks* and Roger Cable TV's *The Prosperity Show*. He has instructed tax courses for Ryerson University and the Institute of Chartered Accountants of Ontario. Brian is a frequent speaker at tax and financial planning seminars. Brian has two income-splitting vehicles: Tara, 10, and Andrew, 13.

Suzanne Schultz, CA, CFP, is an Associate Vice President at AIC Group of Funds, where she provides tax education and advisory services to financial advisors and their clients. Suzanne has authored courses on corporate taxes and trusts for CCH Canadian Limited, has written columns for *The Globe and Mail*, and also makes regular appearances on various Canadian television and radio programs. She is a sought-after speaker and enjoys teaching others through seminars, courses, literature, and media appearances. Suzanne is a graduate of Dalhousie University and completed her CA designation while working for KPMG. She has also completed the CICA's in-depth tax course and is a member of the Canadian Tax Foundation. Aside from her career, Suzanne enjoys a busy family life with her husband, Kevin, and sons, Carter and Ben.

Leigh Vyn, CA, CFP, is an Associate Vice President of AIC Tax Smart Services, where she plays an essential role in providing financial advisors across Canada with a broad range of tax and estate planning services. She has written articles for CI mutual funds and *The Globe and Mail*'s Report on Business. She has also co-authored courses on trusts and corporate tax for CCH Canadian Limited. Leigh has become a frequently requested speaker, and has made numerous television appearances. Leigh received her Honours Bachelor of Commerce at McMaster University, in Hamilton, Ontario. She began her accounting career at KPMG and then went on to obtain her CA designation. Leigh has also completed the CICA's in-depth tax course, and is a member of the Canadian Tax Foundation.

Authors' Acknowledgments

With four authors contributing to this book, we'd like to recognize the following people for their assistance: First, a special thank you to Kathy Stradwick for keeping us organized and ensuring that all of our deadlines were met.

A sincere thanks to our editor, Michelle Marchetti, and the staff at John Wiley & Sons Canada for helping to make *Tax Tips For Canadians For Dummies* such a success. We'd also like to thank them for helping us transform what is normally a very dry subject into one that is fun to read and easy to understand.

And finally, we'd all like to thank our families for their patience and support while we wrote this book.

Publisher's Acknowledgments

We're proud of this book; please send us your comments at canadapt@wiley.com. Some of the people who helped bring this book to market include the following:

Acquisitions and Editorial

Associate Editor: Michelle Marchetti

Developmental Editor: Leah LeDrew

Copy Editors: Sandra Braun,
    Susan Morton Stewart

Production

Publishing Services Director:
    Karen Bryan

Project Manager: Elizabeth McCurdy

Project Coordinator: Robert Hickey

Layout and Graphics: Pat Loi

Proofreader: Bonnie Maitland

Indexer: Belle Wong

John Wiley & Sons Canada, Ltd.

    Bill Zerter, Chief Operating Officer

    Robert Harris, General Manager, Professional and Trade Division

Publishing and Editorial for Consumer Dummies

    Diane Graves Steele, Vice President and Publisher, Consumer Dummies

    Joyce Pepple, Acquisitions Director, Consumer Dummies

    Kristin A. Cocks, Product Development Director, Consumer Dummies

    Michael Spring, Vice President and Publisher, Travel

    Suzanne Jannetta, Editorial Director, Travel

Publishing for Technology Dummies

    Andy Cummings, Acquisitions Director

Composition Services

    Gerry Fahey, Executive Director of Production Serviceds

    Debbie Stailey, Director of Composition Services

Contents at a Glance

Table of Contents

Part III: Tax Preparation Tips: Claiming Deductions and Credits 163

Chapter 10: Tips for Deductions to Calculate Net Income 165

Introduction

• •

*O*kay, we know what you're thinking. This is a tax book. How fun a read can it be? How can it possibly keep my attention? How will I ever get through enough of this tome to learn what I need to prepare my tax return accurately and on time? We're pretty good mind readers, aren't we? But you're only right on one account: this is a tax book. You'll be pleasantly surprised, though (amazed and astounded, really), to find that this book does hold your attention, and you don't have to pore over it from start to finish to get out of it what you need to do your taxes. As for the fun part, well . . . we promise this will be more fun than a root canal!

Why Buy This Tax Book?

Like most *...For Dummies* books, this one is easy to read. And reading from cover to cover isn't necessary. In fact, a good way to use this book is to simply dive in to the particular topic you need help with — that's what the Table of Contents and the Index are for, Dummy. Sorry, we won't make that assumption about you. The truth is, very intelligent people like you all across Canada are reading this very same book, as you read this. We understand. Taxes are a tough topic, and you should feel no shame about needing help in preparing your return!

This is the 2004 version of *Tax Tips For Canadians For Dummies*. We're sure you'll find that the book lives up to the *...For Dummies* reputation. This book is full of expert advice tipped off with a little humour. Very little humour, actually. But hey, some is better than none.

Excuse us while we give ourselves a collective pat on the back, but we really couldn't have assembled a better team of authors to put this book together. Each author is a chartered accountant with considerable expertise in tax matters. Their combined years of experience span more decades than an accountant can count. Each author contributed hours of work to this project. Trust us, at the hourly rates these folks charge, this book is a deal. The bottom line? You can't beat the advice you get in this book, and the value is outstanding.

Your Tax Road Map

By now you've probably had a glance at the Table of Contents. If so, you'll notice that the book has been divided into five parts:

Part I: Getting Ready to File

This part of the book helps you understand Canada's tax system, including our tax rates, and our provincial tax systems too. We also talk about how to organize your receipts and other tax information, and the various ways to file your return (no it's not good enough to simply dump your receipts in an envelope and mail them to the tax collector!).

Part II: Tax Preparation Tips: Reporting Income

What type of income do you earn? Believe it or not, it can make a huge difference in how much tax you pay each year. Perhaps you're an employee receiving salary or wages, or maybe you're retired and receive pension income or income from your registered retirement savings plan (RRSP). And let's not forget about investment income. Your investments can generate interest, dividends, rents, royalties, capital gains — or losses. In this part, we look at how the various types of income are taxed, and how to report them on your tax return.

Part III: Tax Preparation Tips: Claiming Deductions and Credits

Here's the real reason you bought this book, right? You'd like to know about all the tax deductions and credits you're entitled to. Part III covers in detail the many types of deductions and credits available. Chances are that a number of the tax deductions and credits don't apply to your situation — but you'll want to make sure that you claim those that do, and take advantage of the tax relief you're rightfully entitled to.

Part IV: After You've Filed Your Tax Return

After you've filed your tax return, what's next? You sit and wait to hear from the tax collector to see whether you've bypassed the long arm of the tax auditors one more time, right? Not quite. In Part IV we talk about your notice of assessment, filing objections to your assessment, and fixing any mistakes after you've filed. We also discuss dealing with the CCRA.

Part V: The Part of Tens

Every book should have a place for a top ten list. Enter The Part of Tens—Part V. You will find invaluable tidbits of useful information in this favourite part of *...For Dummies* books. Specifically, we cover the ten major tax changes that have taken place for 2003, the top ten ways to reduce your risk of an audit, and more. We also wanted to include the top ten chocolate chip cookie recipes we've stumbled across, and the top ten verbal insults for 2003, but the publisher thought these lists would best belong in other books. So, we focussed solely on tax issues.

Icons Used in This Book

 This nerdy guy appears beside discussions that aren't critical if you just want to know the basic concepts and get answers to your tax questions—that is, if you're using the book as a quick reference days before your return is due (you wouldn't do that, now, would you?). However, actually reading these little gems of information can deepen and enhance your tax knowledge. You'll be the tax-savviest person around the office water cooler.

 The bull's eye marks the spot for smart tax tips and timesavers to help you get your tax return done quickly and with a minimum amount of pain. This is definitely the icon to look for if you're pulling an all-nighter on April 29th.

This is a friendly reminder of stuff we discuss elsewhere in the book or of points we really want you to remember.

Don't make these common, costly mistakes with your taxes! Aren't we nice folks to point them out?

This highlights tax provisions that went into effect in the 2003 tax year.

Part I
Getting Ready to File

The 5th Wave   By Rich Tennant

"That? That's Schedule X. We've never had to use it. But if anyone actually discovers how to grow money on trees, the CCRA's got a form to get their fair share of the leaves."

In this part...

This is the beginning, so sit down and get comfortable! You'll be glad to know that in these first few chapters, there are very few numbers and complicated calculations. Instead, we're going to ease you in gently: Have you ever wanted to know how Canada's tax system works? And how, in the midst of all the paper, you figure out what forms to fill out? If so, you've come to the right place. We'll also give you some handy pointers on how to stay organized, or for all you procrastinators out there, how to become organized in the first place. And for those of you who are not do-it-yourselfers, we'll let you know when it's okay to throw in the towel and call for help!

"Isn't it appropriate that the month of the tax begins with April Fool's Day and ends with the cries of 'May Day!'"

—Robert Knauerhase

Chapter 1

Canada's Tax System and Rates

● ●

● ●

*T*hough confusing at times, Canada's income tax system has two straightforward purposes. One, of which we are all quite aware, is to obtain dollars to finance government expenditures. A second purpose, which is not as obvious as the first, is to encourage certain expenditures by Canadians. That's right, our government cuts you a tax break when you spend money in ways that they approve of. In other words, income tax legislation acts as a tool for the government's desired fiscal policies.

Let's look at a few examples. The government wants to do the following:

✔ **Encourage you to save for retirement.** There are favourable tax rules for registered retirement savings plans (RRSPs). For more on these tax-friendly plans see Chapter 10, line 208.

✔ **Encourage you to go to post-secondary school.** Tuition fees are eligible for a tax credit (Chapter 12, line 323), as is interest incurred on student loans (Chapter 12, line 319). Don't forget that an education credit (Chapter 12, line 323) is allowed to both full-time and part-time students.

✔ **Encourage you to work.** If you have kids who need to be taken care of, a deduction is available for child-care expenses (Chapter 10, line 214).

✔ **Encourage you to invest in shares.** Dividends from Canadian corporations are taxed at a favourable rate (see Chapter 13), and only one-half of the capital gain (see Chapter 7) on a sale of investments is subject to tax. Moreover, if you borrow to invest, the interest you incur is generally tax deductible (Chapter 10, line 221).

The government also recognizes that some of us incur additional costs to earn income, due to disabilities, illness, and living in remote locations. Therefore, the income tax rules include tax savings provided by the following:

✔ The disability tax credit (Chapter 12, line 316)

✔ The medical expense tax credit (Chapter 12, line 330)

✔ The northern residents tax deduction (Chapter 11, line 255)

The government wants you to give to charities — hence, the charitable tax credit (Chapter 12, line 349).

And finally, you can get a federal tax break by contributing to your favourite federal politician or party. Read about the political tax credit (Chapter 13, lines 409 and 410). Tax breaks are also available for contributions to provincial and territorial politicians and parties (Chapter 14). We agree with you — the political tax credit seems to be a little self-serving for the politicians.

Make use of the various tax incentives in your spending, investing, and lifestyle decisions — *and save tax*!

You Have the Right to Pay Less Tax!

You have the right to arrange your affairs to minimize the tax you pay. A U.S. federal judge, Learned Hand (1872–1961), is often quoted:

> *There is nothing sinister in so arranging one's affairs as to keep taxes as low as possible. Everybody does so, rich or poor, and all do right. Nobody owes any public duty to pay more than the law demands.*

Canada's tax system is based on self-assessment. Each of us has the responsibility for ensuring our tax return includes all necessary information for reporting income, claiming tax deductions and tax credits, and, finally, calculating our tax liability. In complying with the tax laws, we all have the right to pay as little tax as is *legally* possible. We stress *legally*. Planning to minimize your tax is legal. Tax evasion is not! Throughout this book we offer many tips on how to minimize the tax you will pay. All these tips are legal, of course — all work within the tax law, not against it. We stand behind the tips we offer, based on the tax law and the currently proposed changes. Remember, however, that as tax laws change, some tips will no longer be valid — and new tips will apply. (Okay, we're done with the disclaimer now.)

Tax evasion occurs when you purposely understate the amount of income tax you should pay. This can occur when you don't report all your income, or when you overstate tax deductions and credits to which you are entitled. At worst, tax evasion can result in a charge being laid under the *Criminal Code* (which often means jail time). This is scary!

Tax planning is a continual process. With the ever-changing economy and tax legislation, and the investment vehicles available in the market, planning to minimize your taxes is a continual process. There are many opportunities for tax planning when there is significant change in your life — a new job, a new child or grandchild, a new marriage or the end of one, a relocation, a business start-up, a business sale, retirement, death of a family member, and so on.

The Provincial and Territorial Tax Systems

To make taxes a little more confusing, we all have more than one tax collector to deal with. Canada's constitution gives income taxing powers to both the federal and provincial governments. (Somehow the territories get covered in there too.) In Canada, taxpayers are liable for both federal and provincial/territorial taxes. With the exception of taxpayers in Quebec, individuals need to deal with one tax collector — the Canada Customs and Revenue Agency (CCRA). The CCRA administers the tax system for our federal government and allthe provinces/territories — except Quebec. Taxpayers in Quebec need to deal with both the CCRA (for federal taxes) and the Ministère du Revenu du Québec (for Quebec taxes).

Taxes in Quebec

Unlike the other provinces and the territories, Quebec has its own tax return — form TP.1-D-V. Residents of Quebec on December 31, 2003, must separately file a 2003 federal tax return and a 2003 Quebec tax return. The Ministère du Revenu du Québec administers the Quebec tax system. Their Web site is www.revenu.gouv.qc.ca and they offer service in English and French.

Many of the federal tax rules discussed in this book also apply to the Quebec return. However, Quebec does have some of its own unique rules and calculations. So, if you need to complete a Quebec return this year, you have a little more work ahead of you than those of us who can get by with simply completing the federal return. See Chapter 14 for more information on Quebec's income tax.

My Taxes Are How High?

There's no doubt about it — Canada is a high-tax nation — which means all the more reason to ensure the taxes paid by you and your family are minimized. Take advantage of the tax saving tips in this book, plus ensure you take advantage of all the tax deductions and credits available to you. Canada's income tax system is a progressive tax rate system. The percentage of your income that goes to fund your tax liability increases as your income increases. This is easily illustrated. Take a look at the four federal tax brackets in Table 1-1.

Table 1-1   2003 Federal Income Tax Brackets and Rates (Provincial and Territorial Taxes Not Included)

Tax Brackets	Tax Rate
$0 to $32,183	16%
$32,184 to $64,368	22%
$64,369 to $104,648	26%
$104,649 and over	29%

As you can see, the greater your taxable income through the four federal tax brackets, the greater the percentage of tax that is applied to that additional income.

The tax rates in Table 1-1 are only the federal tax rates, and do not include provincial/territorial income taxes (see Chapter 14). When your taxable income falls into the top federal tax bracket (that is, greater than $104,648), your combined federal and provincial/territorial tax rate on the portion of your taxable income in the top tax bracket can be as high as the tax rates summarized in Table 1-2. However, the tax rates in the charts shown are before any tax credits (except the basic personal amount) that may be available to individuals. These tax credits are discussed in Chapter 12. Your tax liability is based on your taxable income. Once the liability is calculated, it is reduced by tax credits available to you.

Table 1-2	2003 Top Tax Rates (Federal and Provincial/Territorial Taxes Combined)		
Province	**Salary & Interest**	**Capital Gains**	**Dividends**
British Columbia	43.7	21.9	31.6
Alberta	39.0	19.5	24.1
Saskatchewan	44.0	22.0	28.3
Manitoba	46.4	23.2	35.1
Ontario	46.4	23.2	31.3
Quebec	48.2	24.1	32.8
New Brunswick	46.8	23.4	37.3
Nova Scotia	47.3	23.7	31.9
Prince Edward Island	47.4	23.7	32.0
Newfoundland	48.6	24.3	37.3
Northwest Territories	42.0	21.0	28.4
Nunavut	40.5	20.2	26.5
Yukon	42.4	21.2	28.6

Note: Figures are current to February, 2003

As the above table indicates, *capital gains* (the excess of sale proceeds over the cost of an asset) are the most tax-efficient sources of income because they are taxed at the lowest rate. Dividends come in second. (If you are not taxed at the highest rate you might find that dividends are taxed at a lower rate than capital gains in your province.) Remember when we talked about how our government cuts you a tax break when you spend money in ways that they approve of? That's why dividends and capital gains are given preferential treatment.

Tallying up your effective tax rate

Your effective tax rate is the percentage your tax is of your total taxable income. It is easy to calculate. It is simply your tax liability (after you have taken all the tax credits you are entitled to) over your taxable income.

$$\frac{\text{Tax liability}}{\text{Taxable income}} = \text{Effective tax rate}$$

Take a look at Micha's 2003 tax return. Micha lives in Thompson, Manitoba. Her taxable income is $53,000. She calculates the tax on the $53,000 and then reduces the amounts for any tax credits she is entitled to. After these credits are deducted, her federal/Manitoba tax liability is $14,493. Her effective tax rate is then 27.3 percent ($14,493/$53,000).

The calculation of your effective tax rate takes into account that portions of your income are taxed in different tax brackets. The effective tax rate calculation "averages" the rates of tax paid in these brackets. The more income you have taxed in the highest tax bracket (taxable income in excess of $104,648), the higher your effective tax rate.

Calculating your marginal tax rate

When tax geeks talk about marginal tax rates, they are talking about the tax rate that applies to your next dollar of taxable income.

Assume your taxable income is $110,000. You are clearly in the top tax bracket. Further assume you live in Alberta. If you were to earn $1 of additional interest income, you would pay 39¢ in tax on this. In other words, your marginal tax rate is 39 percent (see Table 1-2 in this chapter). On an after-tax basis, that extra dollar of income leaves you with only 61¢, or 61 percent. This is referred to as your after-tax rate of return. It can be calculated as:

$$1 - \text{Your marginal tax rate} = \text{Your after-tax rate of return}$$

The calculation of your marginal tax rate ignores that portions of your income were taxed in different tax brackets and subject to different tax rates. The marginal tax rate is focused on your *next* dollar of taxable income — not your overall taxable income.

The marginal tax rate is an easy way to assess the impact of a raise. With a marginal tax rate of 39 percent, you know that if you receive a $10,000 raise you will only be taking home an additional $6,100. When looking at investment returns from alternative investment opportunities, ensure you compare after-tax rate of returns.

A marginal tax rate can also be used to calculate the tax savings that a tax deduction will provide. Again assume your taxable income is $110,000 and you live in Alberta. You are wondering what the impact would have been if you had contributed $5,000 to your RRSP and taken a deduction on your 2003 return. Your taxable income would have been reduced to $105,000 by the $5,000 RRSP deduction. You know your marginal tax rate on that $5,000 would have been 39 percent. The tax saving you would enjoy if you were able to deduct the $5,000 RRSP contribution is $1,950 ($5,000 multiplied by 39 percent)! You can clearly see why there is so much talk about the tax-saving qualities of RRSP contributions!

Chapter 2

Getting and Staying Organized

. . . .

In This Chapter

▶ Understanding the necessity of keeping good books and records

▶ Knowing how long to keep your records

▶ Dealing with the loss of information slips and receipts

▶ Taking a look at the Merchant Rule

. . . .

Do you want to know the secret to making sure you claim every deduction you're entitled to? To saving money when you have a tax preparer do your tax return? To surviving a CCRA audit unscathed? We'll tell you: Keep good records!

That is all there is to it, really! In this chapter we give you our tried, tested, and true methods of keeping things organized — methods that will save you time and money, not to mention headaches!

Did you know that when dealing with the CCRA, the burden of proof is on you to provide support for the deductions you have claimed? The CCRA is considered by law to be correct unless you can prove otherwise. This is one case in which you are guilty until proven innocent.

Keeping Good Books and Records

You may think that by filing a tax return for the year you've absolved yourself from any further CCRA requirements. Unfortunately that's not true. You see, the CCRA requires every person who is required to pay or collect taxes, or who is carrying on a business in Canada, to keep books and records. The requirement means you have to keep information pertaining to your taxes in case the CCRA asks to see this information in the future. If reviewed by the CCRA, the books and records must enable the CCRA to determine your taxes payable for the year and must be supported by source documents to verify the amounts reported.

Make sure you keep all source documents pertaining to your tax return. These include such documents as the following:

- ✔ Sales invoices
- ✔ Purchase invoices
- ✔ Cash register receipts
- ✔ Written contracts
- ✔ Credit card receipts
- ✔ Delivery slips
- ✔ Deposit slips
- ✔ Cheques
- ✔ Bank statements
- ✔ General correspondence

When deciding what type of source document to keep, consider this: What type of document will best verify your tax records? The stronger the evidence, the less likely it is that your tax records will be rejected by the CCRA. Remember, the original bill is best, the CCRA will not always accept cancelled cheques and credit card statements as authentication of an expense.

Setting up your record-keeping system

In our experience, the number one reason people end up paying more tax than they have to is because they keep lousy records. We know that taming the paper tiger is no mean feat. What follows are our best suggestions to make your tax organization and preparation tasks much easier.

Save all receipts and records that you feel you might be able to use, especially those in the list above. It is much more difficult to recover receipts that have been thrown away than it is to ceremoniously toss out whatever unnecessary paper you have left after your tax return is complete.

Our favourite method of organizing tax information is in an accordion file (you could also use file folders or envelopes). You can pick up any one of these at any office supply store. Label each section by expense category. Use the categories listed on the tax form you will be completing; for example, charitable donations, medical expenses, office supplies, parking, advertising, and so on. As you collect receipts throughout the year, periodically sort them into the proper category. When it comes time to file your tax return, all you have to do is take out the receipts, add them up and enter the total on the tax form. Voilà!

You may also want to consider organizing your tax information by the tax schedules you have to file; that is, Statement of Real Estate Rentals, Capital Gains and Losses, Statement of Business Income and Expense. If your tax return is uncomplicated, it might be sufficient to have one file for each year; as you receive your tax information throughout the year, just put it into the file. This will save you from tearing your house apart looking for that investment statement or charitable receipt you were using as a bookmark last June. Keep a copy of the tax return you filed for that year and your Notice of Assessment, once received, in the same file folder.

Even if you end up hiring a tax accountant to prepare your tax return for you, you will save money if you sort and organize your tax information before you hand it over. (Hint: Accountants prefer organized clients! Just ask us.)

Your friend the computer

Your computer can be a huge help in tracking your tax information each year. There are a number of software packages available that do an excellent job. There are many software packages out there, each with its own merits. Speak with a knowledgeable software salesperson before purchasing, to make sure you get only what you need. There is no sense in buying an expensive, state-of-the-art accounting package if you are only going to use one or two components.

We recommend the software packages Quicken and Microsoft Money for tracking personal and small business expenses and QuickBooks for tracking the expenses of larger businesses. These packages will help you do everything from tracking your investment portfolio to balancing your chequebook to monitoring payroll. Using a software package to enter your data means more of a time commitment up front, but when you need the records for tax time, the figures will be added up and ready to go.

If you do use a computer to do all your record keeping or if you have other valuable papers, it makes sense to store a recent backup of your computer files and those valuable papers, or copies of them, off-site. That way if you suffer a fire or other disaster, all will not be lost.

Record-keeping timebombs

Look out for these special situations:

- ✔ **Automobile expenses:** If you are claiming automobile expenses for a vehicle used for both business and personal purposes, you must keep a log to support the vehicle's business use, detailing dates, number of kilometres driven, and destinations.

- ✔ **Charitable receipts:** A charitable receipt from a registered charity is the only support accepted by the CCRA for a charitable donation. Cancelled cheques and ticket stubs will not be accepted. And if you want to claim a tax credit, ensure you are donating to a registered charity — ask to see a registration number if you're not sure. The registration number must appear on the receipt.

How Long Should I Keep My Tax Records?

One of the questions we are most frequently asked is "How long do I have to keep my records and receipts?" The answer according to the CCRA is six years. The books and records must be kept in Canada at your residence or place of business. Remember, these books and records must be made available to the CCRA should they ask to see them.

Even though after six years the CCRA can't go back and audit your tax return — unless fraud is suspected, in which case all tax years are free game — you will need to keep purchase receipts and investment statements for assets you still own. You may need those records as proof of ownership if you ever have to make an insurance claim or if you sell the asset. And you may need proof of its cost in the future if the gain or loss must be reported on your tax return.

If a particular tax year is under objection or appeal, you should keep your books and records on hand until the objection or appeal has been disposed of and the time for filing a further appeal has expired. It would be a shame to throw out your books and records, only to have legitimate tax deductions denied down the road.

Missing Information Slips and Receipts

Employers and other issuers of information slips are generally required to send you your slips by the end of February in the year following the year in which you received the payment. This includes slips such as T4s, T5s, and slips from the government. However, T3 slips are often not available until after March 31. If you are missing any slips, call the issuer for a new one.

Giving the CCRA your best estimate

If, after you've made a reasonable attempt to obtain your slip, you are still "slipless," you should estimate your income and related deductions (that is, CPP, EI, income tax, union dues) and report them on your tax return. Your pay stubs are a good way to make this estimate if it is your T4 that is missing. Attach a note to your return stating you were unable to obtain your slip and summarize the estimated amounts. You should also give the name and address of the person or organization that should have issued the slip.

You must still file your tax return before the April 30 filing deadline (June 15 if you or your spouse is self-employed) even if you know information is missing. Attach a note to your return explaining what is missing, detail any estimated amounts, and get it in on time! This is especially important if you owe money, since you will be charged a late filing penalty if the return is late, and interest if your balance owing is not paid by April 30.

Missing receipts

Receipts for some deductions, such as RRSP contributions, charitable donations, and medical expenses, must be attached to your tax return when it is filed (assuming you are paper-filing your return). If these receipts do not accompany your return, processing will probably be delayed and your deductions may be disallowed. Remember, the onus is on you to prove all your income and deductions!

If your receipts are missing, call the person or organization responsible for issuing them, to obtain another copy. If you cannot get another copy before the April 30 tax return filing deadline, you should still file your return on time. You can forward the slip to the CCRA when it does finally arrive. Alternatively, you can simply leave the deduction off your tax return and file an adjustment to your tax return once you receive the receipt.

Some other types of receipts don't have to be attached to your tax return. For example, if you have claims for union dues, tuition fees, or child care expenses, the receipts aren't attached to your return when it is filed. However, be aware that the CCRA does regular "reviews" of these types of credits and deductions, so you should still ensure you have the proper documentation on hand should the CCRA ask to see it in the future.

 Don't think you can get away from keeping receipts and other supporting documentation because you are NETFILING, TELEFILING, or EFILING your return. The CCRA can and does often ask to see the support!

What to Do If the Dog Really Did Eat Your Tax Records

Your worst nightmare has come to life — you're being audited! And to top it off, Sparky has eaten some of your tax receipts. Does this mean you'll lose out on all your legitimate tax deductions? Not necessarily. The CCRA does understand that these situations can occur, and will give you the benefit of the doubt (sometimes) if you can show them reasonable proof of your income and deductions.

Reconstructing missing or damaged tax records

If the CCRA does come calling, and you simply don't have the tax records you need to support your tax deductions, all is not lost. There are other ways of proving your claims were legitimate. It may take you some time to reconstruct records, but when you consider the alternatives (additional tax, interest, and penalties on disallowed deductions from an audit), the time you spend will be well worth it. The simplest way to reconstruct missing tax records is to ask for new ones. For example, if you know you bought a number of prescriptions this year but can't find your receipts, go back to your local pharmacy and ask them for a printout of your expenditures for the year. You will be surprised at how many deductions you will be able to reconstruct simply by asking for duplicate receipts.

If you've disposed an asset this year but you do not have a record of its original cost, either because you lost the relevant documents or because the asset was a gift, there are several ways to establish a cost figure:

✔ Look in newspapers from the year you purchased or were given an asset to determine what similar assets were selling for. Your local library should have old newspapers on file or on microfiche.

✔ If trying to find information on a property, consult with the local real estate board. They usually keep historical data on property in the area. You could also go to the property tax collector's office in your municipality. Their assessed values for the property might be of use.

✔ If you inherited an asset, the easiest way to establish its tax cost to you is to check the deceased's final tax return to see at what price they were deemed to have disposed of the property to you. This disposal price is the same as your tax cost.

✔ Call your financial advisor for help. Your advisor will keep back records of your financial affairs and may be able to help you find the cost of your shares, mutual funds, or other assets managed by him or her.

If it is your business records that have been lost or destroyed, you can re-create many of your expenses using the following tactics:

✔ Get copies of your phone, utility, credit card, rent, and other bills from the companies that issued the bills. It shouldn't be too difficult to get an annual statement from a major vendor.

✔ It is possible to obtain duplicate bank statements from your bank (all for a small fee, of course!) that will help you to establish income for the year and some of your expenses.

✔ Automobile expenses may be reconstructed based on a reasonable estimation of what it would cost to run your type of vehicle. The dealer from whom you bought your car might be helpful in estimating these costs.

✔ Look at your previous years' tax returns to establish your expenses in prior years and also your profit margins. If you have lost those too, you can obtain copies of previous years' returns by request from the CCRA.

The Merchant Rule

Our discussion would not be complete if we didn't highlight the Merchant Rule. This rule comes out of a Canadian tax court case in which a lawyer attempted to deduct certain expenses for which he had no receipts. The CCRA disallowed all of the expenses on the grounds that the taxpayer had no support for his claims and that it was therefore impossible to determine how much had actually been spent. The case was appealed and the taxpayer won. The courts had established the rule of *reasonable approximation*. In other words, for an expense to be deductible the taxpayer need only establish that it was *reasonable* to conclude that he had incurred the expenses and that the amounts claimed were *reasonable* in the circumstances.

A similar case in the U.S. courts involved George Cohan, who deducted $55,000 in business-related entertainment expenses in 1921 and 1922. The judges in the Cohan case arrived at the same conclusion. In response to the Cohan decision, U.S. Congress changed the law to make sure taxpayers could no longer deduct expenses without receipts or support. Presently, Canada's Parliament shows no interest in following this U.S. lead.

Are we saying that you no longer have to keep receipts to support your tax deductions? Of course not! However, keep Mr. Merchant and Mr. Cohan in mind if ever you are under the watchful eye of the CCRA and have no receipts to prove your expenses. As they've shown us, if you can otherwise corroborate your deductions, you may be entitled to tax deductions even if you have no traditional receipts. But be prepared for a fight.

Chapter 3

Going Over Your Preparation Options

C hances are, if you're reading this chapter you've already determined that yes, you need to file a tax return, and yes, you need to do it now. So, now what? Do you prepare your return yourself, or do you throw in the towel and hire someone to do it for you? This chapter gives you some handy advice on when to file your own return, and when you should seek help. We will also discuss various options for filing your return.

Be sure that you read through this book regardless of whether you decide to prepare your return yourself or hire someone to help you out. Not only does it provide you with some handy hints so that you don't make any mistakes, but it may also give you some ideas about deductions and credits you might not know are available.

Using Your Computer to Tally Up Your Taxes

Have you ever thought of preparing your tax return using your computer? Think about it. No more adding machines, or the dreaded smell of liquid paper. No more tearing through the forms when you've erased the amount on line 150 one too many times. Tax preparation software makes sense for those of you who have already dived into the world of preparing your own return. And even for those of you still sitting on the fence, tax preparation software may be the answer to your phobia.

The perks and perils of going the techno route

There are a number of advantages to using software to prepare your tax return. The favourite, of course, is automatic recalculation. When one number on your return changes, the program updates all relevant forms and recalculates your final tax bill. Another advantage is that most software packages are dummy-proof. Most programs are set up so all you need to do is find the window that corresponds to the particular slip you have, be it a T4, T3, T5, or so on and fill it in based on what appears in your boxes.

Computers aren't people. They can't look at numbers to determine if they're reasonable, or if they're correct. No computer will tell you to think again before deducting as a business expense your all-inclusive trip for two to Jamaica.

Shopping for tax software

There are several programs available to help taxpayers deal with the headaches that April so often brings. Here is one of the more popular packages:

  ✔ **QuickTax:** Gather up your receipts and answer the simple questions posed by QuickTax. The program then puts the information on the forms where it belongs. QuickTax will review your return when you're finished and even alerts you to any missed deductions or credits. QuickTax has extra features such as "what if" scenarios, an auto lease versus buy analyzer, and RRSP planners. QuickTax also has a Web-based program you can use to prepare and NETFILE your tax return. Check out `www.quicktax.ca`.

QuickTax is Canada's number one best-selling tax software.

Here are some other lesser-known Canadian tax preparation software packages available for 2003 that you might want to have a look at:

- **GriffTax:** If you are a Mac user, have a look at `www.grifftax.com`. GriffTax has NETFILE capability and has been around since 1985.

- **Sim Tax:** This "shareware" program (meaning it's free!) is available at `www.simtax.com`. This program is slated to be available in January 2003 after some development issues last year. Both Canadian and U.S. tax returns can be completed using Sim Tax.

- **Tax Man:** This program can be downloaded for free at `www.winsite.com`. Although you can't NETFILE or do Quebec tax returns, you can print out the CCRA-accepted forms, including business rental, and employment expense forms to mail in to the CCRA.

- **Dr Tax-UFile:** Another on-line program with NETFILE capabilities. This program is a retail program based on Dr. Tax, a program used by some professionals. Check it out at `www.ufile.ca`.

- **H&R Block:** Not only can you have H&R Block do your tax return for you, but also they have an on-line program where you can do your own taxes and NETFILE it. Go to `www.hrblock.ca` for more information.

Surfing Your Way to Tax Help

So it's 11 p.m. on April 30, and you need help. What do you do? Well, if you're lucky, you may find the answers to some of your questions via the Internet. There are several Web sites available that provide handy, up-to-the-minute tax tips. Let's take a look at our top picks.

- Ernst & Young, `www.eycan.com`. This Web site provides you with the latest tax changes, as well as tax calculators. There are also a number of "Tax Alerts" on various tax subjects, budget analyses, and even a downloadable booklet on managing your personal taxes.

✔ Deloitte & Touche, www.deloitte.ca. The daily tax highlights provided on this Web site will ensure you don't miss any of the tax changes. Be sure to keep your eye open for TaxBreaks, Deloitte and Touche's bi-monthly newsletter on personal and corporate tax and their helpful booklets or guides on various tax subjects.

✔ KPMG, www.kpmg.ca. You'll find out all the latest tax changes by visiting KPMG's site, and reading their tax publications including the *Canadian Tax Letter*—an easy-to-read newsletter on current developments in corporate and personal taxation.

✔ PricewaterhouseCoopers, www.pwcglobal.com. Visit the publications area of the Tax Services part of the site, for guides on specific tax subjects. You can also visit the Tax News Network area of the site for all the latest tax information.

✔ BDO Dunwoody, www.bdo.ca. This site is chock-full of tax information ranging from tax facts and figures for each province, to weekly tax tips to in-depth bulletins on many specific tax topics.

✔ The Department of Finance, www.fin.gc.ca. This is where you go to get the information straight from the horse's mouth—so to speak. All the tax changes and updates start here. So if you want the changes the minute they happen, go to this site. Be aware that you'll find a lot of technical information here. So you may want to wait until one of the other sites interprets the changes for you.

When to Get Help from the Tax Collector

Believe it or not, the CCRA is an excellent source for information. Not only can you download a copy of the income tax package, and request additional forms, this site also contains detailed information on all of the most frequently requested topics. Visit the CCRA Web site at www.ccra-adrc.gc.ca.

The TIPS service

If your question relates to your personal tax situation, the CCRA has set up an automated service called Tax Information Phone Service (TIPS). There is also a TIPS on-line service available. TIPS offers the following choices:

- ✔ **Telerefund:** This function tells you the status of your income tax refund.

- ✔ **Goods and Services Tax/Harmonized Sales Tax credit:** Select this and you'll find out if you are eligible to receive the credit, and when you can expect to receive your payment.

- ✔ **Canada Child Tax Benefit:** This service tells you if you are eligible to receive the benefit and when you can expect to receive your payment.

- ✔ **RRSP deduction limit:** Want to know your RRSP contribution limit for the year? TIPS has your answer.

- ✔ **General tax information:** Services include general tax information for individuals, as well as those operating a business, and recent tax and benefit information. General information is available 24 hours a day, 7 days a week.

If you require any of this information, call 1-800-267-6999 or go to the CCRA's Web site at `www.ccra-adrc.gc.ca/services/tipsonline/menu-e.html`. The service is entirely automated, so you will need your social insurance number, date of birth, and the amount you entered on line 150 of your prior year's income tax return.

Visiting your local Tax Services Office

If you can't find the information you need on the Web site or through TIPS, you should try contacting your local Tax Services Office in person or by phone. The TSOs are open Monday to Friday (except holidays, of course), 8:15 a.m. to 4:30 p.m. To find the location of your nearest TSO, visit the CCRA's Web site, and click "Contact us" at the main menu.

Enquiring by phone

Agents are also available to answer your questions by phone, Monday to Friday (except holidays), 8:15 a.m. to 4:30 p.m. To accommodate the flood of calls during tax season, these hours are extended until 10:00 p.m. weekdays, and include weekends from 9:00 a.m. to 1:00 p.m. from late February to April 30. Contact the CCRA by phone at 1-800-959-8281.

If you would like someone else to call the CCRA on your behalf, be sure that you've completed and mailed consent form T1013 to the CCRA. This form gives the CCRA permission to discuss your tax affairs with someone other than you.

Making the Most of Tax Pros

If your plumbing is broken, do you immediately call the plumber, or do you try to fix it yourself? For some, calling for help is the last resort and this is how they feel about preparing their own tax return. Sometimes, however, it's a good idea to admit defeat and hire someone before you get yourself into trouble.

Be sure you have accumulated all the information necessary before sending it to your preparer. If you have a business, your best bet is to summarize all your revenue and expenses ahead of time. This is one way to cut down your fee and ensure no relevant information is omitted.

Hiring someone may be a good idea if you need some tax planning advice. Sometimes the additional fees you pay may actually be recovered in saved taxes! However, be careful whom you hire for tax planning, since some individuals are more competent than others.

Questions to ask your tax professional

You'll see when you look in the Yellow Pages that there are dozens of pages of accounting firms and businesses that specialize in tax. Finding a reputable tax professional is kind of like finding a mechanic — you've got to be careful. In your initial meeting, the tax professional should ask a lot of questions about your situation. Here's a list of questions to ask your "tax professional" to ensure they can handle your situation.

- ✔ **What services do you offer?** Some tax professionals only prepare tax returns, while others will help you with other matters such as retirement planning or estate planning.

- ✔ **Have you worked in this area before?** If you have your own business, or are an avid investor, make sure your professional has worked with similar situations before. Many firms have specialists in particular areas, while some may be used to working with employees who only have a T4 and RRSP slips.

- ✔ **Who will prepare my return?** Unless you're dealing with a sole practitioner, the person you're speaking to will not necessarily prepare your return.

  Don't be alarmed if you have a junior staff member prepare your return — this is common practice and can actually save you preparation fees. However, ensure that your tax professional reviews it for errors.

- ✔ **What is your fee structure?** Most tax professionals charge by the hour, so make sure you ask up front for the hourly fee, as well as for an estimate of the time your project will take to complete.

- ✔ **What qualifications do you have?** Many tax professionals are Chartered Accountants, and many are also Certified Financial Planners. Those specializing in tax should also have completed a two-year in-depth tax course offered by the Canadian Institute of Chartered Accountants.

EFILING Versus Paper Filing

You're now at the point where your tax return is complete. Now what? If you've hired someone to prepare it for you, you have the option of EFILING your return. EFILE is an automated system that allows approved electronic filers to electronically deliver individual income tax return information to the CCRA.

You can't EFILE your tax return yourself. You must first have your return prepared by an approved electronic filer. Most businesses that offer tax preparation services are registered to EFILE returns.

Who can EFILE?

The majority of Canadian taxpayers can electronically transmit their return. People who *can't* EFILE include non-residents, people who came to Canada during the year, people who have declared bankruptcy, and people who have to pay income tax to more than one province or territory.

What are the benefits of EFILING?

Most people like EFILING their return because they get their assessment and refunds faster. In fact, the wait is cut to two weeks from the usual four to six, if you're a procrastinator and file towards the end of April. If you're one of those who file in the middle of March, you may actually see your refund in just over a week! As well, since electronically transmitting your return saves the CCRA from having to manually input your data, it reduces the likelihood of data entry errors. Last but not least, EFILING saves you a stamp.

Are my chances of audit lower if I EFILE?

No. EFILED returns are selected for review using the same criteria as paper-filed returns. So if you're worried about an audit, don't think you can reduce your odds by EFILING your return. And if you don't like having any contact with the CCRA after you file your return other than a report card called the Notice of Assessment, then we don't suggest you EFILE. You see, since no supporting documentation is sent to the CCRA when you EFILE, the taxman may contact you asking for backup information for some of your claims. The most common requests are for medical and donation receipts. The CCRA tries to select only returns for which they think there is a higher probability of non-compliance, but this is not always the case. Don't panic, however, if you receive a request to send more information. It doesn't mean you're being audited.

TELEFILING

With TELEFILE, you don't need to have someone else prepare and file your return. You can electronically file your own return. All you need is a touch-tone phone and an invitation to TELEFILE. The system accepts income tax information such as employment income, pension income, interest income, RRSP contributions, and charitable donations. The more complex returns would take more telephone time, and often the CCRA needs to see supporting documentation in order to process them. Only those individuals who file the T1S return instead of the longer T1 return are eligible for TELEFILE.

The T1 Special or T1S is sent to individuals who are wage and salary earners only, students, seniors, and filers who file only to obtain tax credits. When individuals eligible to use TELEFILING receive their tax package from the CCRA, they will also receive a special invitation, along with an access code and instructions on how to use the system.

NETFILING

Now more than ever, Canadians are doing everything from banking to buying cars to planning the family vacation over the Internet. So why not file your income tax return over the Internet? NETFILE allows eligible individuals to file their income tax returns through the Internet.

The CCRA has set up a Web site for people eligible to NETFILE. This Web site provides step-by-step details on how to NETFILE, as well as the requirements that must be met. Be sure to visit it at www.netfile.gc.ca.

Before you can NETFILE your return to the CCRA, you must first prepare your return using certified tax preparation software. Basically, all this means is that the software will save your return in a format that the CCRA can read. A listing of approved software is available on the CCRA's Web site at www.netfile.gc.ca/software-e.html and includes the following programs:

- ✔ GriffTax
- ✔ UFile.ca
- ✔ QuickTax
- ✔ TaxWiz
- ✔ Cutetax
- ✔ TAXcel
- ✔ MyTaxexpress

Where to Get Forms and Other Information

The package that's sent by the CCRA in mid-February contains only the most commonly used forms. If you didn't receive a package or need additional ones, you can pick one up at the post office or the TSO nearest you. If you find that you need a form not contained in your package, getting the forms has never been easier!

You have three options. You can visit your local TSO and pick up the form there, download the form from the CCRA's Web site, or request to have the printed form mailed to you.

Part II
Tax Preparation Tips: Reporting Income

The 5th Wave   By Rich Tennant

"And just how long did you think you could keep that pot 'o gold at the end of the rainbow a secret from us, Mr. O'Shea?"

In this part...

Here's where we get into the good stuff. Contrary to popular opinion, every type of income you earn belongs somewhere on your tax return. Unfortunately, it doesn't all belong on one line. Here's where all the various schedules and forms come into play, and where the confusion may begin. That's why we always say: Start with the identification section, ease into the rest of the return, and be thankful you only have to complete your T1 return once a year.

This part walks you through the various types of income that typical taxpayers may have. In the traditional ...*For Dummies* format, we've managed to make this as simple and painless as possible. So whether you're an employee, a business-owner, an investor, or retired, this part's for you!

"The hardest thing in the world to understand is income tax!"

— Albert Einstein

Chapter 4

Tips for Employment-Related Income

● ●

In This Chapter

▶ Defining employment income

▶ Establishing the difference between employee and self-employed

▶ Using taxable and non-taxable benefits to your best advantage

▶ Tips for dealing with commission income

▶ Dealing with other employment income

● ●

*F*or many Canadians, much of their time is spent at work. There are farmers and bankers and teachers and bus drivers among us, plus professions that many of us have yet to imagine. But the one thing that we all have in common is that we go to work to get paid so that we have income to enjoy the rest of our lives. And, much to the chagrin of many Canadians, employment income is where we pay the bulk of our taxes. But don't despair, with some planning and a better understanding of how the CCRA views employment income, we just might be able to help you end up with a few more dollars in your pocket after all is said and done.

What Is Employment Income?

Employment income includes all amounts received in a year as salary, wages, commissions, director's fees, bonuses, tips, gratuities, and honoraria. You should report all these items — which, in most cases, have been reported by your employer on your T4 slip in box 14 — on line 101 of your personal tax return. This includes commission income, which is reported again on line 102. You should record any income from the list above that is not reported on your T4, but was received by you, on line 104 "Other employment income."

Employee Versus Self-Employed

Are you your own boss? For obvious reasons many of us like to think so, but this is yet another question that the CCRA wants answered. Plainly stated, the CCRA wants to know, are you an employee or are you self-employed? For many of you the answer may be simple, but for others, it's not so obvious. In fact, you may consider yourself to be self-employed, but the taxman may think differently. You see, the CCRA makes the distinction between self-employed and employed based on several factors or tests. And make no mistake about it, this distinction can make a huge difference in your taxable income. If you are an employee, the *Income Tax Act* restricts the expenses that can be deducted from your employment income. If a deduction is not specifically mentioned in the Act, the answer's simple — it's not deductible. Self-employed individuals do not have these same restrictions.

 If possible, in most situations it's advantageous to arrange your business relationship so that you are an independent contractor rather than an employee. This is because independent contractors are entitled to claim deductions for many expenses not deductible by an employee. See Chapter 9 for details.

 Wondering how to set yourself up as an independent contractor? The CCRA has a guide entitled *Employee or Self-Employed?* (RC4110) that identifies the factors they look at to determine your status. These include:

✔ How much supervision or control does your "boss" have?

✔ Do you work your own schedule as opposed to having to comply with instruction as to when, where, and how work is to be performed?

✔ Does your employer furnish the tools needed for the job, or do you furnish them yourself?

✔ Were you hired to do one job with no pre-determined continuous relationship?

 Self-employment is not for everyone, since it comes with its own pitfalls. As a self-employed person, you'll be responsible for paying the employer's share of CPP, which will effectively double your payments. As well, before leaping at the opportunity to become your own boss, remember, if the company turns sour, there will be no EI or severance waiting for you. And, of course, you won't be entitled to any employment benefits such as medical or dental coverage if you are not considered to be an employee.

Taxable Benefits and Non-Taxable Benefits

An employer will sometimes provide other benefits for your work in addition to your paycheque. These are often referred to as *perks!* The majority of the benefits you receive from your employer are considered to be taxable income, whether or not they are received in cash (for example, certain automobile allowances), or in kind, like an all-expense-paid holiday.

Taxable benefits

Even though you may not be pleased that some perks offered by your employer are taxable, a taxable benefit will usually be more financially advantageous than if you had to pay for the benefit yourself. For example, if your employer pays group term life insurance premiums of $4,000 for you annually, and you are taxed on the amount at 40 percent, you will only pay tax of $1,600—that's much less expensive than your having to pay this amount out of your after-tax income.

The following items are some of the more common taxable benefits that may show up on your T4 slip, along with some tips to use these benefits to your best advantage:

- ✔ **Stock options.** The difference between the price you pay (also known as the exercise price) and the market value of the shares on the exercise date is taxable to you. However, this benefit *may* be reduced by one-half if certain conditions are met. See Chapter 11 for details.

- ✔ **Interest-free or low interest loans.** You are taxable on the difference between the actual interest rate charged and the CCRA's "prescribed rate." These rates are set quarterly and can be found on the CCRA's Web site at www.ccra-adrc.gc.ca.

  If the loan was to help you relocate and purchase a home at least 40 kilometres closer to a new work location, the interest benefit on up to $25,000 of loan is deductible for up to five years!

- ✔ **Club dues.** If your employer is willing to pay for your dues to a recreational, sporting, or dining club, ensure that you can show the membership is primarily to your employer's advantage (think networking and sales prospecting!). If this is the case, the benefit will not be taxable to you.

✔ **Car allowances.** If your employer is giving you an allowance to help defray the cost of your vehicle, ensure you receive a per-kilometre reimbursement. If you receive a lump sum allowance that is not based on a per-kilometre rate, you will find yourself with a taxable benefit. The good news is that even if the allowance is taxable, you may be entitled to deduct some of your auto expenses if you use your car for business purposes. See Chapter 11 for details.

✔ **Company cars.** If you are provided with a company car, you will have a taxable benefit (called a standby charge), whether or not you use the car personally! In addition, if your employer pays for operating costs of the car (such as gas, insurance, or maintenance) you will also have an operating benefit charged to your income!

Think twice about accepting a company car as part of your compensation. You see, you'll be required to pay tax on two separate benefits: the standby charge (which will likely be as high as 24 percent of the cost of your car each year!) and an operating benefit. Even though the value of your car is reduced as soon as you drive it off the lot, your standby charge stays the same each year. The car's depreciating value is ignored in calculating the standby charge. Thanks but no thanks!

Measures announced in the 2003 Federal Budget propose to reduce the standby charge if personal driving does not exceed 20,000 kilometres in a year and the automobile is used more than 50 percent for business purposes

✔ **Employee profit-sharing plans.** Your employer should provide you with a form T4PS detailing the amounts to include in your income. Among other amounts, this will include amounts received by the plan from your employer and income earned in the plan during the year. However, when a distribution is actually made by the plan to you, it will generally be tax-free, since you've already paid tax on the amount received.

✔ **Insurance payments received by you due to employment.** Payments made to you in respect of loss of income under a sickness, accident or disability, or income maintenance plan are taxable if your employer paid your premiums.

Make sure your plan at work is set up so that you pay the premium. That way any disability payments will be tax-free if you ever have to collect.

✔ **Group term life insurance premiums.** These premiums, paid by your employer, are taxable to you.

✔ **Reimbursements and awards.** Such items received because of your employment – for example, paid holidays or incentive awards from employer-related contests – are considered taxable.

✔ **Rent-free or low-rent housing.** If your employer provides you with rent-free or low-rent accommodations the difference between the actual market value of that housing and the amount you are required to pay should be included in your income. There is an exception, however, if your duties are performed at a remote location or at some special work sites. See Chapter 11 for further details.

✔ **Spouse's travelling expenses**. If your spouse joins you on a business trip, you'll probably have a taxable benefit equal to the travelling expenses of your spouse paid for by your employer unless your spouse was primarily engaged in business activities on behalf of your employer.

There's no harm in extending your business trip to include a personal vacation. Since the initial trip was for business purposes, the costs paid by your employer will be tax-free benefits. Of course, this is provided you pick up all the additional costs, other than the trip home, from your extended trip.

✔ **Gifts from your employer.** You can receive two non-cash gifts per year, and if the combined total is less than $500, the entire amount is non-taxable! But watch out — if the total amount of the gifts you receive is more than $500, the entire amount becomes taxable — not just the portion above $500!

Gifts that have been personalized with your name or corporate logo will have a reduced market value. When the award is a plaque, trophy, or other memento for which there is no market, there likely will be no taxable benefit!

✔ **Relocation expenses**. If your employer compensates you for the diminished value or loss on the sale of your home due to relocation, these benefits are taxable to you. The taxable amount is half of the amount reimbursed over $15,000. Better than nothing, we say!

✔ **Frequent flyer programs**. If you use points earned from business trips for personal travel, you'll have to report a taxable benefit for the market value of the points used. The good news (if you can call this "good") is that the value of the benefit is not the normal fare you'd have to pay if you bought the ticket yourself. Due to restrictions on the use of points at the airlines (and boy, are there a lot!), the government will allow you to use the value of the most heavily discounted economy-class ticket sold for the flight.

✔ **Forgiveness of employee debt**. Do you have a nice employer who lent you money? Do you have an even nicer employer who forgave some or all of this debt? In this case, your debt may be gone, but the value of the forgiven amount is taxable.

Non-taxable benefits

And now for the fun stuff—non-taxable benefits! The following are benefits you can enjoy tax-free from your employer. Keep these benefits in mind if you're negotiating your way into a new job or simply at your next compensation review:

- ✔ **Transportation to the job.** Some employers provide their employees with transportation to and from work, for security or some other reason (think black limo with a driver, not city bus with an employer-provided bus pass). Whatever the reason, there will be no inclusion for the value of the benefit in the employee's income. So now you can sit back and enjoy the ride, without worrying about any tax hit.

- ✔ **Food and lodging.** Food and lodging will not be taxable benefits if you were required to work at a temporary site for more than 36 hours consecutively. To qualify, the temporary site must be in a remote place or be farther away than a reasonable daily commute from your residence, and you must keep your usual residence.

- ✔ **Personal counselling.** Not many people know this, but your employer can pay for counselling related to the mental or physical health of you or someone related to you, and you won't have to report a taxable benefit. This may include counselling related to tobacco, drug or alcohol abuse, stress management, job placement, or retirement. Be sure to negotiate these payments with your employer if you find yourself or someone related to you in need of these services.

- ✔ **Computer and Internet services.** The CCRA has said that the provision of home computers and Internet services to an employee, where the primary use is for work or for the employee to become more computer literate, is not a taxable benefit. The CCRA has suggested the employee pay a nominal fee for personal use.

- ✔ **Death benefits.** If you pass away and your employer pays a death benefit to your family, the first $10,000 of that benefit is received tax-free.

- ✔ **Education costs.** Where your employer picks up the tab for education, there will be no taxable benefit in taking the course, provided that you are benefiting your employer. If the course is of "personal interest," it would result in a taxable benefit since it has nothing to do with your work. So, if your employer kindly agrees to pay for your bird-house carpentry course, be prepared for a taxable benefit.

✔ **Parking space.** The fair market value of an employer-provided parking space, minus any amount you pay for the spot, must usually be included in your income. There is no taxable benefit if your employer provides a parking space to you and you use your vehicle regularly during business hours to carry out your duties. Of course, when the spot is in a location where free parking is readily accessible, then there will be no taxable benefit.

Other non-taxable benefits you may receive include:

✔ Employer contributions to pension plans

✔ Employer contributions to private health services plans

✔ Merchandise discounts, if extended to all employees

✔ Subsidized meals, as long as you pay a reasonable charge for those meals

✔ The cost of uniforms, and the cleaning of them

✔ In-house recreational and fitness facilities

✔ In-house day-care services (but not day-care provided by a third party and paid for by your employer)

Commission Income

If you sell goods or negotiate contracts for a living, you may be compensated partially or wholly by commissions. From a tax point of view, you may be considered a commissioned employee, or self-employed (see our discussion of employee versus self-employed earlier in this chapter).

If you are considered an employee, your commissions will show up on your T4 slip.

 Although commissions are separately disclosed on your T4 slip, don't add this amount to your employment income on line 101. You see, box 14 of your T4 includes all taxable employment income you earned, including salary and wages, taxable benefits, and commission income.

 As a commissioned employee, you are entitled to deduct many expenses incurred to earn your commissions. See Chapter 11 for details.

If you are self-employed, you'll have to file special tax forms outlining your commission income and expenses for the tax year. See Chapter 9 for more information.

Other Employment Income

The CCRA asks for certain items to be reported on line 104 "Other employment income" that are not technically employment income.

These items include the following:

- ✔ Royalties from a work or invention
- ✔ GST rebate from a prior year
- ✔ Research grants net of expenses
- ✔ Amounts received from a supplementary unemployment benefit plan
- ✔ The taxable portion of an income maintenance insurance plan
- ✔ Director's fees
- ✔ Signing bonuses
- ✔ Some termination payments and damages for loss of office or employment
- ✔ Executor's fees received for administering an estate

Chapter 5

Tax Tips for Pension Income

● ●

In This Chapter

▶ Making the most of the Old Age Security (OAS) program

▶ Preparing for the OAS "clawback"

▶ Sorting out the Canada Pension Plan (CPP) and the Quebec Pension Plan (QPP)

▶ Understanding other pensions

▶ Handling foreign pension income

▶ Separating non-taxable pension income

▶ Understanding and transferring pension income credit

● ●

*I*f you're like most Canadians under 65 years of age, you're probably asking yourself whether you need to bother with this chapter. We suggest you take the time to read it — you might be surprised by all the ways pension income can be part of your tax picture, even if you are a spring chicken. True, only three lines of the tax return relate to pension income. And reporting OAS, CPP, and other pension income is usually straightforward. In most cases you will be issued an information slip detailing the amounts to be included in line 113 (Old Age Security pension), line 114 (Canada Pension Plan benefits), and line 115 (other pensions and superannuation). So why is this chapter so long? Well, we decided to go further, discussing the various sources of OAS and CPP, and offering you tips on whether you qualify for these payments, how to go about receiving them, and how to pay the least tax on the amounts received. We also delve into the "OAS clawback" and offer you some pension and tax-planning ideas.

First Things First — What Isn't Pension Income?

So let's be clear right off the bat about what this chapter deals with and what it doesn't. Income from a registered retirement savings plan (RRSP) is not considered pension income — we could probably come up with a detailed reason why, but it would add little value to this book. Since RRSP income is not considered to be pension income, we will not go into how RRSP withdrawals are taxed here. (Well, maybe we have space for just a little info — the amount withdrawn is noted on a T4RSP information slip and the amount is included on line 129 of your tax return. Any tax withheld by the RRSP trustee is included on line 437. Much more on taxes and your RRSP can be found in Chapter 10.) RRIF (registered retirement income fund) income is considered pension income. RRIF income is dealt with later in this chapter under the heading "Line 115: Other Pensions"

Old Age Security Pension

Old Age Security, or OAS, pension is a monthly pension payment. It is available to most Canadians aged 65 and over — even if they no longer live in Canada. The amount is adjusted quarterly for increases in the cost of living as measured by the Consumer Price Index (CPI). The maximum monthly OAS pension payment for July to September 2003 was $461.55. The OAS is administered by Human Resources Development Canada (HRDC).

You must apply for OAS!

Applying for OAS

To ensure your OAS payments start on time, you should apply six months before your 65th birthday. A registration kit (ISP 3503) is available from any HRDC office, or you can call 1-800-277-9914. The kit can also be downloaded from the Web site of HRDC at www.hrdc-drhc.gc.ca/isp. You cannot apply on-line. You need to download the form (ISP 3000), complete it, and send it to the address noted on the Web site.

Non-resident recipients of OAS

Payments can be made to addresses outside Canada. If you are not a resident of Canada a "non-resident tax" may be withheld from your payment of OAS. The maximum withholding is 25 percent. HRDC will not withhold any non-resident tax on payments of OAS if you are a resident of the United States or the United Kingdom.

Speed up the receipt of your OAS! Have your OAS payment deposited in any bank account in Canada or the United States.

OAS eligibility criteria

Eligibility for an OAS pension is based on two issues: age and years resident in Canada. OAS pension is not affected by your employment history and you are entitled to receive it whether or not you have retired. Two categories of people are eligible for OAS:

✔ People living in Canada who

- are 65 or older,

- are Canadian citizens or legal residents, and

- have lived in Canada for at least 10 years while adults.

✔ People living outside Canada who

- are 65 or older,

- are Canadian citizens or legal residents at the time they cease to live in Canada, and

- had lived in Canada for at least 10 years as adults.

Not falling into any of these categories? You still may be eligible to receive OAS! Canada has a number of social security agreements with other countries. If you lived in one of these countries or contributed to its social security system, you may qualify for a pension from that country, Canada, or both. Need more information to determine whether you qualify? Contact HRDC at 1-800-277-9914. HRDC'S Web site at www.hrdc-drhc.gc.ca/isp contains a wealth of information. You can also drop into a regional HRDC office. Addresses are on the HRDC Web site.

Are you entitled to a full or partial OAS?

The main criteria in determining whether you're entitled to a full or partial OAS pension is the length of time you've been in Canada. You should qualify for full OAS if the following apply to you:

✔ Lived in Canada for at least 40 years after your 18th birthday or

✔ Were born on July 1, 1952, or earlier and

- Lived in Canada on July 1, 1977,

- Between your 18th birthday and July 1, 1977, lived in Canada for some period of time, or

- Lived in Canada for 10 years prior to your OAS application being approved.

Do you not qualify because you haven't lived in Canada for the past 10 years? Don't fret! You should still qualify for full OAS if

✔ You lived in Canada for the year immediately before your application was approved.

✔ Prior to those past 10 years, you lived in Canada as an adult for a period of time at least three times the length of your absences during the past 10 years. (Go ahead, be confident, do the math!)

If you do not qualify for a full OAS, a partial OAS pension may be available to you. The amount you would receive is based on the number of complete years you lived in Canada after turning 18.

Is my OAS pension taxable?

You bet. The reporting of OAS on your tax return, however, is very simple. If you received OAS payments in 2003, you will receive a T4A(OAS) information slip summarizing the amount paid. You should expect this slip to arrive in January 2004. The amount noted in box 18 is to be included on line 113 of your tax return. Some tax may have been held back on the OAS pension payment to you. If so, this amount will be noted in box 22 of the T4A(OAS). Be sure to include the withheld tax on line 437 of your return.

If you want to reduce the amount of taxes that come due on April 30 each year, you can request that more taxes be withheld from your OAS pension payments.

OAS repayment ("clawback")

The government giveth, the government taketh! Much to the chagrin of seniors, our government believes that those with income in excess of $57,879 do not deserve to receive a full OAS pension. When a taxpayer has received OAS higher than his or her calculated maximum OAS entitlement, the excess amount must be repaid. The amount that must be repaid is equal to 15 percent of net income in excess of $57,879 — stay tuned for an example.

When the OAS repayment program began, the government continued to pay taxpayers their full share of the OAS without considering whether all or a portion of the OAS would have to be repaid at tax time. The amount to be repaid was not calculated until the taxpayer completed a tax return, and was then added to the individual's tax liability. This often came as a shock to seniors, some of whom had already spent all their OAS pension! Since the government gave the funds and then asked for them back, the OAS repayment became known as the OAS *clawback*. The program has since been amended so that monthly OAS payments are reduced to take into account an individual's expected OAS repayment. High-income individuals do not receive any OAS at all. The withholding of an expected OAS clawback adds complexity to tax return preparation. This is discussed below.

After you make an OAS repayment, the CCRA tattles on you. They tell HRDC, which then adjusts your future monthly OAS payments. Assuming you file your 2003 tax return by April 30, 2004, the CCRA should assess you by the end of June 2004. Based on the assessment of your income on your 2003 return, HRDC will adjust your next 12 OAS monthly payments beginning with the July 2004 payment. (Your July 2004 payment may be significantly different from your June 2004 payment.) The adjustment to your monthly OAS payments is made under the assumption that your 2004 net income will be about the same as your 2003 net income. In other words, HRDC expects that you will have to repay all or a portion of your 2004 OAS in an amount that is approximately what you had to repay in respect of the 2003 OAS. Rather than paying you the OAS and then waiting for you to repay OAS as part of your 2004 tax return, HRDC simply reduces the amount of your monthly OAS cheque.

What if your 2004 net income is lower than your 2003 net income to the extent that you did not receive 2004 OAS in the amount you were entitled to? The deficiency is paid to you by decreasing your tax liability (or increasing your tax refund) on your 2004 tax return. Confused? Just remember that the determination of your OAS payments is six months after the tax year for which you just filed a tax return.

Calculation of OAS repayment

Let's work through an illustration of how the OAS repayment (or clawback) is calculated.

Jim turned 65 on January 1, 2003. He applied for OAS six months before his 65th birthday. We have purposely made Jim's income exceed $57,879 to detail the calculation and impact of the OAS repayment on his tax return and tax liability.

Old Age Security (OAS) pension (estimate)	$5,600
Other pension income	$60,000
Interest income	$2,000
Deduction for support payments made to former spouse	($5,000)
Net income before deduction for OAS repayment (line 234 on tax return)	$62,600

Calculation of OAS repayment

Net income before deduction for OAS repayment (as above)	$62,600
Less base amount	$57,879
Excess net income	$4,721
Net income before deduction for OAS repayment (as above)	$62,600
Less repayment — 15% on excess net income (line 235 on tax return)	$708
Net income after OAS repayment (line 236 on tax return)	$61,892

The amount of repayment owing is included in determining your total tax liability or refund. It is included on line 422 of the tax return as part of the calculation of your total tax liability for the year. Depending on your tax position, the OAS repayment may increase your tax owing at April 30, 2004 — or decrease your refund!

Protect your OAS! Once your net income is $94,148 all your OAS will be repaid or "clawed back." Therefore, use the tips in this book to minimize your income and to minimize the OAS clawback.

OAS overpayments

You may have received OAS payments in error during 2003 and previous years. Repayments of these amounts are noted in box 20 of the T4A(OAS) slip. (Note that OAS repayments differ from the "clawback.") Repayments are claimed as a deduction on line 232 of your return to the extent that the amount was included in your income in 2002 and prior years.

Guaranteed Income Supplement (GIS)

The GIS provides low-income seniors in Canada with additional money in addition to the regular OAS pension. The GIS is based on the taxpayer's income and marital status. The maximum monthly GIS from July to September 2003 was $548.53 for a single person and $357.30 for an individual married to an OAS recipient. The GIS payment is included in the monthly OAS pension cheque.

Applying for the GIS and yearly renewal

As with OAS pension, you must apply for GIS. Form ISP-3020 or ISP-3037 "Application for Guaranteed Income Supplement" should be used to apply. The form is available on the HRDC Web site or at an HRDC office. The GIS is renewed annually, since it is based on your income from the previous year. You do not need to reapply each year — just be sure to file an income tax return each year. (Sometimes, HRDC will still send you a renewal form — form ISP-3026 or ISP-3038 or ISP-3039 "Application for Renewal of Guaranteed Income Supplement." If you receive a form, complete it right away to ensure your GIS payments are not held up.)

Is the GIS taxable?

No, but the amount must be reported on your tax return. The T4A(OAS) slip will note the amount of GIS you received in box 21. This is first included in your income on line 146 and then deducted on line 250.

The Allowance

The allowance is additional money paid to low-income seniors with a spouse or common-law partner who receives the OAS and GIS. It is like an early OAS pension. The recipient must be 60 to 64 years of age and meet some residency tests. If you are receiving the allowance, you will receive an annual T4A(OAS) slip. The amount received will be noted in box 21. The amount is not taxable but must be reported on your tax return in the same fashion as the GIS. You apply for the allowance using the same form as for the regular OAS—form ISP-3000.

Allowance for the Survivor

Additional money is paid to low-income seniors aged 60 to 64, if their spouse or common-law partner has died and they meet residency requirements. Like those receiving the allowance, recipients of the allowance for the survivor will receive an annual T4A(OAS) slip. Again, the amount received will be noted in box 21 and is not taxable, although it is still reported on your tax return. Again, form ISP-3000 is used to apply for the allowance for the survivor.

To continue receiving the GIS, the allowance, or the allowance for the survivor, ensure you file a tax return by April 30 each year. See Table 5-1 for a summary of the tax implications of these items.

Table 5-1   The Taxation of Old Age Security (Line 113)

Type of Receipt	*Taxable?*
Old Age Security (OAS) pension	Yes — and it can be taxed up to 100 percent. (See comments above on the "OAS Clawback.")
Guaranteed Income Supplement (GIS)	No — but it must be reported on your tax return .
The Allowance	No — but it must be reported on your tax return.
Allowance for the survivor	No — but it must be reported on your tax return.

Line 114: Income from the Canada Pension Plan (CPP) and Quebec Pension Plan (QPP)

You pay into the CPP or QPP throughout your working life, so you probably would like to know the variety of ways you can benefit from these plans. Table 5-2 lists the variety of amounts that you can receive from the CPP and the QPP:

Table 5-2	Summary of Amounts You Can Receive from the CPP and QPP
Type of Receipt	*Taxable?*
CPP/QPP lump sum benefit	Yes — but a portion may be taxed in a prior year.
CPP/QPP retirement pension	Yes
CPP/QPP disability pension	Yes
CPP/QPP child disability benefit	Yes — but taxed in tax return of child.
CPP/QPP survivor benefit	Yes
CPP/QPP child survivor benefit	Yes — but taxed in tax return of child.
CPP/QPP death benefit	Yes — but taxed in estate.

CPP versus QPP

The Quebec government administers the QPP on behalf of the people of Quebec. HRDC administers the CPP for the remaining nine provinces and three territories. With respect to most issues, the two plans operate in a similar fashion. For simplicity and conciseness, most of this chapter deals with CPP issues.

Reporting your CPP/QPP income on your tax return

Each January, HRDC sends CPP recipients a T4A(P) tax slip. The amount noted in box 20 is to be put on line 114 of your tax return. Figures in the other boxes provide a breakdown of your sources of CPP. None of these figures needs to be reported on your tax return, with the exception of box 16 — the disability benefit. This is to be noted in line 152 of your return, which is just to the left of line 114. Do not add box 152 when calculating your total income; the amount is already included in box 114.

Lump sum CPP or QPP benefit

If you received a lump sum benefit in 2003, all or part of it may be in respect of a prior year. The amount needs to be reported in your 2003 tax return. However, you may qualify for preferential tax treatment. Where the amount related to a previous year is $300 or more, you can have that portion taxed in the year to which it relates. This is beneficial if the tax in the relevant year would be lower than your 2003 tax would be if the amount were included in your 2003 return. This would be the case if you had been in a lower tax bracket in that previous year. The CCRA, based on information from HRDC, will reassess your 2003 return and that of the other year, and advise you of the results on a Notice of Reassessment.

CPP retirement pension

The CPP is a monthly pension paid to individuals who have contributed to:

✔ the CPP or

✔ both the CPP and Quebec Pension Plan (QPP), if you live outside Quebec.

Like OAS, you must apply to receive a CPP retirement pension

Applying for your CPP retirement pension

HRDC suggests you apply six months before you want your retirement pension to begin. A retirement information sheet (ISP-1000A) and application form is available from any HRDC office, or you can call 1-800-277-9914. You can also download the sheet from HRDC's Web site — www.hrdc-drhc.gc.ca/isp. You cannot apply on-line. You need to download the form, complete it, and send it to the address noted on the Web site.

The retirement pension is designed to be paid starting when an individual turns 65. However, you have the option of taking a discounted payment at any time between the ages of 60 and 64. If you defer your pension until you are 66 to 70, your monthly payment will be increased. If you decide to take the pension when you are 60 to 64, you must have stopped working, or you must be earning less than the monthly maximum CPP retirement pension. In 2003 this was $801.25 per month.

 Once you begin to receive CPP you are permitted to work as much as you like and your pension amount will not be affected. However, you can no longer contribute to the CPP.

 To find out how much CPP you are entitled to at different start dates, you can contact HRDC. Simply fill out form ISP-1003 "Estimate Request for Canada Pension Plan (CPP) Retirement Pension," with alternative start dates. The closer you are to the date you want your pension to begin, the more accurate the estimate will be. The form is available at any HRDC office or via the Web site: www.hrdc-drhc.gc.ca/isp

 As with the OAS, you may qualify for a CPP retirement pension that is calculated based not only on contributions you have made to the plan, but also on contributions you have made to another country's social security system. This is good news if you were only in Canada for a short while before you retired but had previously worked and paid social security taxes to another country.

Taking your CPP retirement pension early

If you decide to start your CPP retirement pension before you are 65 years of age, the payments are reduced by 6 percent for each year (actually .5 percent per month) that you are under 65.

Increasing your CPP retirement pension

If you elect to start receiving your CPP retirement pension after you are 65 years of age, you are entitled to an increased amount — again, 6 percent per year (or .5 percent per month). If you wait until your 70th birthday, your entitlement increases by 30 percent! (The amount cannot be increased more than 30 percent. So waiting until you are 71 or 72 will not get you a bigger CPP pension.)

How do you decide when to start taking your CPP retirement pension?

HRDC suggests that in making your decision, you consider the following:

- ✔ Whether you are still working and contributing to the CPP
- ✔ How long you have contributed
- ✔ How much your earnings were
- ✔ What your other sources of retirement income are
- ✔ How your health is
- ✔ What your retirement plans are, including desired lifestyle

Other benefits offered by the Canada Pension Plan

In addition to the retirement pension, the CPP also provides the following:

- ✔ CPP disability benefits
- ✔ CPP survivor benefits

CPP disability benefits

The CPP will provide you with a monthly pension if you have been a CPP contributor and are considered mentally or physically disabled under the CPP guidelines. Payments can also be made to dependent children. Your disability must be "severe and prolonged." HRDC considers "severe" to mean that you cannot work regularly at any job, and "prolonged" to mean that your condition is long term or may lead to death. The amount paid comprises a flat amount plus a second amount based on the number of years you have contributed to the CPP. The maximum monthly disability benefit in 2003 was $971.26.

If you become disabled, your child under 18 can also qualify for a benefit. Even if your "child" is between ages 18 and 25, he or she will still qualify if enrolled in what HRDC considers a recognized institution — usually a school providing post-secondary education. The maximum amount paid in 2003 was $186.77 per month per child.

You must apply for both CPP disability benefits — the regular benefit and the children's benefit. Application forms are available from HRDC offices or from HRDC's Web site. You should apply as soon as you consider yourself to have a long-term disability that prevents you from working at any job. The government will require you to provide a medical report from your doctor.

CPP survivor benefits

CPP survivor benefits are paid to your estate, surviving spouse or common-law partner, and dependent children. There are three types of survivor benefits.

Death benefit

The death benefit is a one-time payment to your estate. The maximum amount for this benefit is $2,500.

Survivor's pension

Your surviving spouse or common-law partner can receive a monthly pension. The amount of the payment depends on how long you paid into the CPP, your spouse or common-law partner's age when you die, and whether this person is receiving a CPP retirement or disability pension. The calculation is based on what your CPP retirement pension would have been if you had been 65 at the time of death. This amount is then adjusted to take into account the age of your survivor. The maximum amount that can be received is 60 percent of what your retirement pension would have been (2003 monthly maximum is $480.75 or 60 percent of $801.25). To receive this, your survivor must be aged 65 or over at the time of your death. Where your survivor is younger, the payments are lower. If your surviving spouse or common-law partner is under 35 and is not disabled or raising your dependent child, the amount is deferred until he or she is 65 or becomes disabled. The survivor will continue to receive the pension even if he or she remarries.

Prior to a change to the rules in 1987, a surviving spouse who remarried would lose the pension. If this happened to you, contact HRDC to find out whether you are now eligible.

Children's benefit

The children's benefit is a monthly payment to a deceased contributor's dependent children. At the time of the contributor's death, the child must be under 18, or between the ages of 18 and 25 and enrolled full time in a recognized educational institution. The maximum monthly amount in 2003 was $186.71. At least one of the child's parents must have been a contributor to the CPP. A child may get two benefits if both parents are deceased or disabled.

You must apply for CPP survivor benefits. Applications are available at HRDC offices and on the HRDC Web site.

Splitting CPP benefits with your significant other

You and your spouse or common-law partner can apply to receive an equal share of the CPP retirement pension you both earned during the years you were together. You must both be at least 60 years of age, and must request that your CPP be shared or "split" at the time you apply for CPP. CPP sharing or splitting is also referred to as an assignment of your CPP retirement pension. Splitting your CPP does not increase or decrease the overall retirement pension to which you and your spouse or common-law partner are entitled.

Why would you split?

The main reason for CPP splitting is to reduce the combined tax you and your spouse or common-law partner pay. This can be done when you are each in different income tax brackets. Let's take a look at an example to make this a little clearer. Assume your income, before your CPP retirement pension, is about $105,000. This puts you into the top tax bracket. The actual tax you pay will be based on the province or territory you live in. Let's say you live in a province or territory where the top tax rate is 45 percent. Let's further assume that your spouse makes $10,000, excluding his or her CPP retirement pension. At this level of income, the tax rate is about 23 percent. Your CPP retirement pension is $5,000 and your spouse's is $2,000. As illustrated in the following table, you and your spouse will pay an aggregate of $2,710 in income tax on your combined CPP retirement pension.

	You	*Spouse*	*Total*
CPP retirement pension	$5,000	$2,000	$7,000
Tax rate	45%	23%	
Tax	$2,250	$460	$2,710

Let's improve the situation. You and your spouse agree to split your CPP retirement pension. You can see that the tax is reduced to $2,380 — a $330 saving in tax, just by filling out a form!

	You	Spouse	Total
CPP retirement pension	$3,500	$3,500	$7,000
Tax rate	45%	23%	
Tax	$1,575	$805	$2,380

This result is optimal when one spouse is in the highest tax bracket (taxable income in excess of $104,649) and the other spouse is in the lowest tax bracket (taxable income of less than $32,183). The saving is enhanced further when the high-income-earning spouse also receives a CPP retirement pension significantly higher than that received by the lower-income spouse.

CPP and marriage breakdown — splitting CPP credits

CPP credits are used to determine the amount of your entitlement to a CPP retirement pension. Since spouses and common-law partners build up credits during a marriage or common-law relationship, both can share in the CPP entitlements earned while they were together. CPP credits can even be split if only one spouse or common-law partner paid into the CPP. You or your ex or one of your lawyers can apply to HRDC.

CPP or QPP overpayments

If you were required to repay a CPP or QPP amount that was paid to you in error and included in your income, you can deduct the amount repaid on line 232 of your tax return.

Line 115: Other Pensions

The dollar amounts of your various pension incomes are to be aggregated and reported on line 115 of your return. This is fairly straightforward — most pension income will be reported on T4A slips or other tax information slips.

Types of pension income

Here are descriptions of the various types of pension income:

✔ Payments from a former employer's or union's registered pension plan (box 16 of T4A slip)

If you transferred a lump sum from a pension plan to your RRSP, see comments at end of chapter under "Transferring Pension Income"

✔ Payments from an RRIF—a registered retirement income fund (T4RIF slip) and payments from an annuity (T4A slip)

(If you are under age 65, these amounts are to be reported on line 130 of your return—not on line 115. This is so the income will *not* qualify for the pension income credit. The pension credit is discussed briefly in this chapter and then in detail in Chapter 12.)

✔ Certain annuity income

Where you have purchased an annuity with non-RRSP funds, the annuity payments you receive are considered to be part interest and part capital. The capital portion is not subject to tax because it represents a partial return of the purchase price that you funded with tax-paid dollars. The interest portion is usually taxed as "interest" (hey, this makes sense!). However, if you are aged 65 or older, receipts from a "mixed annuity" (an annuity payment in which the interest and capital portion are determined by the tax rules), the interest portion is considered pension income and is reported on line 115.

A *mixed annuity* is the street name for the technical term *prescribed annuity*. The term *prescribed* implies something has been specifically determined by tax rules.

Foreign pension income

Foreign pension income refers to any pension income that is received from a source outside Canada. A common type is U.S. social security paid to a resident of Canada. To receive this you would have worked in the U.S. at some time in your life. If you worked in the U.S. or any foreign country you may have been part of a foreign employer's pension plan. When you retire you are entitled to receive your pension even though you are no longer resident in the country that is making the pension payments. You also may have served in a foreign country's armed forces. If so, you may be entitled to a pension from the respective country. Most foreign pension income is subject to tax — but not all! Immediately below, we discuss various sources of foreign pension income. We also comment on the respective tax issues of each source.

U.S. social security income

The full amount of U.S. social security income you receive is to be included on line 115. Of course, you will need to translate the U.S. dollar amount received into a Canadian dollar amount!

You can translate receipts using the exchange rate as of the day you received the social security payment. Alternatively, you can use the annual average U.S./Canada exchange rate that the CCRA provides. Choose the method that is most beneficial to you — that is, the method that translates into the lowest Canadian dollar equivalent.

On line 256 of your return, you can take a 15-percent deduction of the amount you received in U.S. social security. This results in only 85 percent of your U.S. social security being subject to tax!

Other foreign pension income

The CCRA suggests that you include the foreign pension income on line 115 of your tax return after applying the appropriate exchange rate, and then attach a note to your return indicating the type of pension and its country of origin. If the foreign country withheld tax from your pension payment, do not deduct the tax, but report the gross pension receipt. The foreign tax paid may qualify as a tax credit (referred to as a foreign tax credit) in calculating your tax liability (see Chapter 13).

Canada has a number of tax treaties with other countries. A treaty may adjust the amount of a foreign pension that is taxed in Canada. If you determine an amount is not taxable in Canada, it can be deducted on line 256 of your return. The CCRA can assist you in determining whether any part of your foreign pension is exempt from tax in Canada.

Non-Taxable Pension Income

The following should not be included in your tax return:

- ✔ Capital element of an annuity. If you are receiving annuity payments, a portion is interest and a portion is capital (in other words, a portion is part of your original purchase price or investment). Since you invested after-tax funds, you are not taxed again.

- ✔ Military and civil pensions paid under the

    - *Pension Act* (pension on death of a Canadian armed forces member)

    - *Civilian War Pensions and Allowances Act* (pensions for civilians injured in the Second World War)

    - *War Veterans Act* (pension for veterans, spouses, and dependent children)

- ✔ War service pension from other countries allied with Canada

- ✔ German compensation in respect of Nazi persecution

- ✔ Halifax disaster pension

Pension Income Credit

You can claim a pension income credit amount if you receive certain types of pension income (schedule 1, line 314 of the tax return). The maximum you are allowed is a tax credit amount up to $1,000 of eligible pension income. If your eligible pension income is less than $1,000, your credit amount will be equal to the amount of eligible pension income. For complete details, see Chapter 12, line 314.

You should remember that if you incur legal fees to establish your right to a pension benefit, the fees may be fully or partially deducted on your tax return. If so, deduct fees paid on line 232 of your return.

Transferring Pension Income

The tax rules let you, within limits, transfer lump sum pension amounts from one registered pension plan (RPP) to another RPP or to your registered retirement savings plan (RRSP). The transfer is tax-free if the funds are transferred directly from one plan to the other. In other words, you don't actually see the money—only the financial institutions do!

If the funds are directly transferred, there will be no income inclusion in your tax return and no need for you to take an offsetting deduction. The institutions involved should not issue you a T4A slip or any kind of tax information slip. You may want to transfer funds when you change jobs or take early retirement. You will often have the choice of leaving the funds or moving them elsewhere — perhaps to a new employer's pension plan. (In practice, we find this form of transfer rare. Most individuals request a transfer to an RRSP.) Your decision to move the funds will rest on the confidence you have in the RPP's investment advisor versus the confidence you have in your ability to take control of the funds (with your own investment advisor's help) through a self-directed RRSP. But be forewarned, if you transfer the funds from an RPP to an RRSP, don't expect to be able to take the funds out of the RRSP (even if you want to pay tax on the RRSP withdrawal). Most provincial pension rules require the funds to be put in a "locked-in" RRSP. This often means you can't get at the funds until you are at least age 60.

The value of your portion of your employer's RPP that you plan to transfer to an RRSP is often referred to as the "commuted value."

Chapter 6

Tips for Investment Income

• •

• •

So you might glance at the notes above and think that this chapter will be really light reading — well, as light as it gets for a tax book, of course. Only two lines on your tax return — how much can there be to know? Don't kid yourself, tons of important information is tied to lines 120 and 121. In this chapter we will look at the taxation of dividends, interest, and other investment incomes, along with the tax treatment of loans from corporations to their shareholders and employees. We will also examine the taxation of income from a trust and briefly discuss the implications of distributions from registered education savings plans. Let's dive right in . . .

Line 120: Dividends

A *dividend* is a distribution of a company's profits to its shareholders. A dividend comes from the retained earnings of a company after all expenses and taxes have been paid. You need to remember the after-tax part, especially when you distribute the profits to shareholders. When calculating the total tax paid, it is important to recall that both the corporation and the taxpayer have paid tax on this money. Too often we meet with owner-managers who only want to receive dividends (as opposed to salary) from their corporations because the tax rate on dividends is less than that on salary. Needless to say, when the total corporate plus personal tax paid is calculated they are quite disappointed to learn that they haven't discovered a new loophole in the tax system!

Whether or not you should receive dividends or salary as compensation depends on a number of factors including your marginal tax rate, the tax rate inside the corporation, and whether or not you want to generate any RRSP contribution room. As a general rule, for those individuals already in the top tax bracket who have maxed out their RRSP contribution room, it doesn't make a significant tax difference if you receive dividends or salary. If you own your own corporation and are wondering how to structure your compensation, be sure to visit a tax professional who can "crunch" some numbers for you.

In some cases it is possible to pay no tax on dividends received because of the basic personal exemption and the dividend tax credit. In some provinces you may be entitled to receive up to $29,000 in dividends and not pay any tax. Of course, this assumes that you have no other sources of income. The amount of tax-free dividends you are entitled to will depend on your province of residence, since the tax rates will differ. Be sure to visit your tax professional to find out the maximum amount you can receive in dividends and still manage to avoid the taxman.

Canadian source dividends

Canadian source dividends — that is, dividends from a Canadian resident corporation — receive special treatment when it comes to paying dividends to residents of Canada.

The treatment involves including the entire dividend in income and then grossing up or adding an additional 25 percent of the dividend into your income. This grossed-up dividend is then entitled to a dividend tax credit that reduces the gross-up by two-thirds of the one-quarter gross-up amount. Confused yet? Read on and we will explain it all.

The concept that drives most of the complicated rules in taxation both in Canada and abroad is called the "concept of integration." At its core is the idea that the total tax paid by a corporation and its shareholders should be the same tax paid by an individual who carries on the same business directly without a corporation. By using a separate tax entity — a corporation — and passing the profits to the shareholder, the shareholders pay tax once at the corporate level and again at the individual level. The theory of integration proves that although there are two levels of tax, the total tax bill is no higher than if the profits had been earned personally.

Let's work through an example. Corporation A and sole proprietor B run a successful typewriter and Telex repair business. Both entities make $1,000 in the year 2003. As shown in Table 12-1, if there were no integration, the following would happen:

Table 12-1	Non-Integrated Tax System	
	Corporation A	*Sole Proprietor B*
Income	$1,000	$1,000
Corporate tax at 20 percent	$200	$0
Income after corporate tax	$800	$1,000
Dividend	$800	$0
Personal tax at 40 percent	$320	$400
Cash remaining after tax	$480	$600

Clearly, if this were the case, no one would want to earn income through a corporation. After all, one could retain more cash after tax by running a sole proprietorship. Since it is not the government's intention to put corporate shareholders at a disadvantage when it comes to earning income, it created an elaborate system to level the playing field.

The system of calculation

The playing field was leveled by using the dividend gross-up and dividend tax credit system.

✔ Dividends from taxable corporations resident in Canada must be included in the income of an individual and grossed up by 25 percent (that is, multiplied by 1.25).

✔ A federal and provincial dividend tax credit is then calculated to offset the grossed-up dividend. The federal tax credit is two-thirds of the 25-percent gross-up. Calculated another way, the tax credit is 13.33 percent of the grossed-up dividend or 16.66 percent of the actual dividend paid.

Let's say Tom receives a $10,000 dividend from IM Canadian corporation, a Canadian resident corporation. For tax purposes, we will assume Tom has a high income and pays federal tax at a marginal 29 percent, and provincial tax at a marginal 14 percent with a dividend tax credit of 6.25 percent, as shown in Table 12-2.

Table 12-2	Integrated Tax System
Dividend received	$10,000
Gross-up (1.25 × $10,000)	$12,500
Federal tax (29% × $12,500)	$3,625
Less dividend tax credit (0.66 × $2,500)	($1,667)
Net federal tax payable ($3,625 – $1,667)	$1,958
Provincial tax (14% x $12,500)	$1,750
Less provincial dividend tax credit (6.25% × $10,000)	$625
Total tax	$3,083

As you can see, the net result of this calculation is that Tom pays about 30-percent tax on the dividend income. When this 30 percent is added to the tax the corporation has already paid, the total tax equals the tax an individual would have paid if he or she had earned the money directly instead of through the corporation.

When you receive a T3 or T5 slip reporting your dividend income for the year, you will notice that the slip has boxes that contain both the actual amount of dividends and the taxable amount of dividends paid. Be sure to include only the taxable amount of dividends on your tax return.

Stock dividends and stock splits

A *stock dividend* is a dividend that a corporation pays by issuing new shares instead of cash.

The rules for a stock dividend mirror those for a cash dividend. The only difference, of course, is you owe tax, but don't have any cash to pay the bill! The company paying the stock dividend will issue you a T5 slip showing you the amount of dividend to report on your tax return. If the company is a Canadian resident, the gross-up and dividend tax credit rules we just discussed will apply.

Be aware that a stock dividend and a stock split are not the same thing. A *stock split* is simply dividing your shares into more shares with no change to the company's share capital. A stock dividend is the result of an increase in the share capital of the paying corporation. No tax is owed on stock splits, while substantial tax can be owed on stock dividends.

Suppose Helen owns one share of ABC Corporation. The paid-up capital of her one share is $100. If the company has a two for one stock split, she would have two shares with a paid-up capital of $50 each, and no tax to pay. If instead the corporation issued a stock dividend of 100 percent, she would end up with two shares with a paid-up capital of $100 each, and tax to pay on a $100 dividend.

Foreign Dividends

Foreign dividends are dividends received from non-resident corporations. These dividends are treated in a different manner than Canadian source dividends.

✔ These dividends are not subject to the gross-up and dividend tax credit procedure.

✔ These dividends are included in income at their full amount. Even if the originating country withheld tax on the dividend, the full amount — not the dividend minus the tax withheld — is included in income.

✔ The dividends must be converted to Canadian dollars when received.

✔ Tax withheld on a foreign source dividend can be recovered by claiming a foreign tax credit. The maximum credit that can be claimed is 15 percent of the dividend (although it's possible that your credit could be less than this if you have a relatively low net income in the year and would be subject to less than a 15 percent tax rate on that dividend in Canada). After entering the full dividend amount including the amount withheld in Part II of schedule 4, you will need to work through schedule 1, to determine your foreign tax credit.

If the withholding tax exceeds the 15 percent allowable (or the amount of Canadian tax otherwise payable on that income), you can deduct the excess from your income.

✔ All dividends are included in income in Canada. Even if the dividend you received is not taxable in the country of origin, Canada does not recognize the non-taxability of dividends of other countries.

✔ If you have interests in foreign property with an original cost of more than $100,000 (in total) at any time in the year, you will need to file form T1135 "Foreign Income Verification Statement." On this form you must describe the property, the original cost, and the nature of the income earned. You must file this form with your personal tax return.

✔ If you or a group of Canadians own 10 percent or more of a foreign company, you will be required to file an information return T1134.

✔ Similar information returns must be filed if you have a 10-percent or more beneficial interest in a foreign trust.

The reporting rules for foreign-owned investment properties are complex, with numerous penalties for deficient or incomplete information. If you are in this situation, you'll require good professional advice.

Claiming dividends received by your spouse

If your spouse or common-law partner receives dividends from a Canadian resident corporation but has income that is too low to use the dividend tax credit, there is an election available to help. This election allows the higher-income spouse to transfer the dividends to his or her return. Once transferred, the dividends will be grossed up and the dividend tax credit can be claimed.

Why would you want to do this? At first glance, you'd think this would result in more tax, since the higher-income spouse is paying tax at a higher rate. But by transferring income out of the lower-income spouse's hands, you may be increasing the spousal credit that the higher-income spouse can claim. The increase in the credit, together with the fact that the higher-income spouse can use the full dividend tax credit, will offset the higher tax rate paid.

There are several restrictions on this election that you should consider:

✔ Only dividends received by your spouse can be transferred. Dividends received by other dependants are not eligible.

✔ Only dividends received from taxable Canadian corporations (that is, dividends eligible for the 25-percent gross-up) may be transferred.

✔ All the spouse's eligible dividends must be transferred. Partial transfers are not allowed.

✔ You can only make the election if you increase your spousal credit by transferring the dividends to your income. Alternatively, if you create the spousal credit by making the transfer, you will also be allowed to make the election.

If your spouse has low income, and you are claiming him or her as a dependant, and he or she earns dividends that are eligible for the gross-up and dividend tax credit, you should consider transferring those dividends to you and including them in your income.

If you are 65 years of age or older, transferring your spouse's dividends to your return could reduce your age credit if it brings your net income above $28,193.

Non-taxable dividends

Believe it or not, there are such things as non-taxable dividends. Really, there are. Read on.

Capital dividends

Dividends paid from a private corporation's capital dividend account will be non-taxable in the hands of the shareholders. What is the capital dividend account? Well, it's a special surplus account where companies accumulate income that is non-taxable. These non-taxable incomes include the following:

- ✔ Non-taxable portion of net capital gains

- ✔ Capital dividends received from other corporations

- ✔ Untaxed portion of gains on the disposition of eligible capital property

- ✔ Proceeds of life insurance less the adjusted cost base of the policy received by the corporation

Capital dividends received from private corporations are non-taxable and should not be included in the income of the receiving shareholder.

If you have your own investment holding company, check with your accountant to see if you have a capital dividend account. Since investment holding companies will generally earn some capital gains over the years, you may have the opportunity to pay yourself tax-free dividends from your company! Work with your accountant, though — there are special forms to fill out.

Don't confuse a capital dividend with a capital gains dividend. Capital gains dividends are *taxable* dividends paid by mutual funds or investment corporations.

Line 121: Interest and Other Investment Income

Interest is the consideration paid for the use of money belonging to someone else. The problem with interest is that it is taxed at the same high rate as employment and business income. This rate, as you know from Chapter 1, is much higher than the dividend or capital gains rate. With this as a motivation, many individuals and businesses have spent time and effort to structure transactions to make it appear that the income reported is of a capital or dividend nature rather than interest. To combat these efforts the *Income Tax Act* has deemed many transactions to be on account of interest, and has brought in requirements on when and how these transactions are to be included in income.

How to report interest income

Paragraph 12(1)(c) of the *Income Tax Act* requires taxpayers to include in income "any amount received or receivable by them in the year as, on account or in lieu of payment of, or in satisfaction of, interest." Simple, eh? Actually, what this means is that taxpayers can't get away with not reporting interest income just because they haven't received any payment.

Section 12(4) of the *Income Tax Act* specifies that individuals must report interest on debt obligations using the accrual method. *Accrual* simply means that interest is included in income as earned, not as received. Take Sarah, for example. She owns a $1,000 bond that earns interest of 10 percent, or $100 every year. However, Sarah only receives the interest every three years. Unfortunately, the CCRA doesn't care when Sarah receives the money; every year in her tax return she must report the $100 earned.

Types of interest income

Interest income falls into one of two broad categories: regular interest or compounded interest. *Regular interest* is interest paid on a regular basis during the term of the investment. This interest is usually reported annually to the investor on a T5 slip. *Compounded interest* is interest that is reinvested throughout the term of the investment. Once earned, the interest is added to the principle so that you can earn interest on your interest. The reporting of this type of interest is not as easy or straightforward as the regular interest.

Methods of reporting interest income

Depending on when you purchased your investments, the recording and reporting of interest can vary dramatically. The following section outlines the different reporting methods of interest income.

Interest on investments made after 1989

This is the easy one. All interest earned on debt must be accrued and included in income on an annual basis. All issuers of debt instruments are required to issue information slips to investors detailing their annual income.

Interest on investments acquired before 1990 and after 1981

Interest earned on debt during this period can be reported in several different ways at the option of the investor:

✔ Interest can be accrued and reported on an annual basis, as above.

✔ Interest can be recognized as received.

✔ Interest can be reported as it becomes receivable. Receivable interest is interest that has been fully earned, and you have a full legal right to claim it.

✔ Interest can be accrued and reported on a triennial basis from the date of acquisition — that is, interest earned on compounding investments need only be reported once every three years, starting from the year of acquisition. For example, if you bought a compounding investment in 1982, the first time you would have had to report interest would be 1985. The next time would be 1988.

 For compounding investments, you are required to use the three-year reporting rule if you do not choose one of the other options. The first reporting date will be December 31 of the third year after the debt obligation was issued. For example, if the investment was issued any time in 1985, the first reporting date was December 31, 1988.

If you receive interest from different types of debt obligations, you may report income from each using any of the above four methods, as long as they are consistently used from year to year. Once you choose to stop reporting interest on a cash basis, you are not permitted to change back to the cash method for that particular investment.

Administratively, the CCRA takes the position that similar investments must report their income in a similar way. For example, if you report interest on a government bond using the annual accrual basis, all government bonds must be reported the same way.

Interest on investments acquired before 1982

Contracts acquired before 1982 are deemed to be issued on December 31, 1988, provided they have been held continuously since 1982. The first three-year anniversary for income recognition will be December 31, 1991, or the day the investment was disposed of, whichever comes first.

Special reporting methods for certain investments

Certain investments have their own special reporting methods. These methods must be considered when making investment decisions, as they may have a significant impact on your final tax calculation.

Annuity contracts

Annuity contracts acquired after 1989 are subject to annual accrual reporting. If the annuity was acquired before 1990 and the premiums paid were fixed, then the triennial method must be used. If the payments were not fixed, the annual reporting method is required.

Investments acquired at a discount

The difference between the face value of the investment (value at maturity) and the purchase price is generally considered interest, and will be included in income at maturity. Investments that sell at a discount include T-bills. If you cash in the investment prior to maturity, you may have a capital gain or loss, in addition to interest income. See Chapter 7 for further information.

Stripped bonds

For investments in stripped bonds, you must report a portion of the total interest earned in income over each year of ownership. The interest must be accrued and reported as at its anniversary day (the day the stripped bond was initially issued and each one-year anniversary thereafter). For example, if you purchased a four-year stripped bond on August 1, 2003, and will earn $1,000 of interest in total on the stripped bond, you are not required to report any interest income in 2003, but in 2004 will report $250 (interest from August 1, 2003 to July 31, 2004 — the anniversary date).

Indexed debt obligations

Indexed debt obligations contain a provision that adjusts your return up or down depending on the effect of inflation — that is, if you are to receive 6-percent interest and inflation is running at 3 percent, the obligation will pay 9 percent to compensate for the effects of inflation. For indexed debt obligations with a fixed interest rate, you must report the interest and the adjustment factor annually and include both in income.

Canada Savings Bonds

Canada Savings Bonds have their own unique reporting rules. Here we review several types of bonds and the tax implications of holding them.

- ✔ **R bonds:** Interest on the R bond is paid and reported annually on a T5 slip until the bond matures or is disposed of.

- ✔ **C bonds:** Interest on C bonds (Compounding bonds) is not received until the bond is cashed. However, all interest must be reported annually and is taxable each year (this applies to **Series 45** bonds and up).

If you purchase Canada Savings Bonds using the payroll purchase plan, the interest charged by your employer is deductible at line 221 as a carrying charge.

Other Special Rules

- ✔ Banks and investment companies generally will not issue a T5 slip if interest earned is less than $50. You must determine how much interest was earned and report it yourself.

- ✔ Interest earned on tax refunds must be included in income in the year it was received.

- ✔ You must report interest income on joint accounts in the same proportion as your contributions to the account, regardless of whose name appears on the T5. For example, if you and your spouse have a joint account, and you contribute 60 percent of the funds, you must report 60 percent of the interest income.

Interest on foreign source income

Interest from foreign sources is subject to many of the same rules as dividends from foreign sources we talk about earlier in this chapter.

- ✔ The interest income must be converted to Canadian dollars when received.

- ✔ The full amount of the interest must be included in your income regardless of whether or not you received all the funds (for example, because tax was withheld at the source country).

- ✔ A foreign tax credit can be claimed for taxes withheld by the source country.

- ✔ If the withholding tax paid to the source country is in excess of 15 percent of the income (or your Canadian tax otherwise owing on that income if your tax rate is less than 15 percent), you may deduct the excess from your income. This deduction is done on schedule 4 under "carrying charges (specify)." The same rules as were explained in the foreign dividend section determine how much foreign tax credit can be claimed.

- ✔ For investments made after 1989, interest earned but not paid on a regular basis must be accrued and included in income on an annual basis.

- ✔ For investments made before 1990, you may use the three-year accrual method.

If you had to accrue foreign interest into your income but have not yet received money on account of that interest, consider signing waivers with the CCRA for the years in question. By signing the waivers, you keep these years open and will be able to claim the foreign tax credit when the interest payments are eventually received by filing a T1 Adjustment. See Chapter 15 for more information on waivers and filing T1 adjustments.

Shareholder and employee loans

Shareholder and employee loans have been the focus of numerous court challenges and legislative changes over the years. The primary concern the government has with these arrangements is that, if structured correctly, they can become vehicles for corporations to distribute all their profit and retained earnings to shareholders and employees on a totally tax-free basis. By extending no-interest indefinite loans, the corporations could give you all the money you wanted with no tax implications to you or the company. Banning these loans altogether is not the answer. The government recognizes that in certain situations loans from a company to an employee or shareholder are necessary for the successful operation of the business. With the above parameters in mind, the government has formulated tax legislation that allows corporations to extend loans when necessary, but which places very restrictive rules on these loans in an attempt to prevent a tax-free extraction of earnings.

The rules that we will discuss extend not only to shareholders and employees, but also to related individuals, companies, trusts, partnerships, and so on. Through years of experience, the CCRA has seen many variations of the general theme of getting money out of a company with no tax paid, and is therefore prepared to challenge anything that falls outside the strict interpretation of the rules.

In general, you must include all loans to shareholders or persons who are not dealing at arm's length with shareholders in the income of the shareholder or the non-arm's length person in the year the loan was made. The same rules apply if you become indebted to a corporation in some manner — for example, you buy a vehicle from the company and pay for it with a promissory note. This being tax, there are exceptions to this general rule. Where would we be without exceptions?

General exceptions to the rule

Shareholder loans will not be included in income in the following situations:

- ✔ The indebtedness is between non-resident persons.

- ✔ The loan is made in the ordinary course of business of loaning money, provided that bona fide repayment arrangements are made at the time of the loan. This exception prevents loans to shareholders of banks or other financial institutions from being included in their income.

- ✔ The loan is repaid within one year from the end of the corporation's taxation year. For example, if the loan is made in 2003 and the corporation's year-end is December 31, 2003, the loan must be repaid by December 31, 2004, to avoid the entire amount being included in the shareholder's 2003 income.

The loan cannot be part of a series of loans and repayments. This means you can't repay the loan, then take out another loan — in theory, you really haven't paid back the original amount. The CCRA will ensure that if you use this strategy, you will be required to report the amount of the loan in income.

Specific exceptions to the rule

The *Income Tax Act* allows loans to be made to shareholders who are employees, under the following very specific conditions:

- The loan is made to an employee who is not a specified employee — that is, one who owns less than 10 percent of the shares of the corporation.
- The loan was made to an employee to assist him or her in acquiring a home for his or her own occupation.
- The loan was made to an employee to assist him or her in purchasing previously unissued shares of the corporation.
- The loan was made to an employee to assist him or her in acquiring a motor vehicle required to perform duties of employment.

    For these exemptions to be valid, two conditions must also be met:

- The loan arose because of the employee's employment and not because of his or her shareholdings. In simpler terms, the loan must be available to all employees, or at least all employees of a particular class (for example, management), not just shareholding employees.
- There must be a bona fide repayment arrangement in place. This means that there must be an agreement in place for the loan to be repaid within a reasonable period of time.

Where loans are made to a shareholder to purchase a home, to purchase treasury shares of the corporation or to buy a car, the principal amount of the loan will not be included in the shareholder's income, provided the loan was made to the shareholder in his or her capacity as an employee and bona fide arrangements were made at the time of the loan for repayment within a reasonable period of time.

For owner-managers it may be difficult to prove that the loan was made because the person was an employee, not a shareholder. The CCRA has said that it is their view that loans made to a person will be by virtue of his or her shareholdings in the corporation where the shareholder can significantly influence business policy. Nevertheless, an employee-shareholder may be able to have the loan excluded from income if he or she can establish that other employees who perform similar duties and responsibilities for a similar-sized employer — but who are not shareholders in that employer-corporation — received loans or other indebtedness of similar amounts under similar conditions.

Forgiven loans

If a loan or debt is forgiven, the forgiven amount is a taxable benefit and is added to the income of the shareholder or employee in accordance with the debt forgiveness rules.

If you are the beneficiary of a forgiven loan, you should consult a tax professional. In certain situations, the debt forgiveness rules can be complicated.

Imputed interest on shareholder and employee loans

If you receive a low-interest or no-interest loan because of your shareholding or past, present, or future (there's a catch-all!) employment, you will be deemed to have received a benefit from employment. The taxable portion of the benefit is equal to the difference between the interest paid in the year (or within 30 days after the year-end) and the prescribed interest determined by the CCRA. This rate is updated quarterly and can be found on the CCRA Web site at www.ccra-adrc.gc.ca.

A loan received solely because of your shareholding will be included in income if it is not paid back before the second year-end of the corporation making the loan. For the period that the loan is outstanding before the second year-end, an interest benefit will be included in your income if the interest rate charged is below the prescribed rate. If the loan is then taken into income, the interest benefit will be reversed for the years of inclusion. Loans made to a shareholder in your capacity as an employee can escape the income inclusion if the loan falls into one of the above exceptions. However, this loan will still be subject to the imputed interest benefit if the interest rate charged is below the prescribed rate.

Let's say that Dale receives a loan from his employer for $100,000 at 0-percent interest on January 1, 2003. Dale is not a shareholder and therefore does not have to meet one of the exemptions to avoid income inclusion. The loan is outstanding until December 31, 2003. Assuming a prescribed rate of 4 percent, what is Dale's interest benefit? Dale will be deemed to have an interest benefit of $4,000 ($100,000 × 4 percent). This amount will be added to Dale's 2003 income. Any interest Dale paid on this loan would have reduced the benefit.

If Dale had used the funds to earn income from business or property, or to purchase an automobile or aircraft for use in employment, he would be allowed an offsetting deduction equal to the interest benefit.

Remember that if you receive a loan from your employer, try to arrange to pay the interest portion on January 30 of the following year. This will save you some cash in the current year and still keep you onside in terms of interest payments.

Special situations

Loans for the purchase or relocation of a home are given special treatment when it comes to calculating the interest benefits.

- ✔ **Home loans:** If the loan is made to you as a home purchase loan, the rate used to calculate the imputed interest benefit for the first five years will never be greater than the prescribed rate at the time the loan was made. When the five years are over, the continuation of the loan is considered a new loan, and the prescribed rate in effect on that day will be the maximum rate charged for the next five years. For example, Maureen receives a home purchase loan on January 1, 2002, at an interest rate of 0 percent. On January 1, 2002, the prescribed interest rate is 3 percent. Over the next five years, Maureen's taxable benefit will be calculated using a prescribed rate that could be less than 3 percent but will never be more.

- ✔ **Home relocation loans:** If the loan is a home relocation loan — that is, a loan to help you purchase a home that is at least 40 kilometres closer to a new work location — you will receive a special deduction in the calculation of the interest benefit. The benefit for the first five years will be reduced by an amount equal to the interest imputed on $25,000 (assuming your loan is at least $25,000). In effect, the benefit on the first $25,000 of the loan will be deducted from the income inclusion.

Registered Education Savings Plan Income (RESP)

RESPs are quickly becoming one of the most popular ways for Canadians to save for a child's education. In a nutshell, here's how they work: A person (usually a parent or grandparent but it could be someone else) places funds in the plan for the benefit of a child. Although there is no tax deduction for RESP contributions (like the one for RRSPs), funds within the plan can grow tax sheltered. It is not until funds are withdrawn from the plan that tax is payable, and it's important to note that only the *growth* in the plan is taxable.

The investment income earned by an RESP is not taxable in the hands of the contributor. Instead, the income becomes taxable income of the student when he or she removes the money for educational purposes. The advantage of having the tax paid by the student is that the student probably has little or no other income, and the tax will be payable at the lowest marginal tax rate. So, if you're a student and received a tax slip this year from an RESP, you'll have to report the income on your tax return.

Distribution from an RESP

If the beneficiaries of the RESP do not attend an institution of higher education, the contributions and the income earned from these contributions (accumulated income payments) can be returned to the contributor. While the initial contributions can be withdrawn tax-free, the accumulated income can only be withdrawn under certain circumstances:

- ✔ The plan must have existed for at least ten years.
- ✔ The beneficiaries are at least 21 years of age and will not be attending an institution of higher learning.
- ✔ The contributor must be a resident of Canada.

If these requirements are met, the contributions and the accumulated income can be withdrawn. This withdrawal will be taxable in the hands of the contributor, and will be subject to a hefty penalty tax.

If the RESP is not used within 25 years of its initiation, it will automatically be returned to the contributor. Any income returned (under any circumstance) to the contributor will be hit with a special penalty surtax of 20 percent on top of the regular tax payable on this income. The surtax can be partially avoided if you transfer the accumulated income directly to an RRSP (among a few other planning techniques). The maximum amount that can be transferred is $50,000. In order to transfer funds to your RRSP, you will have to have sufficient RRSP contribution room. If the contributor passes away, the contributor's spouse can use the RRSP transfer option.

File form T1171 "Tax Withholding Waiver on Accumulated Income Payments from RESPs" to avoid tax being withheld on amounts that will be transferred directly to your RRSP.

Example: Simon contributed the maximum amount of $42,000 to his son Jacuzzi's RESP. By the time Jacuzzi realized that he did not want to go to university, the plan had been in existence for 20 years and he was 25 years old. The value of the plan had grown to $142,000.

Simon decided to end the RESP and take back the contributions plus the accumulated income. At the time Simon decided to take back the money, he had $55,000 in unused RRSP deduction room. How much income will Simon have to pay the 20-percent surtax on?

Amount withdrawn		$142,000
Return of Contribution		$42,000
Amount to include in income		$100,000
Less the lesser of		
a) Amount Simon contributed to his RRSP	$55,000	
b) Lifetime RRSP transfer limit	$50,000	$50,000
Net income subject to tax and 20-percent surtax		$50,000

Other Investment Income

Line 121 of your income tax return is designed to capture all interest and other investment income. Believe it or not, there are still other forms of investment income on which we have not yet touched. In this section we highlight some of the more recognizable forms of other investment income you may have to claim on your tax return.

Mutual funds

Mutual funds are groups of assets managed by professionals. The assets managed can range from real estate to mortgages to stocks and bonds. Investors in mutual funds receive T5s if they invested in a mutual fund corporation, or T3s if they invested in a mutual fund trust. The income that is distributed to the mutual fund's unit holders retains its identity, which means that income earned as dividends by the fund is still regarded as dividends when it is distributed to the investors. As a result, investors can receive interest, dividends, capital gains, foreign income, or capital dividends from a mutual fund trust. Only capital gains and dividends (not interest or foreign income) can be distributed to investors of mutual fund corporations. If you invest in foreign mutual funds and receive payments from these funds, the payments will be classified as regular income. The shares of mutual funds are capital property that will generate capital gains or losses on disposition.

Foreign fund payments do not retain the characteristics of the underlying assets when paid to Canadian investors. Therefore, amounts received will be fully taxable here in Canada. If any tax is withheld by the foreign country, this tax is eligible for a foreign tax credit.

Very often, funds automatically reinvest distributions to the fund holders in new shares of the fund. In these situations, although you never see any of the cash, you will be taxed on the income distributed. This is why you may have received a tax slip this year even though you didn't see any cash coming into your account. Be sure to keep track of the reinvestments since they will increase your adjusted cost base and can help minimize capital gains when you eventually sell the investment.

Royalties

Royalties are payments you receive for the use of your property. This income can be classified as business or investment income, depending on its nature. Royalties received for writing a book are business income, while royalties received for the use of property you purchased are investment income.

Annuities

Annuities are amounts payable on a periodic basis according to a contract, will, or trust. Report the interest income earned from an annuity at line 121, unless the recipient is 65 years of age or older and receiving retirement income, in which case you report the interest at line 115.

Labour-sponsored venture capital corporations

Labour-sponsored venture capital funds are sponsored by organized labour to provide venture capital to start-up businesses. Investments in the funds generally offer special tax credits both federally and provincially. Investments can be withdrawn at any time, but penalties usually apply if money is withdrawn before eight years. If successful, the fund could generate the same income streams mutual funds provide to their investors.

Exempt life insurance contracts

Offered by insurance companies, exempt life insurance contracts allow you to pay life insurance premiums and make deposits to a tax-sheltered investment account (up to certain limits). The investments are allowed to grow tax-free inside the plan and can be withdrawn tax-free if they form part of the death benefit paid to the beneficiary. Alternatively, funds can be withdrawn tax-free as a loan against the policy (if the loan is obtained from a third-party bank — not the insurance company), which is then repaid from the death benefit. However, be careful when money is removed from a life insurance policy during the insured's lifetime — tax could result. Universal life insurance is one of the most popular types of exempt life insurance that can be used for investment purposes.

Income of a trust beneficiary

In the simplest trust, the total income equals any income generated by the assets held by the trust less any deductions for amounts paid to the beneficiaries of the trust. Income is paid to a beneficiary when the recipient receives the payment or when a payment has been allocated to the beneficiary to which they have a legally enforceable right to receive the payment (i.e., the income is paid or payable to the beneficiary).

Income of the beneficiaries

Amounts deducted from the trust's net income that are paid or payable to the beneficiaries are taxed on the beneficiaries' personal tax returns. This income is reported on a T3 slip. The income retains its original identity even after being paid to the beneficiaries. The term *retaining its identity* means that income that was earned as dividends by the trust remains as dividends in the hands of the beneficiaries. This flow-through of income allows beneficiaries to take advantage of the dividend tax credit on dividends from Canadian corporations or the foreign tax credits on foreign source income. Beneficiaries are also allowed the capital gains deductions on qualified farm property and qualified shares of a small business corporation, provided the trust is resident in Canada. Trusts are also permitted to pass on non-taxable dividends that, when received by the beneficiary, are excluded from income. The only exception is net capital losses, which do not flow through to the beneficiaries.

Chapter 7

Tips for Capital Gains and Losses

• •

In This Chapter

▶ Calculating a taxable capital gain or loss

▶ Sorting out capital gains versus ordinary income

▶ Understanding types of capital property

▶ Understanding capital gains exemptions

▶ Dealing with cumulative net investment losses

▶ Getting a handle on the capital gains reserve

• •

*I*n this chapter we will provide you with the general information you need to report a capital gain or loss. You'll be treated to tons of definitions and savvy tips to minimize your tax liability. What is a capital gain or loss, you ask? Well, read on.

Line 127: Taxable Capital Gains or Allowable Capital Losses

To calculate any capital gain or loss, you need to know the following three amounts:

✔ The proceeds of disposition

✔ The adjusted cost base (ACB)

✔ The costs related to selling your property

To calculate your capital gain or loss, subtract the total of your property's ACB and any outlays and expenses involved in selling your property, from the proceeds of disposition. The result is your capital gain (or loss). Only 50 percent of the gain is taxable to you (and only 50 percent of a loss is deductible — and only against capital gains!).

Do not include any capital gains or losses in your business or property income even if you used the property for your business.

Calculation of adjusted cost base

The adjusted cost base of a property is usually the purchase price of the property plus any expenses incurred to acquire it, such as commissions and legal fees. The cost of a capital property is its actual or deemed cost, depending on the type of property and how you acquired it.

For example, the cost is normally the amount you paid to buy the asset. However, there are many situations when figuring out your cost is a little more complicated. Here are some examples:

✔ If you make improvements to a capital asset, such as a major overhaul of your family cottage, the cost of these improvements will increase your ACB.

✔ If you inherit an asset, your ACB is the market value of that asset on the day you took ownership of it (although special rules apply if you've inherited the asset from your spouse).

✔ If you are a newcomer to Canada, your ACB is the market value (not your purchase price) of your asset on the day you became a Canadian resident for tax purposes.

✔ If you reinvest distributions, such as dividends, earned on your investments, these reinvestments should be used to increase your ACB.

✔ If you elected to crystallize a capital gain back in 1994 in order to use your lifetime capital gains exemption, your elected amount becomes your new ACB.

Identical properties

If you own "identical properties," you'll have to do a special calculation to figure out your ACB. You may have identical properties if you've purchased shares of the same class of the capital stock of a corporation or units of a mutual fund trust over time. If you've bought and sold several identical properties at different prices over a period of time, to determine your ACB you have to calculate the average cost of each property in the group at the time of each purchase. You determine the average cost by dividing the total cost of identical properties purchased (usually the cost of the property plus any expenses involved in acquiring it) by the total number of identical properties owned.

Partial dispositions of capital property

When you sell only part of a property, you have to divide the adjusted cost base (ACB) of the property between the part you sell and the part you keep.

Graeme owns 100 hectares of vacant land with a cost base of $100,000. He decides to sell 25 hectares of this land. Since 25 is $1/4$ of 100, Graeme calculates $1/4$ of the total ACB as follows:

Total ACB	$100,000
Minus: The ACB of the part he sold ($100,000 × $1/4$)	– 25,000
The ACB of the part he kept	= $75,000

Therefore, Graeme's ACB is $25,000 for the 25 hectares he sold.

Proceeds of disposition

The proceeds of disposition is usually the amount you received or will receive for your property. In most cases, it refers to the sale price of the property. This is fairly straightforward if you are selling property such as publicly traded stocks or mutual funds on the market — the proceeds are the amount you'll receive on the sale.

You may think that just because you haven't received any proceeds from a sale, you have no capital gain (or loss) to report. A common example of this occurs when you gift assets to a family member. In these situations, you may be "deemed" to receive fair market value proceeds at the time the gift (or sale for less than fair market proceeds) took place. It doesn't matter how much cash actually changed hands!

Selling costs

These are costs that you incurred to sell a capital property. You can deduct outlays and expenses from your proceeds of disposition when calculating your capital gain or capital loss. You cannot, however, reduce your other income by claiming a deduction for these outlays and expenses (as you can in the case of a carrying charge deduction on schedule 4). The types of expense that may be used to reduce your capital gain (or increase your capital loss) include fixing-up expenses, finders' fees, commissions, brokers' fees, surveyors' fees, legal fees, transfer taxes, and advertising costs.

Calculation of taxable capital gains

You have a capital gain when you sell, or are considered to have sold, a capital property for more than its ACB plus the outlays and expenses related to the sale of the property. For transactions occurring during 2003, you have to report one-half of your capital gains as income on your return. Capital gains, once reduced to their inclusion amount, are called *taxable capital gains*.

Let's say that in March 2003, Lynne sold 1,000 shares of ABC Public Corporation of Canada for $7,500. She received the full proceeds at the time of the sale and paid a commission of $80. The adjusted cost base of the shares is $3,500. Lynne calculates her capital gain as follows:

Calculation of Capital Gain on Sale of ABC Co. Shares

Proceeds of disposition	$7,500
Less: Adjusted cost base	$3,500
Less: Outlays and expenses on disposition	$80
Equals: Capital gain	$3,920

Because only one-half of the capital gain is taxable, Lynne reports $1,960 as her taxable capital gain on her return.

Calculation of allowable capital losses

You have a capital loss when you sell, or are considered to have sold, a capital property for less than its ACB plus the outlays and expenses related to the sale of the property. For transactions occurring during 2003, you can deduct one-half of your capital losses, or your allowable capital losses, against the current year's taxable capital gains.

Allowable capital losses can only be used to offset capital gains and not other types of income. Losses that cannot be used in 2003 can be carried back three years or forward indefinitely to offset taxable capital gains in those years (and therefore reduce taxable income in those years!).

Capital Gains Versus Ordinary Income

Usually, you have a capital gain or capital loss when you sell or are considered to have disposed of a *capital property*. The question as to whether or not a property is a capital property can be a difficult one to answer. The judgment depends on both the nature of the property and the manner in which the owner manages the property. If the owner intends to realize a profit from the property versus hold the property for the income it produces, the gain or loss realized on sale is treated as an ordinary income gain or loss as opposed to a capital gain or loss.

Often it helps to understand the difference between capital and income in relation to the taxpayer's intention by thinking about the scenario of a tree and its fruit. If the taxpayer bought the tree with the intention of selling the fruit, then any subsequent sale of the tree would be on account of capital. If, however, the taxpayer purchased the tree intending to sell the tree and make a quick buck, then the transaction would be treated as income — and 100 percent of any gain would be taxable.

In deciding whether the gain or loss is on account of income or capital, the tax courts have used the following tests:

- **The period of ownership:** If property has been held for only a short period, it may be considered to have been purchased to be resold and therefore the profits may be treated as income. A property held for a longer period is more likely to be treated as capital.

- **Improvement and development:** Where a systematic effort has been made to make a property more marketable, it may indicate a business of selling properties.

- **Relationship of the transaction to the taxpayer's ordinary business:** The more similar the transaction is to the taxpayer's ordinary business, the more likely it is that the transaction will be treated as income (for example, the sale of a renovated home by a general contractor).

- **Reasons for and nature of sale:** If the sale of a property is the result of an active campaign to sell it as opposed to the result of something unanticipated at the time of purchase, the profits may be considered on account of income.

- **The frequency of similar transactions:** A history of buying and selling similar properties, or of quick turnovers, may indicate the taxpayer is carrying on a business.

Falling offside on one of these tests does not mean the transaction will automatically be considered capital or income. The courts look at the larger picture, and you may have the opportunity to argue either way.

In an ideal situation, you would have your gains treated as capital and your losses treated as income. The reason for this is twofold: one, capital gains are only 50-percent taxable in Canada, while business income is fully taxable; and two, capital losses can only be applied against capital gains, while a business loss can be applied against any source of income to reduce tax. For the average stock and mutual fund investor, this will be difficult. However, if you are planning to sell other types of capital property, it is something to think about.

Types of Capital Property

Capital gains and losses are reported on schedule 3 of your tax return. Schedule 3 is divided into the following sections.

Real estate

The real estate section is used to report a capital gain or loss if you sell any of the following types of property during the year:

- ✔ Vacant land

- ✔ Rental property (both land and buildings)

- ✔ Farm property, including both land and buildings (other than qualified farm property)

- ✔ Commercial and industrial land and buildings

This section should not be used to report the sale of personal use property — that is, your residence or the sale of mortgages and other similar debt obligations on real property. Report these types of transactions under the appropriately named sections (see later in this chapter).

If you sell a property that includes land and a building, you must determine how much of the selling price and original cost relates to each of the land and the building. The sales of these items must be reported separately on schedule 3.

If the building was used in a business or rental activity and you claimed capital cost allowance on the building in any past tax year, your situation is slightly more complex. In addition to a potential capital gain, you may also have recapture or terminal loss to deal with. See "Depreciable property" for more info.

Mutual fund units and shares

This section is used to report a capital gain or loss when you sell shares or securities that are not described in any other section of schedule 3. These shares or securities include the following:

- ✔ Publicly traded shares

- ✔ Units in a mutual fund trust

- ✔ Shares that qualify as Canadian securities or prescribed securities, provided they are not qualified small business corporation shares or qualified family farm corporation shares

- ✔ Shares issued by foreign corporations

This section should also be used if you make a donation of the following properties:

✔ Securities listed on a prescribed stock exchange

✔ Shares of the capital stock of a mutual fund corporation

✔ Units in a mutual fund trust

✔ Interest in a related segregated fund trust

If you donate publicly traded shares or mutual fund units, you'll be deemed to have disposed of them at their current fair market value. Any capital gain that results is just one-quarter taxable — half of the normal inclusion rate of one-half. You'll still receive a donation slip equal to the fair market value of your shares. If you have donated any of these properties to a qualified donee, use form T1170 "Capital Gains on Gifts of Certain Capital Property," to calculate the capital gain to report on schedule 3. If you sold any of the items listed above in 2003, you will receive either a T5008 slip "Statement of Securities Transactions," or an account statement from your investment dealer.

If you own shares or units of a mutual fund, capital gains can arise in two ways:

✔ When you sell your shares or units of the mutual fund, a capital gain (or loss) will result from the difference between your proceeds of disposition and the adjusted cost base of the investment. Report these amounts in the "Mutual fund units and other shares including publicly traded shares" area of schedule 3.

✔ Capital gains realized by the mutual fund from its investment portfolio can be flowed out to you as distributions. You should receive information slips from your investment dealer (usually a T3 or T5 slip) detailing the amounts to be reported in this situation.

Bonds, debentures, promissory notes, and other properties

This section is used to report capital gains or losses from the disposition of bonds, debentures, treasury bills, promissory notes, bad debts, foreign exchange transactions, and options, as well as discounts, premiums, and bonuses on debt obligations.

Treasury bills (T-bills) and stripped bonds

When a T-bill or a stripped bond is issued at a discount and you keep it until it matures, the difference between the issue price and the amount you cash it in for is considered to be interest that accrued to you. However, if you sell the T-bill or stripped bond before it matures, in addition to the interest accrued at that time, you may have a capital gain or capital loss. Before you calculate your capital gain or loss, you have to determine the amount of interest accumulated to the date of disposition. Subtract the interest from the proceeds of disposition, and calculate the capital gain or loss in the usual manner.

Foreign currencies

The foreign currencies section is used to report capital gains or capital losses realized by virtue of fluctuations in foreign currencies on investments you've sold. Provided that the foreign currency transactions are capital in nature (which they generally are if the underlying investment was capital — such as a share), they are treated in the same way as any other capital gain or loss. The only difference is that the first $200 of gain realized is not taxable and the first $200 of loss cannot be claimed as a capital loss. Before deducting the $200 amount from the capital gain or loss determined, all capital gains and losses from foreign currency must be netted and the $200 exemption applied against the net foreign exchange gain or loss for the year.

There is no place on schedule 3 to report your reduction for exchange gains or losses. Therefore, a reduction in the gain can simply be reflected as a reduction in the proceeds of disposition. Remember, if you've increased your loss because of an exchange loss, you must increase your proceeds by the amount of the loss, up to $200.

Mortgage foreclosures and conditional sale repossessions

You may have held a mortgage on a property but had to repossess the property later because the debtor failed to pay all or a part of the amount owed under the terms of the mortgage. In this case, you may have to report a capital gain or a capital loss on this section of schedule 3.

A *mortgagee* is a person who lends money under a mortgage on a property. A *mortgagor* is a person who borrows money under a mortgage.

If, as a mortgagee, you repossess a property because the mortgagor failed to pay you the money owed under the terms of the mortgage, you are considered to have purchased the property. At the time of repossession, you do not have a capital gain or a capital loss. Any gain or loss will be postponed until you sell the property. If you are the mortgagor and your property isrepossessed because you do not pay the money owed under the terms of the mortgage, you are considered to have sold the property. Depending on the amount you owed at the time of repossession, you may have a capital gain, a capital loss, or, in the case of depreciable property, a terminal loss. However, if the property is personal-use property (such as your principal residence), you cannot deduct the loss.

Capital gains from a mortgage foreclosure or a conditional sales repossession will be excluded from net income when you calculate your claim for the Goods and Services Tax/Harmonized Sales Tax credit, the Canada Child Tax Benefit, and the age amount. You should also exclude this income when calculating your social benefits repayment.

Personal-use property

The personal-use property section is used to report capital gains from the disposition of personal-use property. This obviously needs some elaboration.

Many people are not affected by the capital gains rules because the property they own is for their personal use. When you sell such property — for example, cars, boats, and jewellery — usually you do not end up with a capital gain. This is because this type of property generally does not increase in value over the years. In fact, because these items may depreciate in value, you may actually end up with a loss. Although you have to report any gain on the sale of personal-use property (PUP) on your tax return, you are not ordinarily allowed to claim a loss.

To calculate any capital gain or loss realized when you dispose of personal-use property, follow these rules:

- ✔ If the adjusted cost base (ACB) of the property is less than $1,000, its ACB is considered to be $1,000.

- ✔ If the proceeds of disposition are less than $1,000, the proceeds of disposition are considered to be $1,000.

- ✔ If both the ACB and the proceeds of disposition are $1,000 or less, you do not have a capital gain or a capital loss. Do not report the sale on schedule 3 when you file your return.

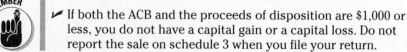

The result? When you dispose of personal-use property that has an ACB or proceeds of disposition of more than $1,000, you may have a capital gain or loss. The bad news is that you have to report any capital gain from disposing of personal-use property. However, the even worse news is that if you have a capital loss, you usually cannot deduct that loss when you calculate your income for the year, including using the loss to decrease capital gains on other personal-use property. This is because if a property depreciates through personal use, the resulting loss on its disposition is a personal expense.

These loss restrictions do not apply under the following circumstances:

- ✔ If you disposed of personal-use property that is "listed personal property" (see the next section); or

- ✔ If a bad debt is owed to you from the sale of a personal-use property to a person with whom you deal at arm's length (in other words, a third party). In this case you can claim the bad debt owed to you as a capital loss; however, your claim cannot be more than the capital gain previously reported on the sale of the property.

If you sell your home — your principal residence — for more than what it cost you, you usually do not have to report the sale on your return or pay tax on any gain (see the "Sale of a principal residence" section of this chapter for more details).

Listed personal property

The listed personal property section is used to report capital gains or capital losses from the disposition of very specific types of property. Listed personal property (LPP) is a type of personal-use property. The principal difference between LPP and other personal-use properties is that LPP usually increases in value over time. LPP includes the following properties:

- ✔ Rare manuscripts or rare books

- ✔ Prints, etchings, drawings, paintings, sculptures, or other similar works of art

- ✔ Jewellery

- ✔ Stamps and coins

To determine the value of many of these items, you can have them appraised by art, coin, jewellery, book, and stamp dealers. Because LPP is personal-use property, the $1,000 minimum proceeds of disposition and adjusted cost base rules apply. See the previous section, "Personal-use property," for more information about these rules.

There is one very important difference, for tax purposes, between PUP and LPP. If losses are generated on the disposition of LPP, these losses are not, well, lost. In fact, the losses can be used to offset gains generated on LPP this year, in the previous three years or in any of the seven subsequent tax years.

Keep a record of your LPP losses that have not expired, so you can apply these losses against LPP gains in other years. An unapplied LPP loss expires if you do not use it by the end of the seventh year after it was incurred.

Depreciable property

Depreciable property is a special kind of capital property on which capital gains must be calculated. *Depreciable property* is defined as capital property used to earn income from a business or property. Common examples are buildings used as rental properties, computer equipment, or office furniture. You can write off the cost of the property as capital cost allowance over a number of years, meaning that at the time the asset is sold, undepreciated capital cost (UCC) will likely be less than the original purchase price. This UCC is a key number in calculating the tax liability on the sale of a depreciable asset.

When you dispose of depreciable property, you may have a capital gain but not a capital loss. But the tax implications don't end there. You may also be required to add a recapture of CCA to your income or you may be allowed to claim a terminal loss.

Recapture of CCA and terminal losses

We'll now do our best to explain the (sometimes complicated) recapture and terminal loss rules. When you sell a depreciable property for less than its adjusted cost base (usually the purchase price), but for more than the UCC in its class, you do not have a capital gain. In these situations you have nothing to report on schedule 3. Generally, the UCC of a class is the total capital cost of all the properties of the class, minus the CCA you claimed in previous years.

If you sell depreciable property in a year, you must subtract from the UCC the lesser of:

✔ The proceeds of disposition of the property, *minus* the related outlays and expenses; and

✔ The capital cost of the property at the time of sale.

If, after performing the above calculation, the UCC of a class has a *negative* balance at the end of the year, this amount is considered to be a *recapture* of CCA. Think of it this way: recapture occurs when you've taken so much CCA over the years that you've actually depreciated the asset, for tax purposes, beyond its true value. The government is now asking for these past tax deductions back. Include this recapture in income for the year of sale. The bad news is, recapture is not a capital gain — it is 100-percent taxable.

If the UCC of a class has a *positive* balance at the end of the year, and you do not have any properties left in that class, this amount is a *terminal loss*. A terminal loss means you didn't depreciate your asset for tax purposes (through CCA) enough, so in the year of sale you get a "catch-up" tax deduction. Unlike a capital loss, the full amount of terminal loss can be deducted from income in that year. If the balance for the UCC of a class is zero at the end of the year, you do not have a recapture of CCA or a terminal loss.

Recapture and terminal losses are not considered to be capital items (which is why they are not reported on schedule 3). Instead, these calculations will be done on the particular schedule you normally calculate CCA on — most commonly a rental or business-related schedule on your tax return.

Let's say that in 1996, Kirk bought a piece of machinery, at a cost of $15,000, for his business. It is the only property in its class at the beginning of 2003. The class has a UCC of $11,000. He sold the piece of machinery in 2003 and did not buy any other property in that class. The chart below gives you three different selling prices (proceeds of disposition).

Calculation of Capital Gain	*A*	*B*	*C*
Proceeds of disposition	$5,000	$15,000	$20,000
Minus: Capital cost	$15,000	$15,000	$15,000
Capital gain	$0	$0	$5,000

Calculation of Terminal *Loss or Recapture of CCA*	*A*	*B*	*C*
Capital cost	$15,000	$15,000	$15,000
Minus: CCA (1996 – 2002)	– $4,000	– $4,000	– $4,000
UCC at beginning of 2003	$11,000	$11,000	$11,000
Minus the lesser of:			
The capital cost of $15,000 and the proceeds of disposition	$5,000	$15,000	$15,000
Terminal loss (or recapture)	$6,000	($4,000)	($4,000)

Example A: Kirk does not have a capital gain, but he does have a terminal loss of $6,000 that he can deduct from his business income in 2003.

Example B: Kirk does not have a capital gain, but he does have recapture of CCA of $4,000 that he has to include in his business income in 2003.

Example C: Kirk has a capital gain of $5,000 and he has recapture of CCA of $4,000 that he has to include in his business income in 2003.

Eligible capital property

Any sale of eligible capital property in 2003 must also be reported on schedule 3.

Eligible capital property is property that does not physically exist but that gives you a lasting economic benefit — for example, goodwill, customer lists, trademarks, and milk quotas.

The taxation rules for eligible capital property are similar to those for depreciable property.

When Does a Disposition Occur?

It may seem silly to have a whole section to explain when a disposition occurs. You would think this is a pretty self-explanatory thing — you sell an asset, so you've disposed of it. But as you've probably discovered by now, tax is not always so straightforward. In fact, you may be surprised when a disposition for tax purposes is triggered.

A disposition usually occurs with an event or transaction where you relinquish possession, control, and all other aspects of property ownership. Simply put, you just sell the asset.

However, you can also have a *deemed disposition* where you are considered to have disposed of property even though you did not actually sell it.

The following are examples of cases, other than an outright sale, in which you are considered to have disposed of capital property:

- ✔ You exchange one property for another.

- ✔ You give property (other than cash) as a gift.

- ✔ You convert shares or other securities in your name.

- ✔ You settle or cancel a debt owed to you.

- ✔ You transfer property to certain trusts (one exception is a transfer to an alter-ego trust).

- ✔ Your property is expropriated.

- ✔ Your property is stolen or destroyed.

- ✔ An option that you hold to buy or sell property expires.

- ✔ A corporation redeems or cancels shares or other securities that you hold (you will usually be considered to have received a dividend, the amount of which will be shown on a T5 slip).

- ✔ You change all or part of the property's use (for example, the change of use of your primary residence to a rental property).

- ✔ You leave Canada.

- ✔ The owner of the property dies.

In some of the instances noted above, you will be deemed to have disposed of your property for fair market value proceeds even though you did not receive any actual proceeds. This, as you might be thinking, may make it difficult to pay the resulting tax bill! Be sure to visit a tax professional to understand the consequences before you cause a deemed disposition.

Sale of a Principal Residence

When you sell your home, you may realize a capital gain. If the property was your only principal residence for every year you owned it, however, you don't have to report the sale on your tax return. However, if at any time during the period you owned the property it was not your principal residence, or you owned more than one property, you may have to report all or a portion of the capital gain and pay tax on it. In this section we'll explain the meaning of a principal residence, how you designate a property as such, and what happens when you sell it.

If after reading this section you need more information, read the CCRA's Interpretation Bulletin IT-120 "Principal Residence."

What is your principal residence?

Your *principal residence* can be any of the following: house, cottage, condominium, apartment, trailer, mobile home, or houseboat. A property qualifies as your principal residence for any year if it meets the following four conditions:

- ✔ It is one of the above properties.
- ✔ You own the property alone or jointly with another person.
- ✔ You, your spouse, your former spouse, or any of your children 18 years of age or younger, lived in it at some time during the year.
- ✔ You designate the property as your principal residence.

The land on which your home is located can also be part of your principal residence. Usually, the amount of land that you can consider as part of your principal residence is limited to one-half hectare (about one acre). However, if you can show that you need more land to use and enjoy your home, you may consider more than this amount as part of your principal residence — for example, this may happen if the minimum lot size imposed by a municipality at the time you bought the property was larger than one-half hectare.

Can you have more than one principal residence?

For 1982 and later years, you can only designate one home as your family's principal residence for each year. If you are married or are 18 or older, your family includes the following: you, your spouse (unless you were separated for the entire year), and your children (other than a child who was married during the year or who was 18 or older). If you are not married or are not 18 or older, your family also includes the following: your mother and your father, and your brothers and sisters (who were not married or 18 or older during the year).

For years before 1982, more than one housing unit per family could be designated as principal residences. Therefore, for these years a husband and wife can designate different principal residences (for example, a house and a cottage) to help minimize capital gains (and taxes) on a sale. After 1982, only one residence per family can be named the principal residence. This makes it important to calculate the potential capital gains on each property you own in order to take maximum advantage of the principal residence exemption.

Disposition of your principal residence

When you sell your home or are considered to have sold it, usually you do not have to report the sale on your return and you do not have to pay tax on any gain from the sale. This is the case if the home was your principal residence for every year you owned it. For many Canadians, this is a no-brainer because they have only one home. However, for those fortunate enough to have a family cottage, or even more than one home, the principal residence exemption is not quite straightforward. Things are complicated further if you didn't actually live in the home, cottage, or whatever during a particular year. If your home was not your principal residence for every year you owned it, you have to report the part of the capital gain on the property that relates to the years for which you did not designate the property as your principal residence.

If you have a loss at the time you sell or are considered to have sold your home, because your home is considered personal-use property, you are not allowed to claim the loss.

If only part of your home qualifies as your principal residence and you used the other part to earn or produce income, you may have to split the selling price between the part you used for your principal residence and the part you used for other purposes (for example, rental or business purposes). You can do this by using square metres or the number of rooms, as long as the split is reasonable. Report only the gain on the part you used to produce income. Don't worry, however, if the income-producing activity was ancillary to the main use of the residence and you have not claimed CCA on the income-producing portion of the home in the past. In these cases, the whole residence can still be considered your principal residence and no portion of any capital gain on sale will be taxable to you. Form T2091 will help you calculate the number of years that you can designate your home as your principal residence, as well as the part of the capital gain, if any, that you have to report.

You only have to include form T2091 with your return if you have to report a capital gain. If all your gain is sheltered by the principal residence exemption, you don't have to report anything on your tax return.

Calculation of the exempt portion of a capital gain on your principal residence

If you sell a property on which all of the capital gain is not tax-exempt, the following formula calculates what portion of the gain is tax-exempt.

$$\text{Exempt gain equals } \frac{1 + \text{number of years the home was designated as principal residence}}{\text{total number of years you owned the home after 1971}} \times \text{gain}$$

Since an individual can only designate one home as a principal residence for any given year, the 1 + in the formula allows you to protect the principal residence exemption when you sell and purchase a home in the same year.

Let's say Tiffany is in the process of moving from Toronto to Vancouver and must sell both her city home and her cottage. She primarily uses the cottage on the weekends to get away from the city smog and traffic. She purchased her city home in 1989 for $120,000, and anticipates that she can sell it for $200,000. She purchased her cottage in 1992 for $100,000, and her realtor assures her that she will get $150,000 for it.

She knows about the principal residence exemption, but isn't sure how it will apply to her since she has owned two homes since she purchased the cottage in 1992.

The first thing Tiffany needs to do is calculate the gain per year from the sale of each property.

	City Home	*Cottage*
Proceeds	$200,000	$150,000
ACB	$120,000	$100,000
Gain	$80,000	$50,000
Number of years	15	12
Gain per year	$5,333	$4,167

Since the city home has a larger gain per year, Tiffany should designate as many years as possible to the city home. Now, initially you would think she should designate 15 years to the city home and none to the cottage. However, remember the formula's 1 + rule. Because of that rule, she should designate 14 years to the city home and 1 to the cottage. The result is as follows:

	City Home	*Cottage*
Gain	$80,000	$50,000
Exemption	($80,000)[1]	($8,333)[2]
Capital gain	$0	$41,667

1. $(1+14)/15 \times \$80,000 = \$80,000$
2. $(1+1)/12 \times \$50,000 = \$8,333$

Sale of Qualified Small Business Shares

You may be eligible to shelter all or a portion of your capital gain (up to $500,000, in fact!) from the disposition of qualified small business corporation (QSBC) shares. The next obvious question is, what is a qualified small business corporation share? A share of a corporation will be considered to be a *qualified small business corporation share* if all the following conditions are met:

✔ At the time of sale, it was a share of the capital stock of a small business corporation, and it was owned by you, your spouse, or a partnership of which you were a member; *and*

✔ At least 90 percent of the company's assets at fair market value were used by the corporation in its active business; or

✔ At least 90 percent of its assets are shares or debts in related corporations that meet the 90-percent rule; or

✔ A combination of assets and shares meet the 90-percent rule; and

✔ Throughout the 24 months immediately before the share was disposed of, while it was owned by you, it was a share of a Canadian-controlled private corporation and more than 50 percent of the fair market value of the assets of the corporation were the following:

  • Used mainly in an active business carried on primarily in Canada by the Canadian-controlled private corporation, or by a related corporation;

  • Certain shares or debts of connected corporations; or

  • A combination of these two types of assets; and

✔ Throughout the 24 months immediately before the share was disposed of, no one other than you, a partnership of which you were a member, or a person related to you owned the share.

You may find it difficult to determine whether your shares qualify for the capital gains exemption. Be sure to visit a tax professional if you think your shares may qualify. Even if they don't currently qualify, it is possible to "purify" the corporation of assets not considered to be active business assets such as cash or investments, so that you will be eligible for this deduction when the time arises.

If you own qualified small business shares, you should consider crystallizing your qualified small business corporation capital gains exemption now — you never know when the Department of Finance might repeal the exemption or when you may fall outside the rules listed above.

Sale of Qualified Farm Property

A special $500,000 capital gains exemption is also available if you sell qualified farm property. The property will qualify if it meets one of two tests (are you surprised?):

✔ The property must be used by you, your spouse, child, or your grandparents in the 24 months immediately before you sell, and your gross revenue from the farming business for a minimum of two years exceeds your income from all other sources.

✔ The property must be used by a corporation or partnership where the principal business is farming, for a minimum of 24 months prior to the sale.

Qualified farm property includes the following:

✔ An interest in a family-farm partnership that you or your spouse own.

✔ A share of the capital stock of a family-farm corporation that you or your spouse own.

✔ Real property, such as land and buildings; and eligible capital property, such as milk and egg quotas.

The farm property must be owned by you, your spouse, or a family-farm partnership. If a corporation or partnership carries on the farming business, the property will qualify if you, your spouse, or your child is an active participant in the business and more than 50 percent of the fair market value of the property is used in the business of farming. Generally, when you dispose of qualified farm property, you report any capital gain or loss realized in the special section of schedule 3. If you dispose of farm property, other than qualified farm property, report any capital gain or loss in the section "Real Estate and Depreciable Property" on schedule 3.

If you transfer farm property to a child it may be possible to avoid tax altogether on the deemed disposition. Consult a tax professional who can determine whether you can take advantage of a "tax-free intergenerational transfer."

Determining whether your farm property qualifies for the $500,000 capital gains exemption is not a do-it-yourself project. The tax rules surrounding farm property are quite complex (definitely not your bedtime reading material). If you are involved in farming, be sure to seek the help of a tax professional. With so many tax perks to farmers, you want to make sure you don't miss out on any that may apply to you!

The Lifetime Capital Gains Exemption

Prior to February 23, 1994, everyone had a $100,000 personal capital gains exemption. This meant that every Canadian could generate up to $100,000 of capital gains during their lifetime (up to this date) and not pay tax on those gains. As the saying goes, all good things must come to an end; therefore, in order to get a final benefit from this exemption, many people elected, on form T664, to use up their exemption and trigger a capital gain. The election increased the adjusted cost base of particular assets owned at that time so that when the property was actually sold, the taxable capital gain was that much less. If you filed form T664, you are considered to have sold your capital property at the end of February 22, 1994, and to have immediately reacquired it on February 23, 1994.

The ACB of your property on February 23, 1994, depends on the type of property for which you filed an election. If you filed an election for capital property, your ACB is usually the amount you designated as proceeds of disposition on form T664. However, special rules exist for flow-through entities, such as mutual funds. The elected amount in this case is known as the "exempt capital gains balance." If you have such a balance, you can use it to offset capital gains distributions made to you annually. These gains do not occur when you sell your investment, but rather are flowed through to you on a T3 or T5 slip. And, if you have an exempt capital gains balance left at the time you sell your investment, it can also be used to offset some or all of your capital gain.

 The exempt capital gains balance can be used to offset annual capital gain distributions only up to 2004. At this time any exempt balance left over is added to the ACB of the units, and will reduce the capital gain when the units are sold.

 If you sold capital property during 2003, be sure to check back to your 1994 tax return to see if you elected to trigger this gain and increase your adjusted cost base. You don't want to report a higher gain than necessary and pay too much tax.

Cumulative Net Investment Loss

The intent of the *Cumulative Net Investment Loss (CNIL)* account is to prevent a person who is taking advantage of various "shelter-type" deductions, from compounding his or her advantage with a capital gains exemption claim. The CNIL account balance is calculated as follows:

Aggregate investment income (for the years ending after 1987)	–	Aggregate investment expense (for the years ending after 1987)

If the result is a negative balance, that amount is your CNIL account balance. If the result is a positive balance, your CNIL account balance is nil.

Why is the CNIL so important? The CNIL account will limit the capital gains exemption allowable on the disposition of QSBC shares and qualified farm property to the extent that you have deducted losses on passive investments. The CNIL account tracks lifetime losses on these types of investments to the extent that they exceed lifetime income from those same investments. (Note: Passive investments are generally investments in assets you acquire neither as trading inventory nor for use in carrying on a business.)

For more information on CNIL and how it impacts on your capital gains exemption, make sure you read through Chapter 11, especially the section called "Line 254: Capital Gains Deduction."

The Capital Gains Reserve

When you sell a capital property, you usually receive full payment at that time. However, sometimes you receive the amount over a number of years. For example, you may sell a capital property for $50,000, receiving $10,000 when you sell it and the remaining $40,000 over the next four years. When this happens, you can claim a reserve. Usually, a reserve allows you to report only a portion of the capital gain in the year you receive the proceeds of disposition. Generally, you cannot claim a reserve if the following apply to you:

- ✔ You were not a resident of Canada at the end of the taxation year, or at any time in the following year.

- ✔ You were exempt from paying tax at the end of the taxation year, or at any time in the following year.

- ✔ You sold the capital property to a corporation that you control in any way.

How to calculate and report a reserve

To claim a reserve, you still calculate your capital gain for the year as the proceeds of disposition minus the adjusted cost base and the outlays and expenses involved in selling the property. From this, you deduct the amount of your reserve for the year. What you end up with is the part of the capital gain that you have to report in the year of disposition.

To deduct a reserve in any year, you have to complete form T2017 "Summary of Reserves on Dispositions of Capital Property." The information provided on the back of the form explains the limits on the number of years for which you can claim a reserve, and the amount of the reserve you can deduct.

If you claimed a reserve in the previous year, include that reserve when you calculate your capital gains for the current year. For example, if you claimed a reserve in 2002, you have to include it in your capital gains for 2003. If you still have an amount payable to you after 2003, you may be able to calculate and deduct a new reserve, which you include in your capital gains for 2004. A capital gain from a reserve brought into income qualifies for the capital gains deduction only if the original capital gain was from a property eligible for the deduction.

The amount of reserve you can take in any particular year is the lesser of the following:

(Proceeds not yet due/Total proceeds) × Gain

$1/5$ of the gain × (4 – # of preceding taxation years ending after disposition)

Did you catch all that? Let's take Finlay, for example. In 2003, Finlay sold capital property for proceeds of $200,000. However, he only received $20,000 up front. The remaining $180,000 is not due until 2004. The adjusted cost base of the property was $150,000.

The total gain from the sale of the property is $50,000 ($200,000 proceeds less cost base of $150,000). However, since Finlay did not receive all the proceeds in 2003, he is eligible to claim a reserve.

In 2003 his reserve is the lesser of the following:

($180,000/$200,000) × $50,000 = $45,000

($1/5$ × $50,000) × (4 – 0) = $40,000

Therefore, in 2003 he can shelter a portion of the $50,000 gain with a $40,000 reserve. He will report only $10,000 of the gain in 2003.

In 2004, he will report another reserve. Keep in mind that he must include the $40,000 reserve he claimed in 2003 in his income for 2004. His 2004 reserve is the lesser of the following:

$$\text{Nil}/\$200,000 \times \$50,000 = \$\text{Nil}$$

$$(^1/_5 \times \$50,000) \times (4 - 1) = \$30,000$$

Therefore in 2004, Finlay cannot claim any reserve and must include in his income the remaining $40,000 of the capital gain.

You do not have to claim the maximum reserve in the year. You can claim any amount up to the maximum. However, the amount you claim in a later year for the disposition of a particular property cannot be more than the amount you claimed for that property in the immediately preceding year.

If you claimed a capital gains reserve in 2000 (or before), the inclusion rate that applied to the portion of the gain reported in the other years will be different from the rate that will apply in 2003. Don't worry. The portion of the capital gain that must be reported in 2003 is only one-half taxable, even if the original gain was subject to a higher inclusion rate.

Capital Gains Deferral on Eligible Small Business Investments

Have you sold shares of a small business corporation during the year? If so, then read on. It is possible to defer tax if you sell certain share investments and then replace those investments with new eligible small business investments.

To qualify for this deferral, you must dispose and repurchase shares of an eligible small business corporation. Generally, this means a Canadian-controlled private corporation that used at least 90 percent of the fair market value of its assets in an active business in Canada.

There are also time limits in place. The 2003 Federal Budget relaxed some of the restrictions on obtaining the deferral. First, you must have held the original shares for more than 185 days. In addition, you must acquire the replacement shares at any time in the year of disposition or within 120 days after the year end.

If you manage to defer your capital gain because of this rule, you must remember to decrease the ACB of your investment. There are a number of calculations that must be done in order to come up with the exact ACB reduction. Take a look at the CCRA's guide *Capital Gains* (T4037) for more information.

The rules for calculating the actual amount of gain you can defer are quite complex (trust us, you don't want us to go into it here). This is one more time where you should strongly consider getting a professional accountant involved.

Chapter 8

Tips for Other Types of Income

*I*n this chapter we will examine sources of income that are generally classified under that ominous title of "Other income." Far from being unusual, some of these sources are encountered by taxpayers on a regular basis. So hold on tight as we dive headfirst into the not-so-weird world of other income.

Line 119: Employment Insurance Benefits (EI)

Amounts received as employment insurance (EI) benefits are included at line 119 of your tax return. These benefits are usually the result of unemployment or maternity leave.

Much to the surprise and chagrin of EI recipients, the government holds back part of your cheques as "tax withheld." The calculation used to estimate your tax generally assumes you will be in the lowest tax bracket and withholds accordingly. The amount in box 14 "Total benefits" of the T4E is the amount to be entered at line 119. The tax withheld in box 22 is deducted at line 437.

Some EI benefits are not included in income. These benefits are payments for a course or retraining program to facilitate reentry into the labour force, and will not appear on the T4E slip.

EI clawback

If you have collected EI benefits in the year, and your net income as determined from line 234 of your income tax return is greater than $48,750, you may be required to pay back a portion of the benefits you've received. The repayment rate is 30 percent of the lesser of

✔ Your net income in excess of $48,750; or

✔ The total regular benefits you were paid in the year.

If you receive maternity, parental, or sickness benefits, you will not have to repay those benefits. This ensures that parents who stay home with their newborn children or workers who are too sick to work are not penalized.

If you are a first-time claimant, you will not have to make any repayments.

If you are required to repay part of your EI benefits, you can deduct the repayment at line 235 "Social benefits repayment" (so you're not taxed on the amount in addition to having to pay it back!). The repayment itself is also reported on your personal tax return, at line 422.

EI premiums

For the year 2003, the maximum annual insurable earnings are $39,000 with a premium rate of 2.1 percent. If you earn $39,000 or more, your employer will withhold the maximum premium of $819 ($39,000 × 2.1 percent). All EI premiums paid entitle you to a 16-percent non-refundable tax credit on schedule 1 of your tax return plus a provincial credit on your provincial tax forms.

If your EI insurable earnings fall below $2,000 for the year, you will receive a full refund of premiums paid for the year. If you over-contribute to EI because your employer withheld too much or because you had more than one job in the year and both employers withheld the maximum, you will likewise receive a refund of your over-contribution.

If you are self-employed, you are not required or permitted to pay EI premiums. Unfortunately, you are also not eligible to collect EI if you find yourself out of work.

Line 122: Limited and Non-Active Partnership Income

The term "limited or non-active partnership" describes a business relationship where you, the minority or limited partner, can invest in a partnership while at the same time avoid being held personally liable for any liabilities of that partnership. (In a regular partnership each partner can be held personally responsible for such liabilities.) Limited partners are not involved in the day-to-day running of the business, but instead are non-active investors. Limited partnerships are often used for tax shelters promoting real estate, oil and gas, films, and so on.

At-risk amount

Tax shelters usually mean tax losses. Be warned, however, that the losses that a limited partner can claim are restricted to the partners' "at-risk amount," unless you've owned an interest in the partnership since prior to February 26, 1986.

Your at-risk amount generally equals the total of your investment, in the partnership, and your share of any profits earned by the partnership each year, less any investment tax credits allocated to you.

The T5013

When a limited partnership earns a profit, or produces deductions or credits that you can claim on your personal tax return, the information is reported to you on a T5013 or a separate statement of income.

Before investing in a limited partnership, ask if it has an Advance Tax Ruling from the CCRA. This document will give you the tax implications of your investment as well as the CCRA's opinion on the tax implications of the partnership's plans.

In the past, not only did investors in limited partnerships have to worry about not being allowed to deduct their losses if they did not have enough at-risk room, but also their losses could be denied altogether if the CCRA said the partnership had no reasonable expectation of profit (REOP)! Talk about a double whammy! Fortunately taxpayers have been fighting this in court, and in 2002, two high-profile cases were heard in the Supreme Court of Canada. Because of the rulings in these cases (*Stewart* and *Walls*), the REOP rule has been thrown out the window if there is clearly no personal element to the loss. What this means for investors in limited partnerships, is that losses will be fully deductible — although you still have to consider your at-risk room.

Line 126: Rental Income

Rental income is earned from renting properties such as a building, a house, a room in a house, an apartment, office space, machinery, equipment, vehicles, and so on. Most types of rental income are considered to be "income from property" and therefore are reported on line 126, although it is possible that you rent out properties as a business, in which case it is reported as self-employment income (see Chapter 9).

Rental income is always reported on a calendar-year basis — that is, January to December. If you co-own a rental property, your share of the rental income or loss will be based on your percentage of ownership. Arbitrary allocations are not acceptable.

Reasonable expectation of profit

The primary motivation of any business should be to earn profit. If you don't earn profit, why are you in business? The reasonable expectation of profit (REOP) principle was the standard the taxman used when examining businesses to determine if yours was a legitimate business or simply a tax shelter. If after examining your rental business the CCRA determined that the business had no REOP, they concluded that yours was not a legitimate business and denied the rental losses.

Due to two precedent-setting cases heard in the Supreme Court of Canada during 2002 (*Stewart* and *Walls*), the REOP test will no longer be a valid reason for the CCRA to deny losses in certain situations. What the court said in these cases was that where an activity is clearly commercial in nature, and there is no personal element, there is a source of income and therefore any losses incurred are deductible by the taxpayer. In other words, so long as there is no personal or hobby element to the activity, losses cannot be denied if there have never been profits, or there may not be profits in the future.

The fact the courts ruled in favour of *Stewart* and *Walls* does not mean the REOP test cannot be used against you. If you are renting out a personal property, such as part of your home or cottage, there is a personal element to your activities (since you are essentially deducting some costs as rental expenses that you would have incurred even if you hadn't rented out part of your premises). What this means is that if you claim losses on that rental activity, the REOP test can still be used to deny your losses.

If you had rental losses denied in prior taxation years because the CCRA said you had no REOP, fight it. You will have to file a Notice of Objection (see Chapter 15) or, if you missed the cut-off date to object, you could ask the CCRA to reassess your tax return for the year(s) in question to allow the losses based on the *Stewart* and *Walls* cases. You have three years from the date on your Notice of Assessment for the tax year(s) in question, to ask for a reassessment before your tax return is statute barred (see Chapter 15).

Undeveloped land

The tax treatment of undeveloped land is a tricky issue. If you rent out this undeveloped land (or even if you don't!), you need to ensure that you do not run afoul of the rules.

Deductibility of interest and property taxes

If you rent out vacant land, you will only be allowed to deduct the interest and property tax to the extent of the net rental income earned on the land (that is, income after other expenses are deducted). In other words, you cannot use the interest and property tax to create a loss on vacant land not used to produce income. If, on the other hand, the land is used or held in carrying on a business, or if the land is held primarily for the purpose of gaining or producing income, the interest and property tax can be deducted in excess of earned income. This distinction allows land under buildings and land used in a business (for example, a parking lot) to avoid the interest and property tax restrictions.

Capital assets

If the vacant land is considered a capital asset, the non-deductible interest and property tax will be added to the cost of the land. This will reduce the capital gain on sale when the land is eventually disposed of.

Inventory

If the vacant land is held as inventory (such as when you're in the business of buying and selling land for a profit), the non-deductible expenses will be added to the cost of the inventory, thus reducing your income when you eventually sell the land.

Real estate rentals — what's deductible, what's not

Unlike vacant land, real estate rentals can create losses. Here is a list of the most common expenses incurred that may be deducted against rental income:

- Mortgage interest
- Property tax
- Insurance
- Maintenance and repairs
- Heat, hydro, water
- Accounting fees
- Condo fees
- Landscaping
- Office supplies
- Fees paid to find tenants
- Advertising
- Management and administration fees
- Salaries or wages paid to take care of property
- Legal fees to collect rent or prepare rental documents
- Lease cancellation fees (amortized over the remaining term of lease to a maximum of 40 years)
- Mortgage application, appraisal, processing, and insurance fees (deducted over five years)

> ✔ Mortgage guarantee fees (deducted over five years)
>
> ✔ Mortgage broker and finder fees (deducted over five years)
>
> ✔ Legal fees related to mortgage financing (deducted over five years)

Soft costs

If you are constructing, renovating, or altering a building to be used for rental purposes, soft costs such as interest, legal fees, property tax, and accounting fees must be added to the cost base of the building and amortized (see discussion on capital cost allowance later in this chapter). This accumulation of costs must continue until the building is finished or 90-percent rented out. After that point you can deduct the expenses for tax purposes on either your rental or business statement.

If you own one rental property in addition to your principal residence, you can deduct motor vehicle or travel expenses to conduct repairs and maintenance or to transport tools and material to the rental property, provided the property is located in your general area of residence. If you own only one rental property (and no other residence), you cannot deduct travel expenses to collect rent; this is considered a personal expense. Also, you cannot deduct travel expenses for a property outside your area of residence.

If you own two or more rental properties, you can deduct all the above expenses plus travel to collect rents, supervise repairs, and generally manage the properties. The properties can be located anywhere, not just your area of residence.

Real estate commissions or legal fees paid in connection with the purchase or sale of the property are not deductible as incurred. Instead, they must be added to the cost base of the property.

Renting your own residence

If you rent all or a portion of your home, be careful not to mix personal and business expenses. Obviously, only the proportion of expenses that can be attributed to the rented portion of your home are deductible for tax purposes.

When renting out your own residence you have to determine which expenses relate solely to the rental activity and which ones are shared with the whole house. The ones that are shared need to be allocated to the rental portion.

✔ **Expenses of the rental activity.** Expenses such as advertising, cleaning, and cutting keys are incremental costs of owning and renting the property. These expenses are 100-percent deductible against rental income.

✔ **Expenses shared with rest of house.** Expenses such as taxes, insurance, water, hydro, heat, maintenance, and mortgage interest would have been incurred even if a portion of the house was not rented out. These expenses are allocated between the rental and the rest of the house.

The CCRA accepts two ways of allocating expenses:

✔ Allocate them based on the number of rooms in the house. If the house has ten rooms and two are rented, allocate $^2/_{10}$th of the household expenses to the rental units.

✔ Allocate the expenses based on the square footage. If the house is 2,000 square feet and the rental is 400 square feet, allocate $^{400}/_{2000}$th of the house expenses to the rental portion.

Do not claim capital cost allowance (CCA) when renting out part of your home. The reason? Once you claim CCA against your rental income, the part of your home that is rented stops being your principal residence. This means that when you sell your home, part of your proceeds will be taxable because they are no longer exempt under the principal residence exemption. See Chapter 7 for more information on this exemption.

Capital versus current expenditures

Unless you're a slum lord, you're likely going to incur some expenditures on your rental property. The question is, can you deduct these expenses against your income?

Expenses of a property can be divided into two main categories: current expenditures and capital expenditures. Current expenditures are the operating or recurring expenses that provide short-term benefits. These expenditures tend to maintain or keep the property in the same shape. Examples are repairs and maintenance, landscaping, window cleaning, heat, hydro, property tax, and interest expense on the mortgage. Capital expenditures, on the other hand, are the expenses of purchasing the property or substantially improving it. Capital expenditures are expenses that give lasting benefits that improve the property beyond its original condition.

Capital expenditures are not expensed in the year of occurrence; rather, they are amortized or deducted over time using the capital cost allowance system discussed later in this chapter. Examples of capital expenditures include major repairs to the property such as a new roof, additions to the property, new windows, new plumbing or electrical wiring, new furnace or coal scuttle.

The key concept in determining if a repair is a capital or current expenditure is the concept of betterment. If a repair improves what was initially there, it will be classified as a capital expenditure. If the repair only restores what was there initially, it is a current expense.

Capital expenditures to assist the disabled are fully deductible in the year of occurrence. These expenses are given current expense treatment in an attempt to encourage landlords to install them, and may include the following: installing hand-activated power door openers, installing ramps, modifying bathrooms, elevators, or doorways to accommodate wheelchairs, modifying elevators to assist the blind, and installing telephone devices for the hearing impaired and computer equipment or software to assist people with disabilities.

Capital cost allowance

Capital cost allowance is a method of writing off the cost of a capital item over time since the cost of capital assets cannot be deducted all at once in the year of acquisition. The length of time that the CCRA requires you to "write off" the asset is supposed to represent the time it takes for the asset to wear out or become obsolete. The amount that you are allowed to deduct each year is called the capital cost allowance (or CCA).

How do I determine how much CCA I can claim?

The amount of CCA you claim on a yearly basis depends on the type of asset you own and when the asset was purchased. The *Income Tax Act* puts each type of asset into a specific asset group or "class." Each class has a predetermined amortization rate.

Various CCA classes also have different rules with regard to the treatment of assets in the first year that they are added to the class. Most classes require you to use the "half-year rule" for new additions. This rule allows you to claim only half the normal CCA in the first year an asset is added to a class. This rule was designed to prevent individuals from buying assets the last day of the year and claiming a full year of amortization (too bad!).

How do you know what class to put your capital asset in? The CCRA's guide "Rental Income" has a good discussion on CCA classes. See the CCRA Web site at www.ccra-adrc.gc.ca.

Suppose Andrea buys a building that costs $500,000 and a fashionable chaise lounge that costs $1,000. The building is added to class 1. This class has an amortization rate of 4 percent per year, and the half-year rule applies. The fashionable chaise lounge is added to class 8. This class is amortized at 20 percent per year, and the half-year rule applies.

Year 1	**Building**	**Chaise lounge**
CCA rate	4%	20%
Cost of assets in class	$500,000	$1,000
CCA	$(\$500,000 \times 4\%) \times \frac{1}{2}$	$(\$1,000 \times 20\%) \times \frac{1}{5}$
	= $10,000	= $100
Year 2		
Cost	$500,000	$1,000
Less: Prior year's CCA	$10,000	$100
(Undepreciated capital cost)	$490,000	$900
CCA	$(\$490,000 \times 4\%)$	$(\$900 \times 20\%)$
	= $19,600	= $180
Undepreciated capital cost at end of second year	$(\$490,000 - \$19,600)$ = $470,400	$(\$900 - \$180)$ = $720

You do not have to claim the maximum CCA every year. This is a discretionary deduction, meaning you can choose to claim any amount from zero to the maximum allowed. If you do not owe tax in a particular year, for example, you may not wish to claim CCA that year and instead preserve your deduction for other tax years when you might need it. Remember, though, there is a maximum amount you can claim each year even if you forgo deductions in previous years (no double-dipping!).

The land component of the purchase price plus the land transfer tax, legal expenses, and real estate commissions that are allocated to the land part of the rental property (as opposed to the building part) are not treated the same way as other capital expenditures. These costs are not eligible for amortization using the capital cost allowance system because land does not wear down the way a building or a driveway does.

Separate classes

Normally assets of the same type are put into the same class, or pool, for CCA purposes. What this means is that you basically add together the costs of all like types of assets in order to depreciate them together on your tax return. This makes it much easier than having to calculate CCA separately on each and every asset you buy.

Rental buildings costing $50,000 or more acquired after 1971 need to be placed in separate CCA classes. This means that if you buy two class 1 buildings and they cost more than $50,000 each, they must not be combined into one class 1 group of buildings; instead, they must each be in a separate class 1 group. The reason for this rule is that when buildings are disposed of (usually for a gain), the government wants to recapture (or reverse) the CCA claimed on the building. (If the building was sold for a gain, it obviously did not depreciate, so why allow CCA?) The rules of recapture do not permit the reversal of CCA on an asset if there is still another asset in the same class. By forcing each building into its own class, there is usually guaranteed recapture when the building is sold.

Combining rental income to calculate CCA

You cannot use CCA to create a loss on rental income. The government requires you to combine all rental income and losses from all properties before calculating CCA. In this way, you are prevented from using CCA to create or increase net rental losses. Let's say Jack owns two buildings. Both buildings are in class 1. The income and loss on the rental buildings are as follows:

	Building 1	Building 2
Net income before CCA	$10,000	($15,000)

Since Jack has to combine the income of both buildings, he has a net rental loss of $5,000. Since Jack is in a net rental loss position, no CCA can be claimed on either building without increasing the rental loss. If this rule did not exist, he could claim CCA on Building 1 to bring income to zero and claim no CCA on Building 2. The result would be a net rental loss of $15,000.

Recapture and terminal loss

Recapture and terminal loss are adjustments that you must make when you dispose of assets and find (based on your selling price) that the assets either were not depreciated enough over time, or depreciated too much. To recapture means to reclaim CCA taken in excess of actual depreciation. To claim a terminal loss means to claim additional CCA when actual depreciation exceeds the allowed capital cost deductions. Neither recapture nor terminal losses can be claimed while assets are still in a CCA class (that is if you had more than one asset of the same type being depreciated). When all assets in a class have been disposed of, you will be able to determine if you over- or underdepreciated assets.

Let's say that Lisa sells her class 1 building for $1,000,000. She originally bought the building for $500,000. Over the years, she has claimed $300,000 of CCA. Since this building is the last asset in the class, we can calculate recapture or terminal loss. At the time of sale, Lisa's undepreciated capital cost balance was $200,000 ($500,000 − $ 300,000) = $200,000.

Since the building increased in value and did not depreciate, the CCRA wants to recapture the CCA she claimed in prior years. As a result, Lisa will be required to include $300,000 of recapture in her income for the year of disposition.

Foreign rental income

For tax purposes, you must include in your Canadian income any rental income that you receive on property located anywhere in the world. The same rules and restrictions apply to foreign source rental income as apply to Canadian source rental income, including the CCA rules.

All foreign transactions must be converted to Canadian dollars at the exchange rate as of the transaction date. You can use the average exchange rate for the year if you have income and expense transactions that take place throughout the year.

Any withholding tax or income tax paid to a foreign country is eligible for a foreign tax credit when you calculate your rental income for Canadian tax purposes. See Chapter 13 for more information.

Line 128: Support Payments

The tax rules surrounding support payments have undergone significant changes in recent years. The catalyst for these changes was a high-profile court case, the *Thibaudeau* case. This case argued that the rules on support payments severely disadvantaged the receiving spouse and children since these payments were fully taxable. The court agreed and changed the rules, effective May 1, 1997. Since some taxpayers are still receiving support payments under the old rules, we'll summarize them all below.

Old rules (pre–May 1, 1997)

Under the old rules for alimony and separation allowances, payments received pursuant to a court order are deducted from the payer's income and included in the recipient's income. Once included, this payment makes up part of the recipient's taxable income and is taxed at that person's marginal rate. Obviously because of this additional tax burden, the amount of the support payment available to the recipient is reduced.

New rules (post–April 30, 1997)

For court orders or written agreements made after April 30, 1997, **child support** payments are not deductible from the income of the payer or included in the income of the receiver. The net result is that tax does not reduce the amount intended for child support. On the other hand, **spousal support** payments are deductible from income by the payer, and must be included in the income of the recipient. The new rules go on to say that if a court order or written agreement specifies that an individual must make both child support and spousal payments, the CCRA considers payments are allocated first to child support and second to spousal support. This additional provision ensures that all child support must be paid before the payer can claim a deduction for spousal support, and the recipient has to include spousal support in income.

 If child support is in arrears, the government will not consider any of the future payments from the payer to be spousal support — at least, not until all back child support is paid. This ensures that the recipient will not be taxed on back child support even if the payer calls it spousal support.

If the court order or agreement does not specify separate amounts for child support and spousal support, all payments will be considered child support and will not be taxable to the recipient or deductible to the payer.

What if I'm under the old rules and would like to use the new rules?

Luckily, you and your former spouse can elect to use the new rules even if your court order or agreement predates May 1, 1997. By using form T1157 "Election for Child Support Payments" the recipient and the payer can agree to treat the child support portion of the payments as non-deductible to the payer and not included in the recipient's income. After this election is filed, however, you cannot return to the old rules.

Under what circumstances do the new rules apply?

The new rules apply automatically in any of the following situations:

✔ The court order or agreement is made after April 30, 1997, and before January 1, 1999, but does not recognize any payments made before May 1, 1997, as payments made under that court order or agreement.

✔ The order or agreement is made after December 31, 1998, even if it recognizes earlier payments.

✔ The order or agreement is changed after April 30, 1997, to increase or decrease the amount of support payable.

Taxable support payments qualify as earned income for RRSP purposes.

Specific purpose payments

Specific purpose payments are payments made to third parties on behalf of the spouse or children. Common third-party payments include rent, tuition fees, medical expenses, or maintenance payments on the recipient's residence.

Unlike regular support payments, these payments may not take place at regular intervals, and are often not at the discretion of the beneficiary. Regardless, if the payments are made pursuant to a court order or written agreement, the tax treatment will generally be the same as payments made directly to the spouse 0for spousal or child support.

Specific purpose payments that benefit the child (for example, child's medical bills) are not deductible or taxable if an agreement was made after April 30, 1997.

Line 129: RRSP and RRIF Income

Registered Retirement Savings Plans (RRSPs) are government-sanctioned plans, with many tax-favourable features, that individuals may set up to save for retirement. The most popular features of an RRSP are that you get a tax deduction for contributions you make to the plan, and earnings within the plan grow free of tax — that is, until you make withdrawals. A Registered Retirement Income Fund (RRIF) is created when you convert your RRSP — usually in the year you turn 69 (although it could occur earlier than this). Once your RRSP is converted to an RRIF, you are required to make taxable withdrawals each year. Withdrawals from an RRSP, on the other hand, are optional.

Withdrawals from an RRSP

Amounts can be withdrawn from an RRSP at maturity (at age 69) or before. Funds can also be withdrawn using the Home Buyers' Plan or the Lifelong Learning Plan, on a tax-preferred basis.

Mature RRSP

An RRSP matures when you reach 69 years of age. At this time, the government requires you to convert your RRSP to an annuity or a Registered Retirement Income Fund. Taxable retirement payments must commence the following calendar year.

 You don't have to make any withdrawals from your RRIF in the year you set up the plan. In fact, you can (and should) defer making a withdrawal until December of the year after your RRIF is set up, in order to defer tax for as long as possible.

 It is usually best to delay receiving retirement income from an RRSP until you absolutely need to. The longer it stays in an RRSP earning tax-free income, the better. After all, your RRSP is supposed to be used for retirement.

Withdrawals prior to RRSP maturity

If you withdraw amounts from your RRSP at any time, the amount of the withdrawals is included in your income. In addition, these withdrawals will be subject to withholding tax at source.

In many cases the amount of withholding tax will not be enough to cover your actual tax liability owing when you file your tax return. Therefore, be sure to calculate how much tax you will actually owe (based on your marginal tax rate) to ensure that if the withholding tax taken off is not enough, you keep enough money on hand to pay the taxman in April.

Normally, it is suggested that you only withdraw money from an RRSP in situations where you really need the income, so you can defer the resulting tax for as long as possible. If you do have to make a withdrawal, there are a few simple strategies to save tax in the process:

- **Low-income withdrawals:** Try to withdraw amounts during a year in which you anticipate having a lower income. This will reduce the tax bite when the amounts are eventually included in income.

- **Take out small quantities:** Don't take all the money out at once. Take the funds out in increments of $5,000 or less. This will reduce the withholding tax to 10 percent (if you reside outside of Quebec) and give you more money to use when you need it. When filing your return, you will, of course, need to pay tax at your marginal rate for the income inclusion. If you urgently need the money, however, better to have it in your hands than in the taxman's (as withheld tax).

- **Withdraw over two tax years:** Try to take the money out in two different tax years. By taking funds out at the end of December one year and in January of the next year, you will be splitting the withdrawal over two tax years, thus reducing the tax hit in any one year. In addition, tax will not be payable on the January withdrawal until April 30 of the following year — that is, if you withdraw money from an RRSP in January 2003, additional tax will not be payable on this amount until April 30, 2004.

- **Withdraw RRSP cash from low-income earners:** If you are married, remove money from the registered retirement savings plan of the lower-income earner first. This will reduce the tax paid by the family, since the lower-income earner probably has a lower marginal tax rate and will pay less tax on the withdrawal.

Withdrawals of unused or over contributions to an RRSP

Sometimes taxpayers are a little overzealous when it comes to contributing to their RRSPs. However (as you can imagine), we're not allowed to put as much money as we want into our retirement savings plans — we discuss these contribution limits in Chapter 10. As well, some taxpayers contribute within the allowable limits, but decide for one reason or another not to deduct the contribution on their tax return.

In some cases you may decide to make an RRSP contribution, but not claim the deduction until a future year. When would you do this? Well, this may make sense when you're currently in an unusually low tax bracket. If you save the deduction for a year when your marginal tax bracket is higher, your RRSP deduction will be worth more.

Generally, any withdrawals of contributions to your RRSP, even those that exceed your contribution limit, are reported on line 129 and taxed as income. This is the case even when you withdraw any undeducted contributions to the RRSP! Luckily, there are relieving provisions that allow you an offsetting deduction against these income inclusions (after all, you didn't get a deduction for the contribution — why should you pay tax on the withdrawal).

If you are going to withdraw your RRSP overcontribution, use form T3012A "Tax Reduction Waiver on the Refund of Your Undeducted RRSP Contribution." By submitting this to the CCRA, it will direct your financial institution not to withhold tax on the withdrawal of funds. If you withdraw funds without form T3012A, the issuer of the plan will withhold tax. In this case, use form T746 "Calculating Your Deduction for Refund of Undeducted RRSP Contributions," to calculate the amount of your tax deduction given that you have already paid withholding tax.

Home purchase loans

Although the general rule is that withdrawals from your RRSP are taxable, there are some special circumstances where the government allows you to withdraw funds with no tax. The first situation is when you withdraw money from your RRSP to purchase a home under the Home Buyers' Plan. Of course, your tax obligations aren't over there. You are required to repay your Home Buyers' Plan withdrawals back to your RRSP. If you don't? You guessed it — the shortfall will be added to your income at line 129. To learn more about the Home Buyers' Plan, make sure you read Chapter 10.

Lifelong Learning Plan

As was the case with the Home Buyers' Plan, funds can be withdrawn from your RRSP on a tax-free basis to help you go back to school. This program is called the Lifelong Learning Plan. If funds withdrawn under the Lifelong Learning Plan are not paid back according to the required schedule, they are included in your income at line 129 every year that the payment is missed. Also, if you withdraw the money but do not use it for education, and if you do not return the funds to the RRSP by the end of the calendar year following your withdrawal from the educational institution, the entire amount will be included in income. For more on the Lifelong Learning Plan, read Chapter 10.

Spousal RRSPs

A spousal RRSP is an RRSP that you have contributed to but which names your spouse as the "annuitant." This means that all retirement funds out of this RRSP will belong to your spouse and not to you, the contributor (although you do get the up-front tax deduction). A spousal RRSP is usually used by individuals who have much higher incomes than their spouses and wish to "split" their retirement income rather than have the entire amount included in their income.

A withdrawal from a spousal RRSP has very special rules that seek to dissuade individuals from transferring money to the spouse and then withdrawing it soon after, to take advantage of the spouse's lower marginal tax rate. If these rules are violated, the income will be attributed back to the contributing spouse, which means it will be added to his or her income.

The rules

If your spouse withdraws money from a spousal RRSP that you have contributed to in the year or in the previous two years, the withdrawal will be taxed in your hands and must be included at line 129 of your return. It does not matter if your spouse's name is on the T-slip! For example, if your spouse withdraws money from a spousal RRSP in 2003 that you contributed to in 2003, 2002, or 2001, the withdrawal will be included in your income, not your spouse's.

If the contributor is separated from his or her spouse, or was deceased at the time funds were withdrawn, the government will not attribute the income back to the contributor.

Contribute to a spousal RRSP at the end of the year (instead of on January 1) to reduce the waiting time on withdrawals from three years to just over two.

RRIF income

A registered retirement income fund (RRIF) is the continuation of a matured RRSP. When you reach the age of 69 or wish to receive retirement income, your RRSP can be converted to an RRIF by way of a tax-free rollover. Like the RRSP, the RRIF earns income tax-free inside the plan. An RRIF is different from an RRSP, however, in that you can no longer contribute to the plan, and a minimum income withdrawal must be made from the plan each year following the year in which the RRIF was established. These withdrawals are considered taxable income. If you are 65 years of age or older, your minimum required RRIF withdrawal should be reported at line 115. Income reported at line 115 is eligible for the $1,000 pension amount at line 314. In all other cases, report income from an RRIF at line 130.

Minimum required withdrawals from an RRIF are not subject to withholding tax. However, if you withdraw amounts exceeding the minimum, these amounts will be subject to withholding tax and must be reported at line 130.

In order to defer the tax hit from your RRIF for as long as possible, and if your spouse is younger than you, consider basing your minimum withdrawals on the age of your spouse. This will reduce the amount you are required to withdraw each year, allowing you to defer tax and leave more assets in your RRIF for future growth.

Line 130: Other Income

Line 130 is called the "catch-all," since it's basically used to report income that does not belong anywhere else on the tax return. This section covers some of the most common types of income to be reported on line 130.

Retiring Allowances

Don't be confused by the term *retiring allowance* — it doesn't apply only to payments you receive when you retire. In fact, it also includes what people normally refer to as "severance" or "termination" pay, as well as to a court award or settlement for wrongful dismissal. Legal awards are discussed in more detail below.

Eligible allowance

Retiring allowances are taxable. However, all or a portion of a retiring allowance (your "eligible" retiring allowance) may be paid directly into your RRSP. The portion paid to your RRSP effectively is received tax-free. Confused? Let's take a step back.

When you leave your employer and receive a retiring allowance, a portion of your payment may be able to be paid into your RRSP. If you choose to do this, you include the full amount of the allowance on line 130 — but a deduction is given on line 208 for the amount paid to your RRSP. So, how much can you transfer? Well, that depends on when you started working with your employer and how long you have worked there.

The *Income Tax Act* sets limits on the amount of retiring allowance you can have paid into your RRSP. The limit is calculated as follows:

- ✔ $2,000 per year, or part year of employment service prior to 1996, plus

- ✔ $1,500 per year, or part year of employment service prior to 1989 in which you had no vested interest in any employer's contributions to a registered pension plan, or deferred profit-sharing plan.

Let's suppose Susan left her employer in 2003 and received a $50,000 termination payment. She had started working there in 1985 and had joined the pension plan in 1987.

The amount she can have paid to her RRSP is calculated this way:

$2,000 × 11 years (1985 to 1995)	$22,000
$1,500 × 2 years (1985 to 1987)	$3,000
Eligible portion of retiring allowance that can be paid to her RRSP	$25,000

The amount that can be paid to your RRSP and deducted on your personal tax return is over and above your regular RRSP contribution (or "deduction") limit. You can still make your maximum RRSP contribution in addition to this *special contribution*. It's not critical that the retirement allowance be paid directly to your RRSP. However, you must contribute the funds to your RRSP within 60 days following the end of the year in which you receive the payment. For allowances received in 2003, this means the contribution must be made by March 1, 2004.

The eligible portion of a retiring allowance can only be rolled into an RRSP of which you are the annuitant. It cannot go into a spousal RRSP.

If you don't make the contribution within 60 days following the end of the year, you lose your right to this special contribution. It is a one-time deal that cannot be carried forward.

You can avoid withholding tax by having the eligible portion of your retiring allowance paid directly to your RRSP.

Ineligible portion of retiring allowance

Any allowance received in excess of the amount you can have paid to your RRSP is considered to be an ineligible retiring allowance for purposes of direct payments to an RRSP. This amount is reported in box 27 of your T4A, and you must add this to your eligible retiring allowance and report the total on line 130 of your income tax return.

Here are some things that you may be able to do to help ease the tax burden on any ineligible portion of a retiring allowance:

- Use up any unused RRSP contribution room. You can have your employer send the portion that you are going to contribute directly to your RRSP and avoid any withholding tax. To do this you must show your employer that you have the RRSP contribution room available.

- Ask to receive the retiring allowance payment over a number of years. With a retiring allowance, you're not taxable on it until it's received, so this can help to defer tax to a year where you may be in a lower tax bracket.

What is not a retiring allowance?

Obviously, retiring allowances can be very beneficial when they can be paid on a tax-free basis to an RRSP. It is for this reason that Canadians want to receive retiring allowances when they leave a job. However, it's important to note that not all amounts will qualify as a retiring allowance. A retiring allowance does not include the following:

- A superannuation or pension benefit
- An amount received as a result of an employee's death
- Payments for accumulated vacation leave

✔ A payment made in lieu of earnings for a period of reasonable notice of termination

✔ Payments made for human rights violations under human rights legislation

Scholarships, Fellowships, Bursaries, and Research Grants

Did you receive a scholarship, fellowship, bursary, or prize for achievement in your field of endeavour this year? First off, congratulations! Second, these amounts must be included in your income to the extent that the total for the year exceeds $3,000. (The $3,000 exemption is obviously a little congratulations from the Department of Finance as well.)

The first $3,000 received is not taxable. You should calculate the total amount received in the year, deduct $3,000, and report any balance on line 130 (the $3,000 exemption does not apply to research grants).

What are scholarships and bursaries?

Scholarships and *bursaries* are amounts given to students to help them pay for school — generally a university, college, or similar educational institution. Normally, a student is not expected to do specific work for the payer in exchange for a scholarship or bursary.

A scholarship from your employer given with the condition that you return to work after completing your studies is not a scholarship at all! In fact, you must report the amount received as employment income on line 104. Say goodbye to the $3,000 exemption — 100 percent of this amount is taxable.

What is a fellowship?

Fellowships are like scholarships or bursaries, in that they're given to students to help them pursue their education. The difference is that in most cases they are given to graduate students by a university, charity, or similar body. Normally, fellowships are included in income to the extent that they exceed $3,000, and are reported on line 130. However, when the primary purpose of the fellowship is not education and training but rather carrying out research, the award is considered to be a research grant.

If a student receives a genuine loan to assist in financing education, the loan is not considered to be a scholarship, bursary, or fellowship. In other words, the loan is not taxable. For a genuine loan to exist, provisions must generally be made for repayment within a reasonable time.

What is a prize in my field of endeavour?

A *prize in your field of endeavour* sounds pretty impressive, right? Although we're not talking about the Academy Awards, prizes do come in all shapes and sizes. Prizes that fall under this heading are awarded for success in an area of effort. It is a result of accomplishment, rather than luck. For example, if you achieve the highest mark on your bar exam, the $1,000 you receive will qualify as a prize. In this case, you wouldn't have to report anything on your tax return because up to $3,000 of prizes in your field of endeavour can be received tax-free. Take the $1,000 and enjoy it.

These types of prizes should not be confused with "prescribed" prizes, which are not taxable. That is, even if the prize exceeds $3,000, no tax will result. A prescribed prize is a prize recognized by the public and awarded for achievement in the arts, sciences, or for public service. These prizes are exempt from tax altogether, as long as the amount cannot be considered compensation for services rendered or to be rendered. Although this exemption is aimed at high-profile awards, such as the Nobel Prize, the definition is general enough for other prizes, such as those in recognition of community service, to be exempt from tax.

What is a research grant?

Did you receive a *research grant*, money given during the year to help pay expenses necessary to carry out a research project? If so, you must report any amount you received in excess of expenses in income. Research grants do not qualify for the $3,000 exemption. Grant money received in excess of expenses is classified as employment income and is reported on line 104 of your tax return (not line 130). If you've been given a research grant this year, you should receive a T4A. The amount you receive is reported in box 28, and the bottom of the slip should indicate the amount related to a research grant.

Want more info on scholarships, fellowships, bursaries, prizes, and research grants? Go to the CCRA's Web site and take a look at Interpretation Bulletin #IT-75R3 at `www.ccra-ardc.gc.ca/E/pub/tp/it75r3em/it75r3-e.htm`.

Tuition Assistance Payments

Tuition assistance payments received from the Employment Insurance Commission (EIC) or Human Resources Development Canada (HRDC) are taxable. The amounts are reported on T4E or T4A slips.

There is an offsetting tax deduction to recipients of tuition assistance where funds are received for adult basic education (ABE). ABE includes primary and secondary level education or other forms of training that do not qualify for the tuition tax credit. This includes courses taken to:

- ✓ Finish high school

- ✓ Develop stronger literacy skills

- ✓ Upgrade secondary-school credentials to prepare an individual for specific occupations or fields of higher learning

Death Benefits

A death benefit is an amount paid on the death of an employee to a spouse or other beneficiary, in recognition of service in an office or employment. The first $10,000 of a death benefit paid in respect of any one employee is exempt from tax.

Death benefits paid under the Canada or Quebec Pension Plans do not qualify for the $10,000 exemption.

The spouse gets first use of the $10,000 exemption. If the spouse receives less than $10,000, and there are other beneficiaries who receive funds, the remaining exemption must be split among the other recipients.

Legal Awards

It's a common misconception that legal awards, such as payments for damages, are not taxable. Although it is possible that the payment may not be taxable, this is not always the case. Take, for example, a retiring allowance. A retiring allowance includes an amount received as *a result of loss of office or employment.* So what does this mean? If you received payment from a lawsuit or out-of-court settlement, for whatever reason, and the complaint arose in relation to your employment, this amount is taxable. For example, amounts paid on account of or in lieu of damages — that is, damages for loss of self-respect, humiliation, mental anguish, hurt feelings, and so on — may be a retiring allowance if the payment arose from a loss of office or employment. The easiest way to look at it is like this: If you sue your employer and you receive payment, it's taxable. If you continue to work, it's included in employment income; otherwise, it's a retiring allowance.

If you win a lawsuit and receive payment that's classified as a retiring allowance, you can deduct any legal expenses incurred. But you can only deduct up to the amount of the allowance you include in income. That is, if you can have the entire retiring allowance paid to your RRSP, you can't deduct any legal costs. Any legal costs you can't deduct can be carried forward for the next seven years, to offset any taxable retiring allowance you may receive in the future as a result of the lawsuit.

Some specific legal payments are excluded from income altogether. For example, all amounts received by a taxpayer or the taxpayer's dependants that qualify as special or general damages for personal injury or death are excluded from income, regardless of the fact that the amount of such damages may be determined with reference to the loss of the taxpayer's earnings. Examples of amounts received as a result of personal injury or death include the following:

- ✔ Out-of-pocket expenses such as medical and hospital bills
- ✔ Accrued or future loss of earnings
- ✔ Pain and suffering
- ✔ Shortened expectation of life
- ✔ Loss of financial support caused by the death of the supporting individual.

Foreign Income

Keep in mind that if you're a Canadian resident, you're taxable on your entire worldwide income. So if you received money from another country, and no other line numbers are appropriate for reporting your income, you can include the amount on line 130. Make sure you remember to convert it to Canadian dollars first!

More "Other Income"

Many T-slips you receive will indicate amounts paid to you as "other income." Fortunately, you don't have to remember to include these other types of income on your tax return, since you'll have the slips to remind you. Simply follow the instructions on your T-slips, and you can't go wrong!

Line 144: Workers' Compensation Benefits (WCB)

WCB received as a result of injury, disability, or death must be included in income. This amount is found in box 10 on the T5007 sent to you by the Workers' Compensation Board. This income inclusion is then deducted at line 250 with the net result is that no tax is payable on this income. You might wonder why you have to go through all this trouble to end up in a tax-neutral position at the end of the day. By including the benefit at line 144, you increase your net income, thus reducing your entitlement to certain credits and deductions, such as the Child Tax Benefit and the GST credit. This higher income will also reduce the spousal amount that your spouse can claim for you.

 If you receive money from your employer as an advance of WCB, the employer will usually put the amount in box 14 of your T4. You should subtract this from your T4 and include it at line 144. Be sure to get a letter from your employer explaining the amount. This letter should be submitted with your return.

Line 145: Social Assistance

Social assistance payments (box 11 on the T5007) are included in your income at line 145 and deducted at line 250, in calculating taxable income. Just as with workers' compensation benefits, the net result of social assistance payments is no tax. But (again, just as with WCB), since the social assistance payments form part of your net income, you could have a reduced entitlement to certain tax credits and deductions. By the way, if your spouse has a higher income than you do, the social assistance payments should be included and deducted on your spouse's return instead of yours.

Chapter 9

Tips for Self-Employment Income

. . . .

In This Chapter

▶ Understanding the tax realities of self-employment

▶ Using the accrual method of accounting

▶ Tips for reporting various types of self-employment income and expenses on your tax return

▶ Using capital cost allowance as a tax deduction

. . . .

Self-employment means running your own business. You are an entrepreneur — someone who accepts the risks and enjoys the rewards of business. There are many advantages to self-employment, including the tax savings component. While the tax savings are attractive, most people become self-employed because "they want to be their own boss."

The Tax Implications of Being Self-Employed

You are required to report your business profits (or losses) on your personal tax return if you are unincorporated. This is because a sole proprietorship is not a separate legal entity — it is simply treated as an extension of the owner (the proprietor). On the other hand if you own shares in a corporation, your corporation is required to report its income or loss on its own tax return. In that case your corporation should issue you a T4 for income and a T5 slip for any dividends paid to you in the year.

It is usually easiest to set up any new business as a sole proprietorship. However, once the business starts becoming profitable, you may want to consider incorporating. This is because corporations can benefit from some tax savings (so long as you actually leave profits in the company).

How does self-employment save taxes?

The tax "win" from self-employment is that any expense you incur to build and run the business is generally deductible in computing your business income subject to tax. This is logical since every dollar you earn from the business will be taxed, so every dollar you spend on the business should be tax deductible. If you are running a business and incur a loss, the loss is deducted from other sources of income on your tax return. (An exception to this may be a loss incurred in operating a farm. Farming is discussed near the end of this chapter.)

If your business produces a loss this year but you don't have any other sources of income to use the loss against, consider filing form T1A "Request for Loss Carryback" to offset income you paid tax on in the previous three years. The CCRA will then send you a cheque for some or all of the taxes you paid! You may also choose to carry the loss forward for a maximum of seven years.

Generally, self-employment offers you the opportunity to deduct more expenses than if you were employed, since only certain employees can deduct expenses they incur to do their job. Even when an employee has the opportunity to deduct a lot of expenses, the self-employed person can usually deduct more.

We've all heard stories about self-employed individuals taking advantage of their status for so-called tax savings. Just because you don't receive T4s, T5s, and so on, reporting the income of your business does not mean you can understate your actual income when you prepare your tax return (even if you were paid in cash). You also cannot deduct personal expenses in calculating your business's net income.

Choosing a taxation year-end for your business

As of 1995 all businesses must either adopt to have a calendar year-end (that is, December 31) or make a special election to have an alternative date apply. If you ask us, however, adopting the calendar year-end will save you a lot of hassle.

Most businesses operate on a January 1 to December 31 taxation year. This is the simplest solution in terms of the complexities of reporting your business's income and expenses. If your business is cyclical or seasonal, it may make sense for you to elect to have a non-December 31 year-end. For example, if your business is extremely busy in late December, perhaps because of the holidays, you would prefer the taxation year-end to be later — say, the end of January or February. If you carry inventory, it would be easier to do a physical count at the end of January or February, rather than at the end of December. Besides, it is only accountants who spend New Year's Eve counting inventory!

Once you have filed a tax return with your business's taxation year-end noted, the taxation year becomes fixed. Though it is possible to change a taxation year-end, it can be difficult: first, you must have a pretty good reason for doing so, and second, you have to ask the CCRA for permission! Our advice is that you take your time in determining the appropriate taxation year-end for your business.

The Accrual Method of Accounting

Most self-employed individuals must use the *accrual method* of accounting in reporting their income and expenses earned from self-employment. (Some people prefer the spelling "a cruel method of accounting.") As we will see near the end of the chapter, self-employed individuals earning commission income or involved in farming and fishing have the option of using the cash method of accounting.

In using the accrual method of accounting

✔ Income is recorded as it is *earned* — not when your customer pays you. In most cases you are considered to have earned your income when an invoice is issued. Where, at the end of your business's taxation year, you have invoiced customers but not yet received payment, the sale would be recognized as being earned in the year. The unpaid amount would be considered an "accounts receivable" at the end of the taxation year.

> ✔ Expenses are recorded as they are *incurred* — whether or not
> you actually paid for the expense in the taxation year. Often, the
> invoice date is used to indicate when the business has incurred
> an expense. If you received an invoice from a supplier that was
> dated for a purchase made prior to the taxation year-end, the
> expense would be recorded in your business's taxation year
> as it was incurred in the year. The unpaid amount at the end
> of the taxation year is considered an "accounts payable."

The purchase of an inventory item for resale is not recognized as
an expense or cost of your business until the inventory item is sold.

The Cash Method of Accounting

Another method of accounting is the *cash method*. Income is
reported when cash is received. Expenditures are recorded when
cash is *paid*. The recording of inventory is usually irrelevant when
the cash method of accounting is used. (Again, you will see that a
farm business is an exception. A farmer's "inventory" may need to
be valued — even when the cash method is used. More on this
near the end of the chapter!)

Lines 135 and 162: Business Income

Business income is the first line on the portion of your return
dealing with self-employment income. (Refer to the self-employment section about one-third of the way down on page 2 of the tax
return.) You report the gross income from your business on line
162 and the net income or loss of the business on line 135.

Form T2124 "Statement of Business Activities"

Most self-employed individuals should complete the T2124 tax form
"Statement of Business Activities." The form serves as an income
statement for the self-employed person. All income and expenses of
the business are reported on the form. The "net" amount of income
(income less expenses) is what the self-employed person pays tax on.

You will see that Form T2124 is broken down into a number of sections. Obviously the first step is to fill in the identification section. We think you can handle that. Next, you'll have to fill in the details of your sales and expense amounts for the year. Here are some tips for dealing with some of these items.

✔ **Sales, commissions, or fees (line c, lines 8000 to 8299):** You record your self-employment sales, commissions, or fees earned in the year on line 8299. You are responsible for ensuring the amount recorded is correct. You will not receive any T-slips from your customers indicating how much you have billed them in the year; it is up to you to track and report the correct amount on your tax return. If you are earning self-employed commission income, you may find that some of your customers will send you an annual T4A slip reporting the amount of self-employed commissions paid to you in the year. Even if you do not receive a slip from all your customers, or if a slip reports an incorrect amount, it's your responsibility to ensure you report the correct amount of gross income earned.

The gross income you report should not include any Goods and Services Tax (GST at 7 percent), or Harmonized Sales Tax (HST at 15 percent), and/or provincial retail sales tax charged to customers. These taxes are excluded because they do not represent income of your business — you simply collect these taxes on behalf of the federal and provincial governments.

If a customer provides you with a deposit for goods or services to be provided after the taxation year-end, the deposit is not included in your gross income. The deposit is not yet considered income because the goods or services for which the deposit was received have not been provided as of the end of your business's taxation year.

✔ **Cost of goods sold (lines 8300 to 8518 and line d):** If you purchase goods for resale, the calculation of your cost of goods sold is detailed on lines 8300 to 8518 of form T2124. If your business only provides services, your cost of sales is zero.

✔ **Expenses of your business (lines 8521 to 9270):** You simply detail your expenses on these lines. The amounts noted on these lines are to exclude the GST/HST you have paid on these expenses, assuming your business is registered for GST/HST. If your business is not registered for GST/HST, the GST/HST you have paid in connection with these expenses gets included in the expense totals noted. The CCRA discloses on form T2124 that in reporting your business's expenses, you "enter business part only." This is the CCRA's way of saying, "Do not deduct any personal expenses in computing your self-employment income because it is against the law and you will pay dearly if

we catch you — so watch out." Many of your business expenses will be 100-percent business use. If you advertise your business in the Yellow Pages, it would be fairly difficult to argue that a part of your advertising cost was personal in nature. However, you probably use your car for both business and personal use. Perhaps you operate your business from your home or apartment. If so, the costs of maintaining your "home office" need to be tracked. Only the "self-employment" or business use portion of your car and home office expenses can be claimed on form T2124. We take a look at deducting a portion of your car and home expenses later in the chapter, along with more details on some specific expenses you can deduct.

Doing your taxes will be much less onerous if you keep good records throughout the year. You can use a computer program to help, or even just get a bunch of envelopes and label each with the various expense categories noted on form T2124. As you pay for items throughout the year, simply place your receipts in the envelope and at the end of the year, add them all up!

✔ **Your share of line g above (line h):** If you are operating as a partnership, you put your share of line g on line h. For example, say you have a $33^1/_3$–percent interest in a contracting business that is operated by you and a couple of partners. If line g on your tax return reported $90,000, your $33^1/_3$–percent share would be $30,000. You would enter $30,000 on line h.

If your partnership has five or more partners, the reporting of your share of the partnership's income is very simple. There is no need for you to detail the income and expenses of the whole partnership. On behalf of all the partners, the partnership should have sent the CCRA a copy of the partnership's financial statements detailing the income and expenses of the partnership. The partnership will simply issue you a T5013 slip "Statement of Partnership Income" indicating your share of the partnership's net income. If you receive a T5013, simply report your share of the partnership's net income at line 9369 (net income [loss] before adjustment) on the T2124.

Some of the expenses you can deduct

As we will see, most business expenses are fully deductible in calculating your self-employed income subject to tax. But tax being tax, it is not always that straightforward. In this next section, we comment on some of the more interesting rules dealing with the deductibility of expenses.

Overall deductibility

The general rule is that any expense incurred to operate a business is deductible. To be deductible, the amount of the expense must be "reasonable" in the circumstances. For example, if the business pays your spouse a salary that is in excess of what you may have paid someone not related to you, the excess may be considered "unreasonable" and the CCRA may disallow the deduction.

Salary and payroll costs

In computing the total expenses of your business or partnership, a deduction cannot be taken for salaries, wages, or fees paid to yourself, or amounts you have taken as "drawings." Sole proprietors simply pay tax on the amount of business income that remains after all other expenses have been recorded. If you are in a partnership, the bottom-line income is shared among the partners on a basis as agreed to by the partners.

Self-employed individuals are permitted to deduct one-half of the Canada Pension Plan or Quebec Pension Plan contributions paid for their own coverage as a business expense. The non-deductible half will continue to qualify as a tax credit. See Chapter 12 for more details.

Prepaid expenses

As noted, under the accrual method of accounting you recognize an expense when it is incurred, not when it is paid. Sometimes you pay for something where the benefit, or a portion of the benefit, of the payment will be in a future taxation year of your business. Take a look at your business insurance. Before the "insurance year" commences, a bill is sent out for the full premium. Say your business taxation year was January 1 to December 31. In September 2003 you arranged to purchase business insurance for the first time. You receive a bill for $1,200 to cover your business for the period October 1, 2003 to September 30, 2004. You make the full $1,200 payment in October 2003.

In preparing the T2124 for your business's 2003 taxation year, you can only deduct $300 for the insurance. This is because only one-quarter (the three months of October through December) of the insurance coverage falls into 2003. The remaining nine months (January to September 2004) of coverage falls into the business's next taxation year — January 1, 2004 to December 31, 2004. You will deduct the remaining $900 of the premium on your 2004 tax return.

Meals and entertainment expenses

Generally, only 50 percent of the amount of meals (including beverages) and entertainment expenses are deductible. Why 50 percent? 'Cause that's the rule! So, say you purchased tickets to a Calgary Stampeders game to take clients to — only 50 percent of the cost of the tickets would be tax deductible.

Premiums for health care coverage

If self-employment income is your main source of income, your business can probably take a deduction for the cost of a health care plan. This would be claimed as part of the "other" category at line 9270 of the T2124.

Automobile expenses

Line 9281 is where you report the automobile expenses of your business. If your business needs a car or van that is used 100 percent of the time in the business — say, to make deliveries — the amount included on line 9281 is simply the total of the expenses to keep the vehicle on the road, such as gas and oil, repairs and maintenance, and insurance. As you'll see below, however, some of your automobile expenses will be restricted — even if the entire use of the vehicle is business related.

Reporting automobile expenses gets a little more complicated when you use your own car, since you likely drive your car for both business and personal reasons.

 You can only deduct the "self-employment use" or "business use" portion of your automobile expenses in computing your net income from self-employment. It is essential that you track the kilometres you drive for self-employment and the total kilometres driven in the year so that, come tax time, you will know what proportion of your car expenses can be deducted. In other words:

$$\text{Total car expenses} \times \frac{\text{self-employment kilometres}}{\text{\# of total kilometres}}$$

 If the CCRA has questions regarding the portion of your car expenses claimed on your T2124, they will want to see a log of your kilometres driven for purposes of operating your business. Get in the habit of having a log in the car, documenting where you are going, where you have been, and the kilometres travelled. It will make things much easier if you ever need to respond to a CCRA query.

Car expenses deductible for tax purposes include the following:

- Fuel (gas, propane, and oil)
- Repairs and maintenance
- Insurance
- Licence and registration fees
- Leasing costs
- Interest incurred on a loan to purchase a car

If you own your car (versus leasing it) and you use it at least partially to carry out business activities, you will also be able to claim capital cost allowance or CCA. We discuss CCA in detail in a section later in this chapter titled "Capital Cost Allowance (CCA)."

Restrictions on certain automobile expenses

As noted above, where you are entitled to deduct a portion of your automobile costs, you deduct only the "business use" portion of the expenses. However, certain automobile expenses have a "cap" on how much you can use in calculating the business use portion (even if the business use portion is 100 percent!). Specifically, restrictions have been put on the lease and interest costs in respect of automobiles because the government does not want to permit tax deductions that it considers to be excessive. So if you lease or finance an "expensive" vehicle, you will find the amount you can deduct for your lease and interest costs restricted to maximum amounts. See Table 9-1 for details.

Table 9-1	Maximum Amounts Deductible for Lease and Interest Costs		
Lease/Purchased In	**2001/2003**	**2000**	**1999/1998**
Monthly lease cost	$800	$700	$650
Monthly interest cost	$300	$250	$250

Notes

1. The government reviews these limits annually and announces any changes prior to the end of the year so that taxpayers are aware of the rules in advance of the year in which they apply. The rates are set and released by Finance Canada by press release.
2. All limits are before sales tax. The limits are actually slightly higher when provincial and territorial retail sales tax and GST/HST are added.

The maximum amounts apply *before* you prorate your passenger vehicle expenses between business use and personal use.

Let's look at Angie. Angie is a self-employed commission agent working out of Regina. She sells hair care products to beauty salons. She sells a number of lines for a variety of hair care product manufacturers.

On January 1, 2003, Angie leased a BMW. Her monthly lease cost is $875. Angie uses the BMW 75 percent for her self-employment. The effective tax deduction she will have is the $800 per month maximum (see Table 9-1 above) multiplied by her 75-percent self-employment use. This results in a tax deduction equal to $600 per month, or $7,200 for all of 2003.

We have simplified things here. So don't get thinking you can get around the lease restriction rules by making a big deposit before the lease commences or guaranteeing the car will have a higher value than normal at the end of the lease. Both these ideas would bring your monthly lease costs down. However, the actual calculation to determine the maximum lease costs takes these ideas into account. In fact, one of the calculations focuses on the manufacturer's list price of the car. If the car is considered expensive in the government's eyes, you simply have to live with the restrictions on the amounts you can deduct!

Home office expenses

If you operate your business from your home or apartment (a home office), you can deduct a portion of the expenses related to maintaining the home office workspace. This deduction is particularly attractive because you will find that you can get a tax deduction for a portion of the expenses you must incur anyway, such as monthly utilities, rent, and mortgage interest. However, for the costs to be deductible, you must ensure your workspace meets one of two tests — but not both!

Under the first test, the workspace must be the chief place where your business is carried out. The CCRA offers the example of the contractor who runs his own business. A contractor spends a great deal of time fulfilling contracts at customer locations. However, the business functions of receiving work orders, bookkeeping, purchasing, and preparing payrolls may be done at home. In this case, the workspace would qualify as a home office and the contractor could deduct related expenses.

Under the second test your workspace must be used exclusively to carry out your business activities. (Note that the word *exclusively* was not used in the first test.) In addition to using the space exclusively for these activities, you must use the space on a "regular and continuous" basis for meeting customers or others associated with carrying out your business. In the CCRA's opinion, infrequent meetings or frequent meetings at irregular intervals are not regular and continuous.

You cannot claim home office expenses to "create or increase a loss" from your business. Say your 2003 business expenses (excluding home office expenses) are greater than your 2003 income: you have a loss from self-employment. You cannot claim home office expenses to increase the loss. If your non–home office business expenses do not exceed your income, you can only claim home office expenses to the extent that they bring your "net" self-employment income to $nil — you cannot create a loss. Any home office expenses that can't be used this year can be carried forward for use in future tax years.

Deductible home office expenses

Subject to the restrictions on deducting home office expenses just mentioned, you can deduct the following expenses:

- ✔ Electricity, heat, and water (utilities)
- ✔ Maintenance costs, condo fees
- ✔ Rent
- ✔ Property tax
- ✔ Insurance on your home or apartment
- ✔ Mortgage interest (but not mortgage principal)

You can only deduct the portion of these expenses that directly relate to your workspace. In most cases you can simply take the square feet of your home office space divided by the total square footage of your home to come up with a reasonable percentage.

Capital Cost Allowance (CCA)

The money you spend in operating your business can be classified in one of two ways:

- ✔ **Day-to-day expenditures of running the business:** These expenditures are not considered to have a future value and are therefore "expenses" of your business. Most of these expenses are noted on lines 8521 to 9270 on form T2124. Examples of day-to-day expenditures include salaries paid to employees, office rent, lease payments, bank charges, travel, and telephone.

- ✔ **Capital expenditures:** Capital expenditures are made when you purchase a capital asset — an asset that has an expected useful life that will extend beyond the end of your business's taxation year. Common examples of capital assets are computers, office equipment (photocopiers, fax machines), office furniture, buildings, and machinery. As the value provided by these assets is expected to extend past the end of your business taxation year, you cannot take a full deduction for these expenditures on form T2124. However, as we detail below, you are allowed to deduct a "portion" of the cost of a capital asset for each taxation year it is used in your business. The calculation of the "portion" that can be deducted on your tax return is called capital cost allowance (CCA).

Capital cost allowance, or CCA, is simply tax lingo for "depreciation" and "amortization." These are terms often used by accountants. Remember this next time you are at a party and want to impress someone with your vast knowledge!

Your business can claim CCA on almost all capital assets purchased. One exception is land. And of course, the asset must have been acquired for use in your business — not for personal use.

Eligible capital property (ECP) are assets that do not physically exist. They are referred to as intangible assets and include such items as the purchase of goodwill, a customer or patient list, a marketing quota or government right, and an unlimited franchise, concession, or license. Technically you don't claim CCA on ECP, but there is a special deduction, similar to CCA, allowed. The starting point for the deduction is 75 percent of the cost of ECP. The deduction you are allowed is 7 percent of this amount, on a declining basis each year.

Calculating CCA — the declining balance method

For most types of assets, you calculate CCA using the declining balance method of depreciation. The costs of specific types of assets (which is generally the purchase price but can also include freight costs, duty and customs fees, retail sales taxes, and even GST/HST if your business is not a GST/HST registrant) are grouped together to calculate the CCA deduction. And, you guessed it — the government dictates which "class" those specific types of assets go into.

For example, say your business purchased a meeting room table and bunch of chairs. The table and chairs, both being "office furniture," would be treated as one asset or "pool." CCA is then calculated on the pool balance multiplied by a legislated percentage rate. The remaining "pool balance" is carried to the next year, where again the same percentage is applied to calculate the CCA. Since the pool balance on which the CCA claim is based declines each year, the method is referred to as the declining balance method. This method results in higher CCA deductions in the early years of a capital asset purchase, and lower and lower amounts as the asset ages.

If your business incurs costs to make rented premises more workable, such costs are referred to as leasehold improvements. Leasehold improvements are not depreciated using the declining balance method. Instead, CCA is calculated as the lesser of the following:

1) $$\frac{\text{cost of leasehold improvents}}{5}$$

2) $$\frac{\text{cost of leasehold improvements}}{\text{\# of years in lease + 1 renewal period}}$$

To maximize the speed at which CCA is claimed on your leasehold improvements, negotiate your lease to be a maximum of four years with a renewal period of one year.

CCA is calculated as of the *last* day of your business's taxation year. The CCA calculation is based on the balance of the CCA class at the end of the taxation year. There is no need to do separate CCA calculations for capital assets owned for only part of a taxation year. However, if you were not in business for the full year (say you just started up on September 1), you do need to prorate your CCA for your shorter than 365-day year. In this case you would take your total CCA times 122 days/365 days.

Common CCA classes and rates

For simplicity, the government has assigned CCA class numbers to similar groups of assets (CCA classes).

- ✓ Buildings: Class 1: 4 percent

- ✓ Fences: Class 6: 10 percent

- ✓ Boats: Class 7: 15 percent

- ✓ Office equipment and furniture: Class 8[1]: 20 percent

- ✓ Cars, trucks, computer hardware, and computer "systems" software: Class 10: 30 percent[2]

- ✓ Computer application software, uniforms, linen, dies, jigs, moulds, rental videos, tools under $200: Class 12: 100 percent

- ✓ Manufacturing equipment: Class 43: 30 percent

Notes
1. CCA class 8 is where all capital assets eligible for CCA are included if they do not fall into any of the other CCA classes.
2. There is a maximum amount that can be used for the capital cost of a car in terms of calculating CCA. This is discussed under "Restriction on the maximum capital cost of a class 10.1 automobile."

A CCA example

CCA can best be explained through an example. Let's continue with your business's purchase of a meeting room table and chairs. Remember that the total cost was $1,200. In preparing your tax return for 2003, you know that you cannot deduct the full $1,200 on form T2124 in determining your net income from self-employment. The meeting room table and chairs are good quality (for $1,200? hmm) and probably can be used in your business for several years. In fact, the chairs have a 10-year warranty!

Office furniture is considered a CCA class 8 capital asset with a CCA rate of 20 percent. (You're forced to accept the 20-percent rate whether or not the chairs are expected to last 5 years, 10 years, or 30 years!)

You would think you could calculate CCA as simply 20 percent of $1,200, or $240. However there's a catch — it's a special rule called the "half-year" rule. Let's look at what this rule says.

The "half-year" rule

When calculating CCA for the year in which the asset is purchased, only one-half of the CCA can be claimed (that is, use half the rate you otherwise would to calculate the appropriate claim).

So, the correct way to calculate the 2003 CCA claim on the office furniture is $1,200 × 10% = $120.

Undepreciated capital cost (UCC)

Undepreciated capital cost is the term used to describe the amount of the capital cost at the end of a taxation year to which CCA has not yet been applied. The UCC at December 31, 2003, in our CCA class 8 office furniture example here would be $1,080. It is calculated as follows:

Undepreciated capital cost (UCC) at January 1, 2003 (assumed)	$nil
Capital cost of additions in 2003	$1,200
Capital cost allowance (CCA) claimed in 2003 (1,200 + 20% × 50%)	($120)
Undepreciated capital cost (UCC) at December 31, 2003	$1,080

In 2004, assuming no further purchases or sales are made, CCA of $216 ($1,080 × 20%) can be claimed.

Sale of capital assets

Let's continue with our CCA class 8 office furniture example to show what happens when an asset used in your business is sold. Say you decided to upgrade the meeting room table and chairs in 2004. Your new table and chairs cost $1,700. The old table and chairs were sold to a used office furniture retailer for $750.

When a capital asset is sold, the UCC is reduced by the lower of the following:

- ✔ The original capital cost of the assets sold (remember, this was $1,200)
- ✔ The sale price — the $750 noted above

When an asset is sold, the half-year rule comes into play once again.

UCC at January 1, 2004 (same as at December 31, 2003)		$1,080
Add: Additions		$1,700
Sale of chairs:		
Lesser of:		
Original cost:	$1,200	
Proceeds:	$750	($750)
CCA claim for 2004:		
$1,080 × 20% = $216		
($1,700 – $750) × 20% × 50% = $95		($311)
Closing UCC (UCC at December 31, 2003)		$1,719

As illustrated above, if you purchase and dispose of an asset in the same CCA class during the year, you must net the addition and disposal together before applying the half-year rule.

Recapture and terminal loss

So now you know how to handle the CCA calculation where assets are purchased and sold. You can see that as long as assets are continued to be purchased for a cost in excess of the sale price of previously purchased assets, the UCC will never reduce to $nil. However, what if your business sells *all* the assets in a CCA class and does not replace them? Well, two things can happen:

✔ **You sell all the assets in a class for *less* than the UCC balance.**

Let's assume that in 2004 you decide not to upgrade your meeting room table and chairs. You admit to yourself that you don't like meeting clients, so the best way not to meet clients is to get rid of your meeting room furniture. (Not a good career move, but it works with the example.) Remember, the table and chairs originally cost $1,200. Again, assume you sell the whole set for $750. In this case, the following would happen:

Opening UCC at January 1, 2004	$1,080

(same as UCC at December 31, 2003)

Sale of chairs:

Lesser of:

Original cost:	$1,200	
Proceeds:	$750	
Lesser:		($750)
UCC balance after sale		$330

Since you sold all the assets in this class, you shouldn't have any UCC left — there is nothing left to depreciate. However, you have $330 remaining. What this means is that you didn't depreciate the assets fast enough. Therefore, the taxman lets you make this up, by allowing you to claim the full amount remaining as a deduction. After all, you were only using the rate they set — why shouldn't you get the deduction? The $330 is referred to as the terminal loss and is fully tax deductible as part of your total CCA claim.

✔ **You sell the assets for *more* than the UCC balance.**

What happens if you sell the table and chairs for $1,800? Sounds good, but there is a downfall. Let's look at the calculation again:

UCC at January 1, 2004	$1,080

(same as UCC at December 31, 2003)

Sale of chairs:

Lesser of:

Original cost:	$1,200	
Proceeds:	$1,800	
Lesser:		($1,200)
UCC balance after sale		($120)

See what has happened? Again, you sold everything in the asset pool, so your UCC balance should clear to zero. However, you have a negative UCC balance. This means you've taken too much CCA — the assets did not depreciate as fast as the taxman thought they would. Obviously, the CCRA won't let you have too much of a good thing, so it will ask for the extra CCA that you took back (hence the term recapture) by adding the negative UCC to your income in the year the asset is disposed. Oh, well!

If you sell an asset for more than its original cost, you may also have a capital gain to report. See Chapter 7 for more details.

Restriction on the maximum capital cost of a class 10.1 automobile

The government does not want you driving an expensive car and being able to write off a significant portion in CCA in determining your self-employment income. Therefore, the amount of CCA that can be claimed on an automobile is restricted in certain situations. As you can see in Table 9-2 below, if you buy a car in 2003 that costs more than $30,000, you will only be allowed to use $30,000 as your capital cost. The excess can never be written off for tax purposes. The CCRA periodically adjusts the maximum amount to take into account rising car prices.

Table 9-2   Maximum Amounts on Which CCA Can Be Claimed on Automobiles

Automobiles Purchased In	2001/2003	2000	1999/1998
Maximum capital cost amount for purposes of claiming CCA on an automobile	$30,000	$27,000	$26,000

The above limits are before provincial/territorial retail sales tax and 7-percent GST/15-percent HST. If you purchased a car in Ontario, you would pay an 8-percent Ontario sales tax and the 7-percent GST — a total of 15 percent. The deemed maximum capital cost for claiming CCA on your car purchase in 2003 would be $34,500 ($30,000 × 115 percent = $34,500).

Special rules in calculating CCA on class 10.1 automobiles

There are a few special rules to consider when you're tallying up CCA on your class 10.1 automobile. Have a look to see if any of these circumstances apply to you:

  ✔ CCA on each class 10.1 automobile is calculated on its own. If two cars were used in your business and they both had an actual capital cost above the limits, your business would have two CCA class 10.1 calculations to make. The purchase or sale of one class 10.1 automobile does not impact the CCA calculation of another CCA class 10.1 automobile.

✔ There is no concept of recapture or terminal loss in dealing with CCA class 10.1 automobiles.

✔ The half-year rule is applied in the year a class 10.1 automobile is sold.

Lines 137 and 164: Reporting Professional Income

The term *professional income* refers to the net income earned by a professional. So what's a professional? The CCRA does not provide an exact definition. However, it is fairly safe to say a professional is a person who earns fees from an occupation for which he or she had to go to school for a long time before being "certified," "licensed," or somehow approved to do what he or she does. If you are a professional, you make most of your money from providing services rather than selling goods. The CCRA offers these examples of professionals: accountants, dentists, lawyers, medical doctors, chiropractors, and veterinarians.

Essentially, professionals calculate their net income from their profession the same way as most self-employed individuals calculate their business income. The comments we have made in this chapter so far with respect to calculating business income apply equally to those who report professional income on their tax return.

The main differences in reporting professional income as opposed to business income are as follows:

✔ Form T2032 "Statement of Professional Activities" is used in place of form T2124.

✔ Professionals need to deal with work-in-progress (WIP)

Form T2032 "Statement of Professional Activities"

Form T2032 is similar in design to the T2124. In fact, the numeric line references on the T2032 are identical to those on the T2124. As it is expected that a professional does not sell goods, the T2032 has no section to compute the cost of goods sold.

The income section of the T2032 includes lines to allow you to correctly account for work-in-progress (WIP).

Work-in-progress (WIP)

A unique characteristic of a professional is his or her ability to claim an amount for *work-in-progress (WIP)*. WIP represents a professional's unbilled time. Say what? A professional's fees are usually based on time. The value of WIP is based on a professional's fees that have been earned but not yet billed.

We'll walk you through this one by looking at Caroline, who lives in Windsor, Ontario. She plans to see a lawyer about difficulties she is having with her husband. The lawyer's name is Richard — Rick, for short. Caroline wants to clearly understand her rights under Ontario's Family Law Act. Caroline makes an appointment with Rick. Rick promotes himself as a specialist in family law. Caroline and Rick plan to meet on December 31, 2003. Rick explained to Caroline the meeting would be an hour in length and that his rate is $200 per hour. Coincidentally, the year-end for Rick's practice is December 31. Caroline and Rick meet as planned. At the end of the meeting, Caroline offers to pay the $200. Rick suggests she wait for a bill that he will get to her in mid-January 2004. Caroline agrees — she likes the idea of keeping her $200 a little longer. (A lawyer not taking money? Whassup? The reason will become obvious in a tip noted soon!) After Caroline leaves his office, Rick makes a record of his meeting in a file for Caroline and records the one hour of time in his bookkeeping system. In entering the time, he records $200 of work-in-progress and $200 of fee revenue earned.

As Rick has only recorded the time but has not billed it, the amount is not yet receivable from Caroline. It will become receivable from Caroline once the bill is issued to her in mid-January 2004.

Let's assume that for his year ended December 31, 2003, Rick has billed all his clients with the exception of Caroline. (Yes, this is unrealistic, but bear with us as we try to make a point!) Rick's total fees billed in 2003 are $200,000. On line A of schedule T2032, he reports revenue of $200,200. This is because the lawyer has earned the $200,000 he has billed to his clients *plus* the $200 he has yet to bill Caroline. Remember, under the accrual method of accounting you report revenue on an "as earned basis."

Where a professional has significant work-in-progress, he or she may end up paying a great deal of tax on income for which a bill has not been rendered. The tax rules recognize this problem and permit certain professionals to deduct year-end WIP in calculating their gross income subject to tax in the year. Where WIP was deducted in the prior year, it must be added back in calculating gross income for the current year. This makes sense because if this was not done, fees in WIP at the end of a year would never be recorded as part of gross income for purposes of calculating tax. (The drafters of the tax legislation are smarter than you think!)

Let's continue with Rick. Assume that back at December 31, 2002, Rick's previous tax year-end, he had $50 in WIP.

Rick would calculate his 2003 gross income subject to tax in the following way:

Professional fees — includes WIP — at December 31, 2003 (line A on form T2032)	$200,200
Minus — WIP at December 31, 2003	($200)
	$200,000
Plus — WIP at beginning of taxation year (WIP at January 1, 2003, would equal WIP at December 31, 2002)	$50
Gross income (line 8299 on form T2032)	$200,050

We have seen that WIP at the end of a taxation year is deducted in determining gross income to use in calculating a professional's net income from self-employment. If the professional delays billing clients for services rendered in one year until the next year, he or she will defer the tax payable on those services for one year. This is an especially good tax planning idea when tax rates are dropping from one year to the next. The tax is deferred, plus it is subject to tax at a lower rate! However, the longer you wait to bill, the longer you wait for the cash. Make sure your business's cash flow is okay before considering such a tax deferral strategy.

Lines 139 and 166: Commission Income

If you earn self-employed commission income, you will detail all of your income and expenses on the T2124, just like for any other business. The good news is that if you've already read the section on business income, you're now an expert! There are no additional special rules for commission income.

Just because you earn commission income does not mean that your income has to be reported as self-employment income. Many commissioned salespeople are actually employees. Not sure of your status? If you've received a T4 slip outlining your commissions, you're an employee. Although you'll find you have more tax deductions if you are self-employed, commissioned employees are also allowed to deduct some of their expenditures for tax purposes.

Lines 141 and 168: Farming Income

Lines 141 and 168 are where a farmer reports gross and net income figures. If operating a farm business, which can include activities such as soil tilling, raising livestock, or even beekeeping, Form T2042 "Statement of Farming Activities" is for you!

Method of accounting

If you are a farmer, the cash method of accounting, rather than the accrual method, can be used to calculate the net income of your farm business. If you used the accrual method in a prior taxation year, you can switch to the cash method. However, to switch from the cash method to the accrual method, you need permission from the CCRA.

Form T2042 "Statement of Farming Activities"

Form T2042 serves the same purpose as the T2124 "Statement of Business Activities." The form simply acts as a schedule to summarize the income and expenses of operating a farm. We'll detail some of the unique features of T2042 below.

The Mandatory Inventory Adjustment (MIA — line 9942)

The MIA only applies to those in farming that record their income and expenses on the cash method of accounting.

Why is there an inventory adjustment? The impact of the inventory adjustment rules is to reduce the amount of net loss a farm business can have. (Warning: Do not mix up the inventory adjustment rules with "restricted farm losses." We discuss restricted farm losses later.) Why do the rules work to minimize a farm loss? Like any self-employment loss, a farm loss can be used to "offset" other sources of income you may have — interest, dividends, capital gains, pension, or perhaps employment income or other sources of self-employment income. A large farm loss could significantly reduce your taxable income, which, of course, reduces the tax you pay. You can see why there would be rules to reduce this! In using the cash method of accounting, inventory is ignored. When preparing a T2042 using the cash method of accounting, you deduct the cost of all items purchased for resale — even if they remain unsold at the end of the year.

Say you purchase a number of calves in the year as part of your beef cattle farm operation. You may keep these for a year or a year-and-a-half before they are sold. If you are operating a dairy farm, you may hold onto your cattle for a number of years before they are sold. Under the cash method, the amounts paid are deducted fully in the year purchased. Where significant purchases are made in a year, the farm loss could be, well, significant! (And that's no bull . . . sorry about this one.)

The MIA rules work to minimize the amount of loss that can be claimed when, at the end of the year, products purchased for resale have not yet been sold.

An MIA must be made on your 2003 T2042 if the following exist:

✔ There is a net loss reported on line 9899 of the T2042

✔ At the end of your 2003 taxation year, inventory was on hand.

The MIA is calculated as the lesser of the following:

✔ The net loss reported on line 9899 of the T2042

✔ The market value of the inventory at the end of the taxation year.

You can see that where the farm inventory is at least equal to the loss on line 9899, the MIA will wipe out the farm loss.

Optional Inventory Adjustment (OIA — line 9941)

Like the MIA, the OIA is an addition you make to your line 9899 net income or loss for 2003. The amount would be deducted on your 2004 tax return.

The maximum amount of the 2003 OIA addition is equal to the market value of inventory at the end of the taxation year less the Mandatory Inventory Adjustment (MIA)

Why would someone decrease his or her farm loss by making an OIA? A good question! An OIA serves to decrease the loss. Remember, an OIA added to net income or loss in the year is a deduction in the subsequent year. If the expectations are that the net income of the farm will be higher next year, a deduction may prove more valuable next year because the deduction will be worth more in tax savings when it can shelter farm income subject to tax at a higher marginal rate.

What if you have a loss from your farming business?

A unique rule regarding self-employment income generated from farming is the treatment of losses. If your farm operated at a loss for 2003, the net loss would appear on line 9946 of the T2042. This may not be the amount you carry to line 141 on page 2 of your tax return. Your farming loss may fall into one of these three categories:

- ✔ Fully deductible
- ✔ Partly deductible
- ✔ Non-deductible

As with other self-employment income activities, for your net farm loss to be deductible you must operate your farm as a business. The CCRA considers you to be in the business of farming if there is no personal element to your farming activities and you are running the farm as a commercial endeavour.

Where you are operating your farm as a business, and farming is your chief source of income in a year, your loss would be fully deductible.

Part-time farmer — the "restricted farm loss" rules

When you operate your farm as a business but farming is not your chief source of income in the year, the loss you claim will be "restricted." In other words, the maximum loss you can claim on your tax return will be less than your actual loss — your actual loss will be partly deductible. Any denied loss is called a "restricted farm loss."

The CCRA considers farming to not be your chief source of income when you do not rely on farming alone for your livelihood. Where you have other sources of income, such as employment income or other sources of self-employment income, farming would not be considered your main source of income.

Whether or not your farm loss is fully or partly deductible is a question to answer each year. In some years farming may be your chief source of income and in some years it may not.

The maximum loss that you can claim if farming is not your chief source of income is calculated as follows:

100 percent of the first $2,500 of the loss plus one-half of the remaining loss

The maximum loss that can be claimed is $8,750. If you are mathematically inclined you can calculate that to be able to deduct $8,750 you would need to have at least a $15,000 actual farm loss. Any excess farm loss above the farm loss you can claim is called a restricted farm loss.

A restricted farm loss can be used to reduce any net farm income you may have reported in the three prior years — 2002, 2001, and 2000, or may be carried forward for up to ten years. To carry a loss back (referred to as a loss carryback) to any or all of these years, you must complete a form T1A "Request for Loss Carryback" and file it with your 2003 tax return.

Once the CCRA receives the form, it will apply the loss against the tax return for the year(s) you requested. As this will reduce your taxable income for the year(s), your taxes will also decrease. The CCRA will issue a Notice of Reassessment for the year(s) in which the loss was applied — along with a tax refund cheque!

Even if you are EFILING your 2003 return, the T1A "Request for Loss Carryback" should be paper filed — a fancy word for mailing it in. This allows for quicker processing of your loss carryback request.

When your farm loss is not deductible at all

Where your farm operations are run in a way not considered to be a business, none of your net loss from farming is deductible. As noted above, for your farm to be considered a business, it must not be a personal endeavour, and must be undertaken in pursuit of a profit. When the farm is not being run as a commercial endeavour, and losses are being incurred, the expenses are considered personal expenses and are not deductible at all. No carryback or carryforward provisions are available. Generally, "farmers" in this category include those that do not look to farming as their chief source of income, and only consider farming to be a hobby.

To determine whether or not farming is your chief source of income, the CCRA will look to a number of factors, including time spent, capital committed, and profitability, both actual and expected.

Lines 143 and 170: Fishing Income

In this final section of the chapter we look at the tax rules that apply to those earning self-employment income from fishing.

What does the CCRA consider fishing income? Let's take a close look. This category includes the following:

- ✔ Amounts received from the sale of fish, lobster, scallops, and so on;

- ✔ Amounts received from other marine products: Irish moss, herring scales, herring roe, seal meat and flippers, seaweed, kelp, roe on kelp, and so on.

If your self-employment income is earned from fishing activities, you report your income in the same fashion as do other self-employed individuals — with a few differences. This section highlights some of these differences. As with farming, you can use the cash method of accounting to calculate the net income of your fishing business.

T2121 "Statement of Fishing Activities"

This form is used to report the income and expenses of your fishing business. It again is similar to the T2124 "Statement of Business Activities."

Expenses

Expenses are detailed on page 2 of the T2121. The expense categories provided are customized a little to reflect items of a fishy nature (we had to say that). For example, the expense categories include "bait, ice, salt, crew shares, gear, and nets and traps."

Food

The cost of food provided to your crew when you fish off-shore is deductible. Food provided on-shore is deductible provided you considered the food as a taxable benefit to your employees.

If it is considered a taxable benefit, the value must be included in the employee's total employment income reported on his or her T4 slip. A deduction can still be claimed when you do not consider the food a taxable benefit, provided your boat is at sea for 36 hours.

Nets and traps

Nets and traps are considered to include lines, hooks, buoys, and anchors. Line 9137 on the T2121 is where your fishing business can claim a deduction for nets and traps. However, the full cost of the nets and traps acquired in the year cannot be deducted. The amount that can be deducted is determined under one of two methods.

CCA method

Your business treats its nets and traps as a capital asset and claims CCA. Nets and traps are CCA class 8 capital assets. You'll recall that the CCA rate for class 8 is 20 percent.

Inventory method

Nets and traps are considered inventory. At the end of each taxation year, the value of all the nets and traps is determined. If the value is less than the inventoried cost, a deduction is claimed on line 9137 for the loss in value.

Part III

Tax Preparation Tips: Claiming Deductions and Credits

"Leveling, grading and terracing the land is a deductable expense — for FARMERS Mr. Daniels, not for people with putting greens in their backyards."

In this part...

*N*ow for our favourite part — deductions and credits to reduce your tax. After reading through the last couple of chapters and calculating your income, you may feel like there's no hope, and next year you may as well just hand over your paycheque to the CCRA. Don't fret — there is a light at the end of the tunnel, and it's shining the words "deductions and credits."

These next few chapters may be the most important in the entire book. So highlight, bookmark, and tag these pages! Do anything you have to do to remind yourself of the deductions to which you're entitled: You can be sure that in most cases, the CCRA won't remind you to claim them! After all, a dollar deduction not claimed means more money in their pockets. Pay close attention to these chapters — you don't want to miss a single tip!

"Taxes should be proportioned to what may be annually spared by the individual."

— Thomas Jefferson

Chapter 10

Tips for Deductions to Calculate Net Income

● ●

In This Chapter

▶ Understanding what "net income" is and its importance

▶ Maximizing deductions in calculating net income

▶ Making the most out of RRSPs

▶ Knowing what you can write off for child care expenses

▶ Benefiting from your moving costs

▶ Ensuring you are up to date on the deduction for support payments

▶ Knowing when your legal expenses are tax deductible

▶ Deducting your employment expenses

▶ Getting a rebate of the GST/PST paid

● ●

So what, exactly, is net income — aside from line 236 on your tax return? It is the amount you arrive at when you take your total income (line 150) less the deductions permitted on lines 207 to 235. You would think that this is the amount of income on which you should pay tax. Well, no. The amount you pay tax on is your taxable income from line 260. The calculation of taxable income is discussed in Chapter 11. (Good news, taxable income can never exceed net income!) Why is calculating your net income so important? Even though we don't pay tax based on net income, it is an important calculation. Take a look at what this one calculation influences:

✔ The amount of provincial or territorial tax credits (Chapter 14, line 479)

✔ The amount of GST credit

✔ The amount of medical expenses (Chapter 12, lines 330 and 331) you can claim

✔ The amount of the refundable medical expenses supplement (see Chapter 13, line 452)

✔ The amount of charitable donations (Chapter 12, line 349) you can claim

✔ The amount of social benefits (Chapter 5, Old Age Security; Chapter 8, Employment Insurance Benefits) you must repay

✔ The amount of spousal credit (Chapter 12, line 303) your spouse or common-law partner can claim in respect of you

✔ The amount for an eligible dependant credit amount (Chapter 12, line 305) another may be able to claim for supporting you

✔ The amount available for transfer of your disability amount (Chapter 12, line 318) to another

As you may expect, the lower your net income the better off you are in terms of minimizing your tax liability! Don't miss taking any tax deductions you are entitled to!

Let's walk through the tax deductions available in calculating your net income.

Line 206: Pension Adjustment

Well, this line really doesn't provide a tax deduction. Line 206 is a *disclosure line* only. A disclosure line on a tax return is where there is a requirement to note a figure, but that figure will not have an impact on the calculation of your tax liability or refund. The amount of your pension adjustment does not impact the calculation of your 2003 net income and therefore cannot impact on your 2003 tax liability or refund. Your pension adjustment will reduce your 2004 RRSP contribution limit — the amount that you can contribute to an RRSP in 2004 and get a full tax deduction. Generally, the *pension adjustment* (PA) is the increase in value of your retirement benefits under a *Registered Pension Plan* (RPP) or *deferred profit-sharing plan* (DPSP).

RPPs and DPSPs are plans set up by employers to assist employees in saving for retirement. As the value of your RPP/DPSP increases, the amount you can contribute to your RRSP decreases. The PA is a component used in the formula to calculate your RRSP deduction limit. The pension adjustment reported on your 2003 T4 will reduce your 2004 RRSP deduction limit on a dollar-for-dollar basis.

When you receive your tax assessment from the CCRA after filing your 2003 tax return, you will see your 2003 PA amount is included in the formula to calculate your 2004 RRSP deduction limit. CCRA picks up on your PA from your disclosure on line 206.

Pension adjustment reversal (PAR)

The *pension adjustment reversal* (PAR) is a fairly new concept. A PAR is essentially a statement showing that the pension adjustments (PA) reported on your T4s over the years were too high — your pension adjustments were overstated so your RRSP deduction limits were understated. The PAR simply corrects for the understatement in your RRSP deduction limit. A PAR will often arise when you leave an employer where you were a member of an RPP. If you are entitled to a PAR, your employer will report this to you on a T10 slip. A PAR indicates your RRSP deduction limit is being increased — this is good news!

 Your employer must send you a T10 slip within 60 days after the end of the calendar year quarter in which you left your job. If you left your job in the last quarter, you should receive your T10 slip by January 30.

 Receiving a severance payment? A PAR can be very beneficial as it opens up RRSP room that you can make use of to shelter all or part of the severance from tax. The higher your RRSP contribution, the lower the amount of your severance on which you will be required to pay tax. Caution — don't confuse this tip with the ability some individuals have to transfer a portion of a severance to an RRSP on *top* of their regular RRSP contribution limit. These special rules apply whether or not there is a PAR. Refer to comments below under "Transferring a severance or retirement allowance into your RRSP," in the section dealing with line 208, the RRSP deduction.

How did your RRSP deduction become understated?

 If you are a member of a defined benefit pension plan, your yearly PAs are calculated assuming you will continue to work for the company and continue to participate in the pension plan until the "normal" retirement age for the plan.

If you leave the plan earlier than expected, either due to voluntary early retirement or perhaps forced severance, the assumptions used to calculate past PAs were incorrect. The error is that your estimated share of the pension plan used has been overstated because your share will be less than anticipated. It is a bonus to receive a PAR T10 slip — it opens up more RRSP deduction room.

Take advantage of the opened-up RRSP room as quickly as you can.

Line 207: Registered Pension Plan (RPP) Deduction

Enter on line 207 the amount that *you* paid into your RPP during 2003. The amount you paid into your RPP will usually be noted in box 20 of your T4 slip from your employer. It may also be reported in box 32 of T4A slips you received or on receipts provided by your union or the pension plan itself.

The full amount noted on the tax information slips is usually tax deductible. This may not be the case under the following circumstances:

✔ The amount is greater than $13,500

✔ Your T4 or T4A slip indicates a past-service amount for services provided before 1990

You may be able to deduct an amount that you contributed in a prior year but have not yet deducted fully.

What is past service? The term *past service* refers to work you did for an employer in a prior year that later became pensionable service. (Now it is clear, eh?) Past service can be contrasted with *current service*, which refers to work done for an employer in a current year.

Contributions to your pension plan for past services are considered "past service contributions." (Finally, something that makes sense!) The contributions are generally made to upgrade your future benefits. Past service contributions are often made in a lump sum. People often refer to past service contributions as "buying back service," or buying increased pension benefits — pay some money now for an increased pension down the road.

Ask your pension plan administrator if you are entitled to buy back any service. Based on your age, your years to retirement, length of service, and the dollars involved, it can be beneficial in terms of your future pension entitlement to buy back service!

Contributions for current service and past service for 1990 and later years

Your total contributions for current service and past service for 1990 and later years can usually be found in box 20 of the T4 slips you received from your employer. The full amount is to be included on line 207 of your tax return.

Past service contributions for years before 1990

Your personal circumstances and the amounts you have contributed in the year for current service and for past services provided in 1990 and later years will determine the amount of the pre-1990 past service contributions you can deduct in completing your 2003 tax return.

If your current and past service contributions for 1990 and later years exceeds $3,500, you will find that none of your past service contribution for years before 1990 is deductible on your 2003 tax return. However, all is not lost! Those contributions will be eligible for deduction in 2004 and subsequent years.

Line 208: Registered Retirement Savings Plan (RRSP) Deduction

Next to the ability to sell your house tax-free due to the principal residence exemption (see Chapter 7), the RRSP is Canada's best tax shelter. Yes, we said tax shelter. Many believe a tax shelter is some very creative (perhaps sleazy) tax planning idea available only to the wealthy! Not true. Almost every taxpayer that has a job or is self-employed can take advantage of RRSPs.

What is an RRSP?

To easily understand what a registered retirement savings plan (RRSP) is, think of it as a retirement savings plan that has been CCRA-approved ("registered") and is eligible for the attractive tax features. An RRSP is an arrangement that allows you to save for your retirement on a tax-friendly basis. An RRSP is simply your personal pension plan.

Tax savings provided by RRSPs

The government wants you to save for your retirement. To encourage this, an RRSP offers two main tax advantages:

- ✔ A tax deduction for contributions made to an RRSP
- ✔ Tax-free growth while the funds remain in the RRSP

With an RRSP, no tax is payable until you make a withdrawal from your plan. You hope that the tax payable on RRSP withdrawals will be less than the tax saved when you took the deduction for making an RRSP contribution. This will occur if you will be in a lower tax bracket during your retirement years than the tax bracket you were in when you made your RRSP contributions.

A better idea is to have the withdrawal taxed in your spouse's hands if he or she will be in a lower tax bracket than you are at the time of the withdrawal. This is especially advantageous if you already have significant retirement income (say, pension income from an RPP) and your spouse has little. We know this sounds too good to be true, but you can do it by making spousal RRSP contributions. Spousal RRSP contributions are discussed later in this chapter.

Setting up an RRSP

Are you reading this after December 31, 2003? Don't worry — it is not too late to set up an RRSP and get a tax deduction for 2003! Contributions made to an RRSP on or before March 1, 2004, qualify for a tax deduction on your 2003 tax return. (Neat, eh?)

You can set up an RRSP in many places: a bank, a trust company, or through your investment planner. It is as simple as filling out a form and handing over the money. After you contribute to the RRSP, you will be provided with an "official RRSP receipt." This is what you will use to support the RRSP deduction that you will claim on your 2003 tax return.

Self-directed RRSPs

Banks and trust companies commonly offer deposit-based RRSPs. The money you contribute is usually invested in a number of investment vehicles, although the choice may be limited. If you would prefer more diversity and flexibility in your RRSP investing, you should consider a "self-directed RRSP." Don't worry — "self-directed" does not mean that you are on your own. You will work with your investment advisor to decide which investments are appropriate for your RRSP, given your investment goals and risk-tolerance levels. For example, you may choose a variety of mutual funds, stocks, bonds, other specialty investments, or even cash to hold in your RRSP.

There is an annual cost to maintain a self-directed RRSP, so in order to justify this cost you should generally wait until your RRSP assets reach $20,000 before setting up this type of plan.

RRSP contributions — in kind

Wanna set up an RRSP or contribute to an existing RRSP, but you're short on funds? Well, provided you already own an investment that is eligible for an RRSP, why not contribute the investment itself to your RRSP? This is called a contribution in kind. But be careful. If you contribute an investment that has gone up in value from the time you acquired it, a capital gain (see Chapter 7) will be triggered that will be taxed on your 2003 return. If the investment has gone down in value, you would think you would be entitled to a capital loss. No such luck. Why not? Because the CCRA says so.

If you are thinking about contributing investments that have declined in value, you should sell the investment, claim the loss, and then donate the cash. This way you won't lose out on claiming the capital loss. If you still like that investment, you can even repurchase it immediately inside your RRSP.

What investments are "RRSP eligible"?

Once you put money into an RRSP, the RRSP needs to purchase eligible investments. An RRSP is not an investment in itself. The following is a list of investments that you may hold inside your RRSP:

- Cash, guaranteed investment certificates, term deposits, treasury bills
- Canada Savings Bonds, Canada RRSP Bonds, and Government bonds
- Publicly traded shares and bonds, warrants, options, and Canadian limited partnerships
- Certain private corporation shares where you and your family own less than 10 percent
- Mutual funds, segregated funds, and labour-sponsored funds
- Certain mortgages, including a mortgage on your own home

Gold, silver, other precious metals, and real estate are not eligible investments. If your RRSP holds an ineligible investment, it will be subject to a 1-percent per month tax on the value of the ineligible investment.

How much can you contribute to your RRSP?

Generally, any person who has "earned income" in Canada can contribute to an RRSP. The amount that a person is allowed to contribute to an RRSP is based on a formula involving three amounts, including:

- 18 percent of the person's prior year's "earned income," to a dollar limit maximum set by the Department of Finance (the maximum for 2003 is $14,500);

- the pension adjustment, PA (discussed above at line 206); and

- the pension adjustment reversal, PAR (also discussed at line 206).

Basically, the formula to calculate your current year RRSP contribution limit is this:

Lesser of:	
— (a) 18% of prior year's earned income	$XXXX
— (b) Set maximum limit	$XXXX
The lesser of (a) and (b):	$XXXX
Less: Pension adjustment (PA)	($XXXX)
Plus: Pension adjustment reversal (PAR)	$XXXX
Current year RRSP Contribution Limit	$XXXX

What is earned income and how is it calculated?

The main consideration in determining your RRSP deduction limit is 18 percent of your prior year's "earned income." For purposes of determining your RRSP deduction limit, earned income consists of the following:

- Your salary, including taxable benefits (box 14 of your T4);

- Self-employed business income;

- Rental income and royalty income;

✔ Taxable spouse and child support payments received;

✔ Amounts from supplementary unemployment benefit plans;

✔ Research grants; and

✔ CPP and QPP disability pension (Chapter 5).

In computing earned income, you need to deduct the following:

✔ Union or professional dues deducted on your tax return (line 212);

✔ Employment expenses deducted on your tax return (line 229);

✔ Losses from self-employment (see Chapter 9);

✔ Losses from rental operations (see Chapter 8); and

✔ Support payments deducted (line 220) on you tax return.

Limit set by the Department of Finance

As mentioned earlier, the maximum amount that can be contributed to an RRSP in a given year is limited by earned income and amounts set by the government. The limit for 2003 is $14,500. The limits are scheduled to rise to:

2004	$15,500
2005	$16,500
2006	$18,000

Finding out your 2003 RRSP contribution limit

There are three ways to find out your 2003 RRSP contribution limit:

✔ **Look at your 2002 Notice of Assessment.** You would have received your assessment from the CCRA after filing your 2002 return. Your 2003 RRSP contribution limit is highlighted on the assessment. Any unused RRSP deduction room from prior years is added in to compute your contribution limit.

Although you can carry forward all your unused RRSP contribution room, don't wait to make your RRSP contribution. By contributing today, you'll reap the benefits of an immediate tax saving from your RRSP deduction and tax-free growth while your money is inside your RRSP.

✔ **Call the TIPS (Tax Information Phone Service)** toll-free number (1-800-267-6999) and ask what your limit is.

✔ **Calculate it yourself.**

Overcontributions to your RRSP

Generally, the amount you contribute to your RRSP will be equal to the RRSP deduction you will take on line 208 of your return. However, the total amount you have contributed to your RRSP may exceed the amount you claim as a deduction if you do one of the following:

✔ **You accidentally overcontribute to your RRSP:** You are permitted to overcontribute to your RRSP. However, the overcontribution is not tax deductible in the year it is made. If your overcontribution exceeds $2,000, you will find yourself in a penalty situation as well as having to withdraw the excess contribution. The penalty is 1 percent per month of the overcontribution in excess of $2,000 — that amounts to 12 percent per year!

Many people will overcontribute by exactly $2,000, since there will be no penalty and the funds can earn income inside the RRSP tax-free. Moreover, the $2,000 can be deducted on a subsequent year's tax return where you may not have contributed up to your maximum.

✔ **You don't deduct some or all of the RRSP contribution you have made:** Why would you not take a tax deduction when it is available? Well, you may plan on being in a higher tax bracket in the future. Even though you make an RRSP contribution during the year, you don't need to take the deduction that same year. You can save the deduction for a tax year when the deduction is more valuable.

Spousal RRSPs

When you make your RRSP contributions, you have the option of putting the contributions in your own RRSP, or a spousal RRSP, or a combination thereof. A spousal RRSP is an RRSP to which you contribute the funds, although your spouse is the one who receives the funds when withdrawn. This means your spouse — not you — makes withdrawals from the plan and pays tax on those withdrawals.

Ideally, both you and your spouse should have equal incomes in retirement. You should make a spousal contribution if your spouse will be in a lower tax bracket than you when the money is eventually withdrawn. You see, this way you get the deduction at a high tax rate, and your spouse pays the tax at a lower one.

But beware: if your spouse makes a withdrawal from a spousal plan in the year or within two calendar years of when you last made a spousal RRSP contribution, you — not your spouse — will be subject to the tax on the amount of the withdrawal that relates to contributions you made during this three-year period.

You are not entitled to additional RRSP contribution room in order to make a spousal contribution. The total contributions to your own plan, plus your spouse's, cannot be greater than your total RRSP contribution limit. (The RRSP contribution limit of your spouse does *not* impact how much you can contribute to a spousal RRSP.)

The RRSP Home Buyers' Plan (HBP)

If you wish, you can withdraw up to $20,000 from your RRSP tax-free for buying a home, as long as you or your spouse hasn't owned a home that you occupied as your principal place of residence in the past four years. Your spouse can make use of the HBP too, leaving a potential for $40,000 to go toward the home purchase, provided your spouse hasn't owned a home in the past four years either, and you are purchasing the home jointly. The withdrawal is treated as a loan from your RRSP, to be repaid over a period of no more than 15 years. The first repayment, a minimum of one-fifteenth of your HBP withdrawal, must be paid back in the second calendar year following the year in which you made the withdrawal. If you took out a $20,000 HBP loan in November 2001, for example, you must repay at least $1,333 (one-fifteenth of $20,000) before the end of 2003. If you do not make the repayment, the $1,333 is included in your income. Yikes!

It's easy to make an HBP repayment. You simply make a contribution to your RRSP. On schedule 7 of your tax return, you note the total of your RRSP contributions and then allocate a portion of the contributions to the annual HBP repayment. (It does not qualify for an RRSP deduction because it is simply a repayment of an amount borrowed from your RRSP.) Your remaining contributions are then allocated to the RRSP Lifelong Learning Plan repayment (see below), if applicable, or simply noted as a regular RRSP contribution that is tax deductible in the normal fashion.

If you contribute to your RRSP and then withdraw the funds within 90 days for the HBP, you won't be able to claim a deduction for that contribution. Always allow your contributions to sit for 91 days or more before making a withdrawal under the HBP.

There is no restriction on speeding up your HBP repayment. It makes good financial sense to repay as soon as you can, because the sooner the funds go back into your RRSP, the greater the tax-free growth in value!

The RRSP and Lifelong Learning Plan (LLP)

The LLP works in a similar way to the HBP. Funds can be withdrawn on a tax-free basis to fund full-time education or training for you or your spouse. The maximum withdrawal is $10,000 per year, or up to $20,000 over a four-year period. Funds need to be repaid to your RRSP over a period of no more than ten years. The minimum repayment is one-tenth of the LLP withdrawal. The first repayment is due on the earlier of the following:

> ✔ The second year after the last year you (or your spouse) was able to claim the "education amount" on line 323 of the tax return (Chapter 12)
>
> ✔ The fifth year after your first withdrawal under the LLP

You make your LLP repayments in the same fashion as you would make the HBP repayments noted above. You simply contribute to your RRSP, and on schedule 7 designate what portion of your RRSP contribution is for your LLP repayment.

Transferring a severance or retirement allowance into your RRSP

If you are going to receive a severance or retirement allowance from an employer you worked for before 1996, you may be able to put all or a portion of the payment directly into your RRSP. (Sorry, it can't go into a spousal RRSP.) This is referred to as a "transfer," and is attractive for two reasons:

> ✔ No income tax needs to be withheld on the portion of the payment being transferred directly into your RRSP. A direct transfer means the cheque goes from your employer to your RRSP — you don't even get to touch the money!
>
> ✔ The portion transferred to your RRSP is in addition to your regular RRSP contribution limit. You can still contribute up to your RRSP contribution limit, in addition to the portion of the severance transferred to your RRSP.

It's not critical that you roll your retiring allowance directly into your RRSP — this transfer can be made later. But be sure to make the contribution within 60 days following the end of the year in which you received your payment. If you don't contribute before this time, this special contribution is lost forever!

The portion of your retirement allowance or severance that cannot be transferred directly to your RRSP is available to assist in maximizing your regular RRSP contribution for the year. As noted above, if you left an employer where you were part of an RPP, you may be entitled to a pension adjustment reversal (PAR, T10 slip) that would serve to increase your RRSP contribution limit.

Line 209: Saskatchewan Pension Plan (SPP) Deduction

If you have made contributions to the SPP, you can deduct the least of the following amounts on your 2003 tax return:

- ✔ Amounts contributed to the SPP for yourself or your spouse from January 1, 2003 to March 1, 2004, excluding any contributions deducted on your 2002 tax return.

- ✔ Your 2002 RRSP deduction limit less the RRSP deduction you claimed on line 208, excluding any amounts transferred to your RRSP (that is, a portion of a severance or retirement allowance received that was transferred to your RRSP).

- ✔ $600.

Line 212: Annual Union, Professional, or Like Dues

Since you are taxed on pretty much all your income, it's logical that costs incurred to earn the income are deductible. It is logical — but no one ever said the *Income Tax Act* was logical. One of the deductions permitted is the cost of belonging to a union or to a professional body, or the cost of carrying professional or malpractice insurance. Union dues paid are noted in box 44 of your T4. Fees paid to professional organizations are usually receipted. If your employer pays the fees for your professional memberships or insurance, the employer gets the tax deduction — you don't, even if the receipt is in your name.

If you paid GST or HST on your union or professional dues, you may be able to have the GST refunded to you. Refer to the section near the end of Chapter 13 on the "Goods and Services Tax (GST)/Harmonized Sales Tax (HST) Rebate."

Line 214: Child Care Expenses

Our government recognizes that many of us incur child care expenses in order to be able to work. Our government also acknowledges that you may incur child care expenses in order to be able to go to school to train for a job.

How much is deductible?

Here are the maximum child care expenses that can be claimed per eligible child in 2003:

Disabled child — regardless of age	$10,000
Child under age 7 on December 31, 2003	$7,000
Child aged 7 to 16 on December 31, 2003	$4,000

However, the maximum deductible is restricted to two-thirds of your "earned income." Don't get the definition of "earned income" for purposes of the child care deduction mixed up with the definition for "earned income" for your RRSP deduction. For purposes of the child care expense deduction "earned income" consists of:

✔ Employment income, including tips and gratuities

✔ Self-employment income

✔ Scholarship amounts in excess of $3,000

✔ Research grants

✔ CPP and QPP disability benefits

✔ Government payments under a plan to encourage employment

To claim a deduction for a child, the child must be your child, your spouse's child, or a child dependent on you or your spouse, and one having a net income in 2003 of $7,757 or less. Eligible child care expenses include payments to the following:

✔ Individuals providing child care services. Payments to the child's mother, father, or a related person under 18 are not eligible. Individuals providing child care must provide a receipt with their social insurance number noted. Other child care providers simply need to provide you with a receipt.

✔ Day care, child care centres, and day nursery schools

✔ Schools where part of the fee is for child care (such as before- and after-school class care)

✔ "Day" camps and "overnight" camps

Where payments are made to facilities providing overnight lodging and boarding, such as overnight sports schools, boarding schools or camps, the eligible deductible amount is restricted to:

✔ $175 per week per disabled child of any age

✔ $175 per week per child under age 7 on December 31, 2003

✔ $100 per week per child aged 7 to 16 on December 31, 2003

A common misconception is that "day" camp fees are restricted to the amounts noted above. This is not true. The restrictions only apply where there is overnight lodging and boarding.

Form T778: Claiming a deduction for child care expenses

You will need to complete form T778 "Child Care Expenses Deduction for 2003."

Who gets to claim the deduction?

If a child lives with both parents, the child care expense deduction is claimed by the parent with the lower income. However, as with everything, there are exceptions to this general rule.

Where one of two supporting persons has no net income, the deduction for child care expenses will be "wasted." Where possible, the supporting person should arrange their affairs so the deduction can be maximized. This involves ensuring the lower supporting person has "earned income." As noted above, the deduction for child care expenses cannot exceed two-thirds of earned income. So for a maximum claim, the earned income of the lower net income supporting person needs to be three-halves (or 150 percent) of the eligible child care costs incurred.

Are you the only supporting person? If so, you make the claim for the child care expenses deduction. Can the higher net income supporting person ever deduct child care expenses? Yes! There are instances in which the supporting person with the higher net income can make the claim, because the lower net income supporting person was in one of these situations:

✔ In school. (The school can be a secondary school, college, university, or an "education institution" certified by Human Resources Development Canada [HRDC] for courses that develop or improve occupational skills.)

✔ Not able to take care of children because of a mental or physical disability.

✔ In jail for at least two weeks in 2003.

Also, if you are the higher net income supporting person, you may be able to make a claim if you and your spouse were living apart on December 31, 2003, due to a marriage breakdown, but reconciled before March 1, 2004. A claim will be allowed to you if you and your spouse had been separated for at least 90 days beginning sometime in 2003.

Supporting persons living apart

Where supporting persons were living apart for all of 2003 by virtue of a marriage breakdown (whether a legal or common-law relationship), each is entitled to a deduction for child care expenses. The aggregate claimed by the supporting persons cannot exceed the overall limits noted above.

If you separated from your spouse in 2003 and you are the higher net income supporting person, you can make a claim if you and your spouse were living apart on December 31, 2003. A claim will be allowed to you if you and your spouse were separated for at least 90 days beginning sometime in 2003 and the child care expenses claimed by you were actually paid by you. The claim period is restricted to the period of separation.

Line 215: Attendant Care Expenses

If you suffer from a severe and prolonged mental or physical impairment, you may deduct certain amounts paid to an attendant, provided that attendant is needed to enable you to go to work or school. Form T929 "Attendant Care Expenses" needs to be completed.

To be eligible to claim this deduction, you must have a severe and prolonged impairment that restricts your activities of daily living and is expected to last for 12 months. As with the disability credit amount (Chapter 12, line 316), your doctor needs to complete and sign form T2201 "Disability Tax Certificate," and you must file it with your tax return. If you've already submitted this form to claim the disability tax credit, there's no need to file it again.

Is your attendant required for you to go to work?

Of course, there's a limit to the amount you can deduct. If the attendant is required to enable you to go to work, the limit is the lesser of the following:

✔ Two-thirds of your "earned income" for the year

✔ The qualifying amounts you paid to the attendant during the year. The expenses cannot include any that you're already claiming as a medical expense (Chapter 12, lines 330 and 331) — no double-dipping!

Qualifying amounts include amounts paid to an attendant to enable you to perform the duties of employment, to carry on a business, or to carry out research for which you receive a grant. The attendant must be over the age of 18, and cannot be your spouse.

As it pertains to deductions for an attendant, here's yet another definition of "earned income" (you'd think the CCRA could come up with a new name), the sum of the following:

✔ Net income from a business

✔ Gross employment income

✔ Net research grants

✔ Training allowances paid under the *National Training Act*

✔ The taxable portion of scholarships, fellowships, bursaries, and similar awards (this is net of the $3,000 exemption, Chapter 8, line 130)

Is the attendant required for you to go to school?

If the attendant is required to enable you to attend a designated educational institution or secondary school, the limit is the least of the following:

✔ Two-thirds of your income from other sources (up to a maximum of $15,000)

✔ Two-thirds of $375, times the number of weeks of attendance at the institution or school

✔ The qualifying amounts paid to the attendant during the year

You are able to claim the disability tax credit and up to $10,000 of attendant care ($20,000 in the year of death) as a medical expense. However, you may only claim the medical expense if you have not claimed those same expenses as attendant care expenses.

Unlike the medical expense credit and the disability credit, the deduction for attendant care cannot be transferred to someone else. You need to think about which deductions and tax credits are most beneficial for you in terms of tax savings.

Line 217: Business Investment Loss (BIL)

In Chapter 7, we discuss capital gains and capital losses. A capital loss occurs when you sell an investment for less than you paid for it. A capital loss can only be used to shelter or offset capital gains from tax — it cannot be used to shelter other types of income (say, employment income, pension income, interest, or dividends) from tax.

 If you had a capital loss in 2003 but had no capital gains, the loss can be applied against capital gains reported on your prior three tax returns, or it can be carried forward to be applied against any capital gains that may arise in the future.

A business investment loss (BIL) is a special type of capital loss. A business investment loss, or a portion of that loss, can be deducted in the year incurred, to shelter any type of income — not just capital gains — from tax.

 A BIL occurs when you sell your shares or debt of a small business corporation (SBC), at a loss. A BIL will also arise if you were deemed to dispose of the shares or debt when the corporation became bankrupt, insolvent, or no longer carries on business, and the fair market value of the shares is nil.

 An SBC is a Canadian private corporation with the majority of the ownership in Canadian hands. The corporation must carry on a business in Canada. If the corporation is simply holding investments, it likely will not be considered to be carrying on a business for purposes of the SBC rules. (Refer to Chapter 11 for a discussion on SBCs.)

Calculating the deductible portion of the BIL

Your true loss is reported on line 228 on your return. The disclosure on line 217 is the amount you are entitled to deduct. As in the calculation of capital losses, 100 percent of a BIL is not tax deductible. This is logical since a gain on the sale of an investment is not fully taxable. The deductible portion of a BIL is referred to as an Allowable Business Investment Loss (ABIL).

A loss incurred in 2003 will be 50-percent deductible. The 50-percent rate parallels the percentage of capital gains subject to tax.

If you have used any portion of your capital gains deduction (Chapter 11, line 254), this will reduce the amount of the BIL that you can deduct.

Let's look at an example. In 1999, Abdul lent $100,000 to assist an SBC in starting up a new Internet business. Unfortunately, in July 2003 the corporation went bankrupt, leaving Abdul with nothing. Back on his 1992 return, Abdul had claimed a capital gains deduction to shelter a $10,000 capital gain he had incurred.

Abdul will report a BIL of $100,000 on line 228. However, his actual BIL eligible for a deduction is reduced by the 1993 capital gain that was sheltered from tax by the capital gains deduction. Therefore, his BIL eligible for deduction is $90,000 ($100,000 less $10,000). He can claim one-half of this amount, or $45,000, as his ABIL on line 217. The $5,000 ($10,000 × 50%) that could not be claimed as an ABIL is treated as a regular capital loss.

Line 219: Moving Expenses

If you moved at least 40 kilometres in 2003 to start a job (even if just a summer job), start a business, or for full-time post-secondary education, you may be eligible to deduct at least a portion of your moving expenses.

The eligible moving expenses may only be deducted from your employment, self-employment, or scholarship income earned at the new location. If your 2003 eligible moving expenses exceeded your 2003 income at the new location, the excess can be carried forward for deduction on your 2004 tax return.

What moving expenses are eligible?

Most moving expenses are eligible for a tax deduction. Specifically, they are as follows:

- Travelling expenses, including automobile expenses for you and your family
- Meals and accommodation on the way to the new residence
- Costs of moving your "stuff" (moving van, storage, insurance, and so on)
- Costs for up to 15 days for you and your family for meals and temporary stay
- Cost of cancelling your lease on the old residence

✔ Costs of selling your old residence (advertising, legal fees, real estate commission, and mortgage prepayment penalty if applicable)

✔ Costs of maintaining your old residence when vacant (including mortgage interest and property taxes) to a maximum of $5,000

✔ Legal fees and land transfer fees paid in acquiring the new residence, provided you sold the prior residence as a result of the move

✔ Utility disconnection and hook-up fees

✔ Incidental costs related to the move (for example, costs of changing your address, costs of acquiring new auto and driver's licences)

With respect to automobile and meal costs incurred while moving, the CCRA permits you to either claim the actual costs or to use a flat rate. The CCRA refers to the flat rate system as the "simplified method" — appropriately named, we would say.

For meals, the flat rate is $11 per meal per person to a maximum of $33 per person per day. Where you use the flat rate, you don't need to retain receipts.

The flat rate for automobile travel varies by province or territory. If you don't use the flat rate, you need to track all the costs of operating the car for a year (gas, maintenance, insurance, interest on car loans, depreciation, and so on). You then need to pro-rate the total of these costs by taking the number of kilometres driven for the move over the total number of kilometres driven for the complete year. (Ugh — perhaps too much math to do.)

Flat rates to use in determining automobile costs

The following flat rates are indicated in cents per kilometre:

Alberta	39.5
British Columbia	42.0
Manitoba	41.5
New Brunswick	41.5
Newfoundland and Labrador	43.5
Nova Scotia	41.5
Ontario	43.5
Prince Edward Island	40.5

Quebec	45.0
Saskatchewan	40.0
Northwest Territories	48.5
Nunavut	48.5
Yukon	48.0

Employer-paid or reimbursed moving expenses

You can only deduct moving expenses to the extent that the expenses were incurred by you. You cannot deduct expenses that were paid for by your employer, that you incurred and which were later reimbursed by your employer. On the other hand, if your employer provided you with an allowance, this amount must be included in your income. Make sure you then claim any eligible moving expenses as a deduction.

When possible, always get your new employer to reimburse you for your moving expenses. This is advantageous for a number of reasons:

- ✔ You will not be out any money. Even at the top tax bracket, a tax deduction is only worth less than 50 cents on the dollar. This means that for each dollar you deduct, you save less than 50 cents in tax. Isn't it better to have your employer give you back the full dollar? (The employer can claim a deduction for amounts reimbursed to you.)

- ✔ Some moving costs are *not* tax deductible. You definitely want to be reimbursed for these.

- ✔ You avoid the hassle of detailing all your moving expenses on your tax return, plus you are far less likely to have the CCRA question your return.

- ✔ You do not need to wait for a tax refund to get any of your money back.

The CCRA has stated that your employer can provide you with an up-to-$650 non-accountable allowance as a reimbursement of moving expenses. The allowance will not be considered income provided you certify in writing that you incurred moving expenses of an amount at least equal to the allowance you received.

Coming to or leaving Canada?

In most situations, moving expenses are not deductible if you are moving to or from Canada. (In this situation, you definitely want to have your employer reimburse your moving expenses!) However, if you leave Canada to study full time — say, at a college or university in the United States — your moving expenses may be deductible. These would be deductible against income from scholarships, fellowships, research grants and similar awards that are reported on your Canadian tax return. This assumes that even though you are studying outside Canada, you continue to be a Canadian resident for tax purposes. If you are a full-time student and you came to Canada, you can deduct your moving expenses against these same types of income earned in Canada.

How do you claim moving expenses on your tax return?

To claim moving expenses, complete form T1M "Moving Expenses Deduction." On this form you report where you moved from and to, why you moved, and the specific details and dollar amounts of your moving costs. Oddly, neither the T1M nor any moving receipts need to be filed with your tax return. However, you are required to keep these on hand in case of a CCRA query.

Lines 220 and 230: Support Payments Made

Support is the word that replaced "alimony" and "maintenance" payments a few years back. Support refers both to payments made for spousal support and those made for child support. It is important to differentiate between spousal and child support because each has its own criteria regarding permissible tax deductions.

Line 230 is simply for disclosure. Here you insert the amount of spouse and child support paid. As detailed below, all support payments may not be tax deductible. Enter the deductible portion on line 220.

Whether you receive the support for yourself or for your children, you should refer to Chapter 8, line 128, to determine what is taxable or not taxable in your hands. You will see that the deduction/income inclusion criteria mirror each other. Where one taxpayer has a deduction, one will have an income inclusion. If no deduction is available, there is no income inclusion. If you are paying a lawyer to help you collect support, the fees are likely tax deductible!

Though it can be emotionally unbearable to go through the process of finalizing the agreement, our experience in dealing with many separated and divorced individuals is that the agreement is vital in maintaining some sanity and in ensuring your financial protection. You should contact a lawyer specializing in family law as soon as possible to protect your rights to support, your assets, and your children. (There are various health care practitioners and clergy you can turn to for help with the emotional side.)

Spousal support

Payments to an ex-spouse (including an "estranged" [separated] spouse) are in most cases tax deductible. To support the deduction, you must have a written agreement or court order signed by both you and your ex-spouse that specifically stipulates the amounts to be paid. The payments must be periodic, that is, monthly. Lump sum payments do not qualify for a tax deduction. If there is no agreement or court order, the amounts paid would not be tax deductible. However, it is possible to have an agreement that provides for at least some of the pre-agreement spousal support payments to be tax deductible.

Any payments you have made prior to the date of a court order or a written agreement *can* be considered to have been paid under an order or agreement, and therefore be tax deductible. The order or agreement must stipulate that any prior payments made are considered to have been paid (and therefore are potentially deductible) pursuant to the agreement. Only payments made in the year that the order or agreement is finalized, and the preceding year, qualify for the retroactive treatment. Get the separation agreement drawn up promptly!

Child support

These rules took a dramatic shift on May 1, 1997. There are now three sets of rules, and you need to determine which ones apply to you. Your child support payments may or may not be tax deductible. The three sets of rules are detailed below.

Child support order or agreement made before May 1, 1997

If you are making payments under an order or agreement made before May 1, 1997, your payments are tax deductible. (Your ex-spouse will include the amounts in his or her income.)

Child support order or agreement made on May 1, 1997, or later

Your payments under a May 1, 1997, or later agreement or order are not tax deductible. (They are not taxable in the hands of your ex-spouse.)

Modification of a pre–May 1, 1997 child support order or agreement

If you are making tax-deductible payments under a pre–May 1, 1997 order or agreement, you may find that your payments suddenly cease to be tax deductible under one of the following circumstances:

- ✔ The order or agreement is amended to increase or decrease child support payments (and therefore, considered a new agreement and subject to the new rules).

- ✔ You and your ex-spouse elect to have the newer rules apply to your old agreement.

Line 221: Carrying Charges and Interest Expenses

Certain expenses you incur to earn investment income are tax deductible. Briefly, these are as follows:

- ✔ Investment counsel and management fees (only the portion of these fees related to services for your non-RRSP investments are deductible)

- ✔ Safekeeping, custodial, and safety deposit box fees

- ✔ Tax return preparation fees, if you have income from a business or a property

- ✔ Interest on money borrowed to earn investment income, such as interest and dividends — but not capital gains

Brokerage commissions are not tax deductible as a carrying charge because they form part of the tax cost on the purchase of an investment or reduce the proceeds on the sale. See Chapter 7 for more information on the calculation of capital gains and losses.

Eligible carrying costs and interest are to be detailed in Part IV of schedule 4 "Summary, Carrying Charges and Interest Expenses" of your tax return. The total is then put on line 221.

More on interest that can be deducted

Interest costs are deductible if you've borrowed money to invest in a business or *earn income from property*. Income from property includes interest, dividends, rents, and royalties.

Capital gains are not considered to be income from property. Therefore, if you're earning only capital gains and do not have the legal potential to earn income from property, the taxman may deny your deduction. Keep in mind that if you're investing in stocks or equity mutual funds, there's usually the potential to earn dividends. This will normally be enough to keep your interest deductible.

A high-profile interest deductibility case was ruled on by the Supreme Court of Canada in 2001 that greatly affected the interest deductibility rules in Canada. In this case, Mr. Singleton, a lawyer, attempted to convert non-tax-deductible debt (a mortgage) into a carrying charge. He did this by removing a sum of money from his capital account at his law partnership, used it to buy a house, and then borrowed from the bank to reinject into his partnership. Because there was a trace of the money from the bank loan to his law partnership (where he could earn business income), he deducted the loan interest on his tax return. The CCRA disagreed with this treatment and fought this all the way to the Supreme Court. Thankfully for taxpayers, the Supreme Court agreed with Mr. Singleton's tax treatment. They said that as long as there was a direct trace of the loan to a tax-deductible purpose, the interest on the loan would be deductible for tax purposes. It is not appropriate to look at the "economic reality" of the transactions on a whole, but rather, to look at each transaction individually.

If you currently have non-deductible interest and open (non-RRSP) investments, you may be able to do a "debt swap" similar to what Mr. Singleton did. Here's how it works. You must first sell your investments — watch out for hidden tax liabilities, though. The best investments to choose would be those that have not greatly appreciated in value since you've purchased them, as these will not give rise to a capital gain (and tax bill) when you sell them. The next step is to use the proceeds from the sale of the investments to pay down any non-tax-deductible debt you have, such as mortgage, line of credit, or other loan. Next, take out a new loan with the bank, and use this loan to repurchase the investments you sold. Because there is now a direct trace from the bank loan to a non-registered investment account, the interest you pay on this loan will be deductible on your tax return as a carrying charge! Presto — you've managed to convert non-tax-deductible interest into a tax deduction!

Interest can continue to be tax deductible even if the investment has been sold. This is provided the entire sale proceeds are used to pay down the loan or to purchase another investment.

In the 2003 Federal Budget the government warned us all that it was looking at the rules for interest tax deductibility. (Obviously, the *Singleton* case left a bad taste in its mouth!)

Therefore, take advantage of the "debt-swap" rules immediately in case the rules are changed soon!

Line 224: Exploration and Development Expenses

Did you invest in an oil and gas or mining venture in 2003 or in a prior year? The type of investment may have been called a "limited partnership," a "flow-through share" investment, or simply a "tax shelter." Whatever the term, if you did invest, you are probably entitled to some special tax deductions. One of the attractive features promoted in the selling of oil, gas, and mining investments is the tax write-offs (slang for "tax deductions") available.

If you are contemplating an investment in an oil, gas, or mining venture, be sure you completely understand the risks associated with the investment. A general rule of thumb is that the greater the tax saving, the riskier the investment. Be sure that such an investment falls within your risk-tolerance comfort zone. You should invest based on the quality of the investment — not the tax saving provided by the investment.

Why are these tax deductions made available? Remember that back in Chapter 1 we noted our *Income Tax Act* serves two purposes. The first is to provide cash necessary for the government to operate. And the second is that the *Income Tax Act* is a tool for many government initiatives. The government thinks it is a good idea to encourage oil, gas, and metal exploration in Canada. So the Act contains provisions to encourage this. The Act provides oil, gas, and mining companies with significant write-offs for the following:

✔ Canadian exploration expenses (CEE) – 100 percent deduction

✔ Canadian development expenses (CDE) – 30 percent deduction

✔ Canadian oil and gas property expenses (COGPE) – 10 percent deduction

Since many exploration companies do not have sufficient money to go out and explore for oil, gas, and metals, the Act permits these companies to turn to you for the funds. You are the one actually funding the exploration and development, so you get the attractive tax deductions. This is referred to as the expenses being "renounced" to you. Since "exploration" is the government's main initiative and the exploration phase has the greatest chance of failure, the write-offs are greatest when funds are expended on exploration.

How to claim exploration and development expenses

The promoter of the oil, gas, or mining ventures will provide you with all the information you need. Depending on the structure of the investment, you will receive a T101, T102, or T5013 slip. Instructions are provided on the back of these forms to assist in calculating your deduction.

You do not have to take the maximum deduction. Any amount not claimed will carryover to the following year for potential deduction using the same percentage figures. Why would you not want to take a deduction? Perhaps you expect to be in a higher tax bracket next year, so the deduction will be worth more in tax savings if you wait a year.

Line 229: Other Employment Expenses

As noted earlier, it is logical that if you are taxed on all your employment income, you should be able to deduct all the expenses you incur to carry out your employment duties. Well, this is not always the case. The fact of the matter is that the deduction for employment expenses is very limited. We warn most of you not to even think about the costs you incur in getting to and from work, your wardrobe, your makeup, and getting your hair just perfect.

(Please, no questions on dry cleaning!) Those most likely to be able to deduct employment expenses are those who have "out of the office" sales jobs and those employed in transportation.

For detailed comments on "tax breaks for employees" see section at the end of this chapter.

Line 231: Clergy Residence Deduction

An employed clergyperson may be able to claim a deduction in computing his or her net income in respect to his or her residence. A deduction is permitted where an individual is

- ✔ In charge of or ministering to a parish, congregation, or diocese, or
- ✔ Engaged exclusively in full-time administrative service by appointment of a religious order or religious denomination.

Where a member of the clergy has free accommodation, the value of this benefit is included in his or her income. It is usually reported on a T4. The amount is included in the total employment income noted in box 14 and highlighted separately in box 30. The deduction available is equal to this benefit. Hence the cleric is subject to tax only on the salary component of his or her employment income.

Where free accommodation is not provided, a claim can be made for the amount paid as rent or the fair rental value of the accommodation owned by the clergyperson. The deduction cannot exceed the employment income earned as a clergyperson. If the clergyperson receives a housing allowance from an employer, the allowance is included in income. However, the income inclusion can be offset with the cleric's residence deduction.

Form T1229 — "Clergy Residence Deduction" needs to be completed.

Line 232: Other Deductions

You can deduct a variety of expenses on line 232 if they apply to you. These include certain legal fees, repayments of OAS, CPP, and EI, withdrawals of RRSP overcontributions and unclaimed foreign tax credits.

Legal fees

Tax deductible legal fees include:

- ✔ Legal fees paid to object to or appeal an income tax assessment.

- ✔ Legal fees paid to collect a severance or a retirement allowance or a pension benefit. You can only claim fees up to the amount of the payment received in the year — minus any amount transferred to your RRSP. If you cannot claim all your legal fees in the year paid, they may be able to be claimed over the next seven years.

- ✔ Certain legal fees paid in respect of marital breakdown and spousal and child support.

 CCRA has relaxed its stance on the deductibility of legal fees incurred to obtain spousal support. Previously these fees were not deductible but they are now. CCRA has always permitted a deduction for legal fees to collect child support and has now expanded this to allow a deduction for legal fees incurred to *increase* child support.

 Ensure your lawyer details the bill such that fees for tax deductible services are highlighted!

Repayments of OAS, CPP, QPP, and EI benefits

Sometimes the government sends you too much money. If you have been paid benefits in excess of what you are considered to be entitled to, Human Resources Development Canada (HRDC) — or the Quebec equivalent — will request it back.

If in 2003 you were required to repay any OAS, CPP, QPP, or EI that was included in your 2002 or prior year's tax returns, you can deduct the repayment on line 232 on your 2003 tax return. EI repayments made in 2003 in respect of EI received in 2002 or prior years are noted in box 30 of your 2002 T4E slip.

Repayments of prior year OAS and EI differ from repayments of OAS and EI, referred to as social benefit repayments or clawbacks (see line 235). Clawbacks are repayments you may be required to make in connection with OAS or EI received in 2003 — not receipts from prior years. The amount to be repaid is calculated based on your 2003 income, as per line 234 of your return.

Other deductions

✓ **Withdrawals of overcontributed RRSP amounts:** Remember, if you remove an RRSP overcontribution (discussed under line 208), you will need to include this in your income as with any RRSP withdrawal. Your RRSP holder will issue you a T4RSP slip. The slip will *not* highlight that the amount you are taking out is an overcontribution. The income inclusion can result in double-taxation since you never received a tax deduction for the RRSP contribution (because it was an over-contribution). To prevent double-taxation you can claim a deduction on line 232 for the amount of RRSP overcontribution withdrawn. You will need to file a form T746 "Calculating Your Deduction for Refund of Unused RRSP Contributions" with your tax return.

✓ **Unclaimed foreign tax credits:** Foreign tax credits are discussed in Chapter 13. As detailed in that chapter, you may not be entitled to claim a full foreign tax credit. When this is the case, the amount of foreign taxes you paid in excess of the foreign tax credit available to you may qualify for a deduction on line 232.

Line 235: Social Benefits Repayment

Canada's social welfare programs for seniors, Old Age Security (OAS), and the unemployed, Employment Insurance (EI), have limitations. Essentially, if your income is considered too high, you are required to repay all or a portion of the benefits received.

OAS clawback

The social benefit repayment is in respect of OAS received in 2003. As you may have received the OAS and then were required to repay all or a portion of it back, it is often referred to as a "clawback." The government prefers to use "social benefit repayment" — a far less aggressive term. The clawback of OAS is a calculated amount based on your net income per line 234 ("net income before adjustments") — not per line 236 (simply "net income"). (Yes, it would be clearer if line 234 were titled "net income before social benefit repayment.")

As noted in Chapter 5, Human Resources Development Canada (HRDC) may not even have sent you any OAS in 2003 (or sent you a reduced amount), because it expected that you would be subject to the clawback in 2003 and need to repay all or part of your OAS.

It has made an assumption based on your 2002 tax return. However, you will still get a T4(OAS) slip indicating that you have received the full OAS. While this will guarantee to confuse you, the slip is correct; the amount clawed back from you will be indicated as a tax paid. (Whether HRDC calls it "tax paid" or a "social benefit repayment" on the slip doesn't really matter because it will "all come out in the wash." You will have to trust us and refer to the discussion on the OAS clawback in Chapter 5.)

As you may remember from Chapter 5, you will be subject to an OAS clawback in 2003 if your line 234 net income exceeds $57,879. For every dollar of income above $57,879, you are required to pay back 15 cents of your OAS income.

The $57,879 base amount will be increased in 2004 to keep up with inflation.

You can deduct any social benefit repayment in calculating your net income. This makes sense because the full amount of OAS or EI has been included in calculating your total income. Therefore, since you are not allowed to keep all the income, only the portion that you can keep, if any, is taxed. The amount you need to repay, the "clawed back" amount, is added to your tax liability on line 422 or your tax return.

 If you have received a T4(OAS) slip, ensure that you complete line 235. HRDC may owe you OAS! If it does, the amount is paid to you as part of your tax return — it will decrease your tax liability or increase your tax refund!

 Since the OAS clawback is based on the line 234 net income, you should plan, where possible, to minimize this net income figure. This can be done by reducing your income subject to tax — perhaps by rearranging your affairs to shift investment income to a spouse. Other ways may be to reduce the taxable amount of Canada Pension Plan (CPP) benefits you receive by splitting your benefits with your spouse (refer to Chapter 5) and, of course, by maximizing your RRSP contributions.

El clawback

 Like the OAS clawback, a repayment of EI because your income is considered too high is referred to as a social benefit repayment. This differs from the situation where you have simply been paid too much in EI benefits in the view of HRDC. If in 2003 you were required to repay some of the EI you received in 2002 or prior years, the amount repaid can be deducted on line 232 of your 2003 return. We discussed this earlier.

You will usually need to repay all or part of your current year's EI benefits if your line 234 net income is more than $48,750.

A person who received special EI benefits (maternity, parental, and sickness) will not have to repay those benefits.

The repayment of regular EI benefits required is calculated as 30 percent of the lesser of

✔ The regular EI benefits you received

✔ The amount of your net income in excess of $48,750

Just as with the OAS clawback, any amount of EI to be clawed back is deducted on line 235 ("social benefits repayment") in calculating net income. Since the amount is being repaid, it does not make sense for it to be subject to income tax. Report the amount repaid on line 422 of your tax return. In essence, you are simply adding to your tax liability the EI amount to be repaid.

Tax Breaks for Employees

You may be one of many employees that are required to fund the costs of carrying out your employment duties. These costs can vary from taking prospective customers out to lunch to using your own car for sales calls to perhaps using space in your home or apartment for work purposes. The following will help you if you're in these situations:

✔ Your employer pays you an allowance to cover your expenses but the allowance is included in your T4 employment income. In other words, you pay tax on the allowance.

✔ Your employer does not pay you an allowance. You are simply required to pay your own expenses.

If you fall into one of these categories, you should be able to claim a deduction for at least some, if not all, the expenses you incurred to do your job.

If you do not fall into one of these categories, don't be overly jealous of those who do. Though it is nice to be able to deduct employment expenses, it would be better if your employer simply reimbursed them. The reimbursement would not be a taxable benefit to you. With a reimbursement, you would not be out any money. Your employer would return to you every dollar you spent in doing your job. In deducting employment expenses, the best you can do is receive about a 46-cent refund for every dollar deducted — and this assumes you are in the top tax bracket, which means your taxable income after all deductions (including the deduction for employment expenses) exceeds $104,649.

Who is eligible to deduct employment expenses?

To deduct the expenses you incur to carry out your employment duties, the following must apply to you:

✔ You must be required to pay expenses to earn your employment income (in the CCRA's words, you must be required to incur the expenses under the terms of your employment contract, whether or not you have a written contract).

✔ Your employer must provide you with a form detailing the expenses you are required to incur. The form is T2200 "Declarations of Conditions of Employment." It is completed and signed by your employer — not you.

Form T777 "Statement of Employment Expenses"

The CCRA publishes this form to assist you in gathering and summarizing your employment expenses. This is the form used by the majority of employees. The total of your eligible employment expenses from the T777 is carried over to line 229 on your tax return. A second employee expense form, TL2 "Claim for Meals and Lodging Expenses," is used by employees involved in air, rail, bus, and trucking industries. Another form that can come into play is form GST370 "Employee and Partner GST/HST Rebate Application." Most employees like this form because it works only one way: It assists you in calculating the amount of GST/HST you can recover from the government!

The employment expenses you deduct are to include the GST, HST, and provincial and territorial sales taxes you paid. Do not separate the GST/HST or provincial/territorial sales taxes from the non-tax portion of your expenses. If you lived in Alberta (no provincial sales tax) and purchased $100 of deductible supplies to do your job, you would actually pay $107 when the GST is added. It is the $107 that is included in your employment expenses on the T777.

Where you are eligible to claim a deduction for employment expenses, record keeping is vital for a number of reasons. One, you don't want to miss out on claiming a legitimate expense. If you do, you overstate your tax liability! Two, the CCRA can request employees to provide support for the expenses claimed on their tax return. You do not send in support for your employment expenses with your tax return. The CCRA is usually happy to accept the deduction for employment expenses, provided the support (receipts, invoices, ticket stubs, kilometre log, and so on) is organized and available for inspection should it be requested. Third, you simplify your tax return preparation. Don't even think of bringing a shopping bag (or the infamous shoebox) full of receipts and stuff to an accountant in late April and expect to be pleasantly welcomed!

What's deductible and what's not?

Let's look at an example. Fiona took an industrial sales job with Warton Products Inc. of Stratford, Ontario, on February 1, 2003. Her conditions of employment were that she was to be paid on a commission basis and that she was required to do the following:

- ✔ Pay for her own office supplies (paper, toner, postage, and so on)
- ✔ Pay the salary of her part-time assistant, Katy
- ✔ Provide a home office for her and Katy. Fiona was not provided with a workspace at Warton
- ✔ Provide her own car because the job involved significant travel in southern Ontario

During 2003, Fiona made commissions of $90,000. She paid GST on her expenses when applicable. All her expenses were incurred in Ontario, so she did not pay any HST in 2003.

HST, or the 15-percent Harmonized Sales Tax, is paid on the purchase of goods and services made in New Brunswick, Nova Scotia, and Newfoundland. These provinces are referred to as the "participating provinces" because they are participating with the federal government in integrating the federal Goods and Services Tax (GST) with provincial sales taxes. The other provinces (and the territories) charge the 7-percent GST and their own version of a provincial or territorial sales tax. (Fortunate Albertans pay no provincial sales tax!) The provincial and territorial sales taxes are not integrated with the federal GST. Provincial and territorial sales taxes operate completely separately from the GST and are based on different taxing concepts.

Table 10-1 compares the expenses that can be deducted by an employee earning a salary and those that can be deducted by an employee being paid on a commission basis.

Table 10-1	Can It Be Deducted?	
Expense	*Earning Salary*	*Earning Commissions*
Legal fees to collect wages, salary, or commissions owed	Yes	Yes
Accounting fees for tax return preparation	No[1]	Yes
Advertising and promotion	No	Yes
Entertainment for customers	No	Yes[2]
Food and beverage[3]	Yes[2]	Yes[2]
Lodging and travel	Yes[4]	Yes
Parking[5]	Yes	Yes
Automobile expense	Yes	Yes
Office supplies[6]	Yes	Yes
Uniforms	Yes	Yes
Clothing, dry cleaning, makeup and hairstyling	No	No
Computer or fax purchase	No	No
Computer or fax lease	No	Yes
Cell phone purchase	No	No
Cell phone lease	No	Yes
Cell phone airtime[7]	Yes	Yes
Long distance calls[7]	Yes	Yes
Internet[8]	Yes	Yes
Licences[9]	No	Yes
Salaries to assistants[10]	Yes	Yes
Office rent[10]	Yes	Yes
Home office[10]	Yes	Yes

Notes

1. *An alternative filing opportunity is to claim the accounting fee as a carrying charge on schedule 4. Refer to comments regarding line 221. It deals with the deduction available for carrying charges and interest expenses.*
2. *Only 50 percent of entertainment, food, and beverage expenses can be deducted.*
3. *Food, beverage, and lodging are only deductible if your employer requires you to be away from the municipality or metropolitan area where your employer is located for at least 12 hours.*
4. *You can deduct travel expenses if you were normally required to work away from your employer's business or in different places, and you did not receive a non-taxable allowance to cover travelling expenses.*
5. *The CCRA's position is that parking costs at your employer's office are not deductible because they are considered a personal expense. However, if you need to go to the office before or after seeing a customer, or to work at a different location, we would argue that the parking in these circumstances should be deductible.*
6. *Supplies must be used directly in your work and for nothing else. The CCRA takes the position that this includes "pens, pencils, paper clips, stationery, stamps, street maps, and directories." Supplies do not include items such as briefcases or calculators. Tools are not deductible.*
7. *Restricted to work-related cost of calls and airtime.*
8. *The CCRA's guide "Employment Expenses" is silent on Internet charges. We would expect the CCRA to permit at least a portion of Internet fees if the Internet is needed to do your job. (Hey, you need an e-mail address, don't ya?)*
9. *Annual licence fees are deductible if needed to carry out work (for example, real estate and insurance licences).*
10. *Your employer must specifically indicate on form T2200 that you are required to incur these costs.*

Assuming Fiona spent $5,350 on office supplies and $4,000 for Katy's salary, she would be entitled to a full deduction of $9,350. This is a hint to what comes later. The amount spent on supplies includes 7-percent GST.

Automobile expenses

If you pay your own automobile expenses and are required to use your car to carry out your employment duties, you can deduct a portion of your costs in completing your income tax return. As noted above, your employer would indicate on form T2200 that you need to supply your own car and incur expenses to keep it on the road. Here are some types of automobile expenses that can be deducted:

✓ Fuel

✓ Repairs and maintenance

✓ Insurance

✓ Licence and registration fees

✓ Leasing costs

✓ Interest incurred on a loan to purchase a car

✓ Capital cost allowance (CCA or tax depreciation)

It is only the "employment use" portion of automobile expenses that is included in your deductible employment expenses. The CCRA states that driving only to and from work is personal use — not employment use. However, if you need to go out in your car in the middle of the day (say, to see a potential customer) or perhaps on your way to or from work, the whole trip can be considered employment use.

Remember that Fiona started working at Warton on February 1, 2003. She was required to provide her own car. Fiona used her Honda Civic, which she had leased a few years back. Her lease costs for the period were $3,300 ($300 per month for 11 months). From February to December 2003, Fiona drove the Civic a total of 20,000 kilometres — 15,000 were work-related. Fiona, being ever fearful of a CCRA query, kept a log in her glove compartment that detailed the work trips and kilometres driven. She updated the log daily. Based on the kilometres, you can see that Fiona used her car 75 percent of the time for work and 25 percent for personal use. Fiona can deduct 75 percent of her automobile expenses in calculating her deductible employment expenses.

Do you really need to keep a log of your kilometres driven for employment use? If you are asked by the CCRA to support your automobile expenses, they will ask to see your log of kilometres. So get in the habit of keeping the log in the car. Every time you get in the car, you should make an entry of where you are going, and later where you have been and the kilometres travelled. You will thank us if the CCRA comes knocking!

Let's calculate Fiona's automobile expenses:

Expenses	Dollar Value
Fuel	$2,000
Maintenance and repairs	$1,500
Insurance	$1,100
Licence and registration	$125
Lease	$3,300
Other — car washes	$100
Total expenses	$8,125
Employment use portion	75 percent
Allowable amount of automobile expenses that Fiona can deduct on her tax return	$6,094

Capital cost allowance (CCA) when an automobile is owned rather than leased

In the above example, Fiona leased the car she used to carry out her employment duties. What would the impact be if Fiona owned the car? Before heading back to our example, let's look at something called *capital cost allowance* — CCA for short. It is the tax term for depreciation.

As your car is expected to last more than a year, the cost of your car cannot be completely deducted in computing your employment expenses. However, a percentage of the car's cost allowance (CCA). The first step in determining the CCA you can deduct is to decide whether your automobile is "class 10" or "class 10.1" for CCA purposes. Both CCA classes 10 and 10.1 calculate the maximum CCA that can be claimed at a rate of 30 percent calculated on the declining balance method of depreciation. Where an automobile is purchased in a year, the "half-year" rule applies. This results in a CCA calculation at 15 percent (30 percent × $1/2$ = 15 percent). The determination of whether your car is considered a "class 10" or "class 10.1" automobile is important, as the CCA on class 10.1 automobiles is restricted to a maximum amount. The restrictions on CCA and other automobile expenses are discussed shortly.

There are many, many CCA classes. For example, a building is usually class 1, which has a 4-percent CCA rate. Furniture and most office equipment are part of class 8 with a 20-percent CCA rate. The determination of the CCA class is important because each class has its own particular rules. Most CCA classes have different percentage figures that are used to determine the maximum amount of CCA that can be claimed in a year.

Rather than leasing her Honda Civic, assume that Fiona purchased the Civic in 2003 for $23,000, taxes included. (By the way, this car qualifies as class 10 — therefore, no restrictions apply in calculating CCA.) Let's take a look at how Fiona would calculate CCA for 2003 and 2004.

Before calculating CCA, Fiona would calculate her employee expense deduction for the operating expenses of her car in the same way as above. She would total up the amounts she spent for fuel, repairs, licensing, insurance, and so on. (Of course there would be no leasing costs as we assume here she owns the car!) The total amount of expenses would then be multiplied by the employment use portion. In the preceding example 75 percent was used for the 2003 year. We'll assume the appropriate employment usage figure was also 75 percent for 2004.

The claiming of maximum CCA available, whether for an automobile or any asset on which CCA can be claimed, is optional. A taxpayer (whether employed or self-employed, or perhaps a corporation) may decide to claim less than the maximum CCA or no CCA at all! While at first it may seem odd that a taxpayer would not take maximum advantage of a tax deduction available, there are some logical reasons for this. For example, an employee may benefit by *not* taking CCA in one year because a higher CCA claim will be available next year. Perhaps the taxpayer will be in a higher tax bracket next year. This will result in a greater tax reduction than if the CCA is taken this year.

Table 10-2 summarizes how Fiona would calculate CCA for 2003 and 2004.

Table 10-2	Fiona's Capital Cost Allowance (CCA) Schedule for 2003 and 2004	
Year: 2003		
Undepreciated capital cost (UCC) at January 1, 2003		$0
Acquisitions in year	$23,000	
Subtract – one-half (note 1)	($11,500)	
	$11,500	$11,500
Base for 2003 CCA calculation		$11,500
CCA at 30 percent (note 2)		($3,450)
Add back one-half subtracted above		$11,500
UCC at December 31, 2003		$19,550
Year: 2004		
UCC at January 1, 2004 (as above)		$19,550
CCA at 30 percent (note 2)		($5,865)
UCC at December 31, 2004		$13,685

Notes

1. *This part of the calculation results in only half of the capital cost of the acquisitions in 2003 being depreciated. While the CCA rate is 30 percent, the subtracted amount results in the CCA being only 15 percent — half of 30 percent. This calculation is referred to as the "half-year" rule.*
2. *Remember that Fiona only used her car 75 percent of the time to carry out her employment duties. Therefore, her tax deduction is 75 percent of the CCA calculated. In 2003 — $3,450 × 75% = $2,587.50. In 2004 — $5,965 × 75% = $4,398.75.*

Restrictions on certain automobile expenses

Where you are entitled to deduct a portion of your automobile as employment expenses, you deduct only the "business use" portion of the expenses you actually paid. For most of your expenses, this is true. The amount you pay is the starting point in determining what you can deduct. However, there are three exceptions to this:

✔ Automobile leasing costs

✔ Interest on car loans

✔ Capital cost on which CCA will begin to be calculated. (CCA class 10.1 automobiles are subject to this restriction.)

When these exceptions apply, you will find that the amounts you use to begin calculating your deductible automobile expenses are less than you actually paid.

Maximum amounts for automobile lease, interest, and capital costs

Remember, these maximums apply before you pro-rate your automobile expenses between employment use and business use.

Let's look at Rashid's situation. Rashid is a salesman. On January 1, 2003, he leased a Mercedes. His monthly lease cost is $850. Rashid uses his car 60 percent for work. Rashid expects that his monthly effective tax deduction will be $510 ($850 × 60 percent), or $6,120 per year. He is not worried about the lease cost restriction because he understands the maximum costs for leases commenced in 2003 is $800 (see Table 10-3 below). Rashid is wrong! The effective tax deduction he will have is the $800 per month maximum multiplied by his 60-percent employment use, which results in a tax deduction equal to $480 per month, or $5,760 for all of 2003.

Oh, by the way, we have simplified things here. So don't get thinking you can get around the lease restriction rules by making a big deposit before the lease commences or guaranteeing the car will have a higher value than normal at the end of the lease. Both these ideas would bring your monthly lease costs down. However, the actual calculation to determine the maximum lease costs takes these ideas into account. In fact, one of the calculations focuses on the manufacturer's list price of the car. If the car is expensive, you will simply have to live with the restrictions on the amounts you can deduct! (Also, don't think you can avoid the restrictions because you drive a van or an SUV rather than a car. You'll still be caught by the rules.)

Table 10-3 lists the ceilings for maximum amounts that can be deducted for lease and interest costs, as well as the maximum amount that can be used for capital cost allowance (CCA):

Table 10-3	Restrictions on Automobile Expenses			
		2003/2002/2001	2000	1999
Maximum cost for CCA purposes	1, 2	$30,000	$27,000	$26,000
Maximum deductible monthly lease payment	2	$800	$700	$650
Maximum monthly interest cost	2	$300	$250	$250

Notes
1. All limits are before sales tax. The limits are actually slightly higher when GST/HST and provincial and territorial sales tax are added in.
2. Automobiles that have a capital cost above these limits are considered "class 10.1" automobiles.

Home office expenses

If your employer requires you to provide space in your home or apartment to carry out your employment duties, your employer must indicate this on form T2200, provided to you. If you do maintain a home office, you can deduct a portion of the expenses related to maintaining the workspace. This deduction is particularly attractive, since you'll be getting a tax deduction for a portion of the expenses that you incur anyway, such as monthly utilities and rent.

For the costs to be deductible, you must ensure your workspace meets one of two tests — you don't have to meet both! Under the first test, the workspace must be the primary place where your employment duties are carried out. A sales representative employed by a company may work from home and rarely "go to the office." A part-time night school teacher may not have an office at a school and must plan lessons and mark exams at home.

If the first test is not met, all is not lost. You may still qualify to deduct home office expenses if your workspace is used exclusively to carry out your employment duties. (Note that the word exclusively was not used in the first test.) In addition to using the space *exclusively* for these activities, you must use the space on a "regular and continuous" basis for meeting customers or clients or others associated with carrying out your employment duties. In the CCRA's opinion, infrequent meetings or frequent meetings at irregular intervals are not regular and continuous.

Deductible home office expenses

As Table 10-4 details, an employee paid on a commission basis is able to deduct more home office expenses than an employee paid by salary.

Table 10-4   Home Office Expenses Deductions

	Earning Salary	Earning Commissions
Electricity, heat, and water	Yes	Yes
Maintenance	Yes	Yes
Rent	Yes	Yes
Property tax	No	Yes
Home insurance	No	Yes
Mortgage interest	No	No
Mortgage principal	No	No

Expenses such as telephone and Internet charges are not mentioned here. Though you may think of these as a home office expense, they can be deducted as "supplies" in completing form T777. The CCRA's position is that long distance charges for calls made to carry out your employment duties can be deducted, but that the monthly charges for your residential phone line cannot — not even a portion of them. However, if you have a separate phone line for your employment, the full costs associated with this phone can be deducted.

Transport employees

If you are employed in the transport industry (air, rail and bus travel, and trucking), you and your employer are required to complete form TL2 "Claim for Meals and Lodging Expenses." The total of the amount deductible is to be included on line 229 of your tax return. Like non–transport industry employees, you may be eligible for a GST/HST rebate.

Musician's instruments

In addition to the costs noted above for employees, you're entitled to deduct capital cost allowance on your instrument (Class 8 — 20-percent declining basis), as well as any amounts paid for the maintenance, rental, and insurance of the instrument. To claim these amounts, you must be required, as a term of your employment, to provide your own musical instrument.

Artist's expenses

If you're an employed artist, there are some deductions you'll enjoy in addition to the "regular" employee expenses. The CCRA considers you an artist if you do any of the following:

✔ Create (but don't reproduce) paintings, prints, etchings, drawings, sculptures, or similar works of art

✔ Compose dramatic, musical, or literary works

✔ Perform dramatic or musical work, as an actor, singer, or musician

✔ Belong to a professional artists' association that is certified by the Minister of Canadian Heritage

An artist who earns income from any of the above activities may deduct related expenses incurred to earn this income. Again, these "related" expenses are in addition to the regular employment expenses deductible by all types of employees that are required to incur these expenses as part of their job.

Mechanics' apprentices

A mechanic's apprentice can deduct a portion of the cost of tools acquired in a year on their personal tax returns. Those of you with a "vehicle mechanic in-training" in the family will know what a significant investment these tools are in relation to their income and will likely want to join us in saying, "It's about time!"

Unfortunately, a deduction for the full cost of the tools is not allowed. The amount of the allowable deduction will be the total cost of new tools acquired in a taxation year, less the greater of $1,000 and 5 percent of the individual's apprenticeship income for the year.

Any part of the eligible deduction that is not taken in the year in which the tools are purchased can be carried forward and deducted in subsequent taxation years. You can also claim a GST/HST tax credit for the sales taxes paid on the deductible portion of the tools.

Goods and Services Tax (GST)/Harmonized Sales Tax (HST) rebate

The *Goods and Services Tax* (GST) and *Harmonized Sales Tax* (HST) are consumer taxes. This means that if you incur GST or HST in carrying out your employment duties, you are really incurring it on behalf of your employer's business — not as a consumer. Therefore, the GST or HST should be refunded or rebated to you because it was not incurred for a consumer purchase.

Say you purchase a gift to give to one of your best customers. The actual price of the gift was $100, but you paid $107 when GST was added. (For simplicity, we've assumed you bought this gift in a non-HST province and we've ignored retail sales tax.)

The $7 paid was not in respect of a consumer purchase. Therefore, the $7 should be refunded or rebated to you. This is referred to as a GST rebate. It is calculated using form GST 370 "Employee and Partner GST/HST Rebate Application." You will note the $7 on line 457 of your tax return and it will either decrease the income tax you owe or increase your tax refund!

What if the gift was for your mother? Well, there is no employment aspect to this purchase, so the $7 is not refundable — it becomes a true cost to you because you are acting as a consumer in making this gift purchase. The $7 is not going to be returned to you . . . but your mom will appreciate the gift.

Assessing your eligibility for GST/HST rebate

If you have to pay your own expenses to carry out your employment duties, you are probably able to claim a rebate for the GST and HST included in your expenses. You are not eligible to claim the GST/HST if either of the following applies to your situation:

- Your employer is not a GST/HST registrant
- Your employer carries on a GST/HST-exempt activity, which includes one of the following:
    - Health care (for example, a medical or dental practice)
    - Financial services (for example, banking, insurance, and investing)

Expenses that qualify for the GST/HST rebate

Deduct expenses you paid GST/HST on and deducted on form T777, plus the GST/HST component of the union or professional dues deducted on line 212 of your tax return.

Expenses that do not qualify for the GST/HST rebate

You probably did not pay GST/HST on all your expenses because some did not attract GST/HST.

- ✔ Expenses where no GST/HST was incurred.

  - You may have paid for goods or services that are GST-exempt, such as some membership fees and dues, insurance, licences, and salaries to assistants.

  - You may have incurred employment expenses where no GST/HST was paid because the vendor of the goods or provider of the service was not registered for GST and, therefore, did not charge GST.

- ✔ Personal use portion of employment expenses. You cannot claim a GST/HST rebate in connection with GST/HST paid on the personal portion of your automobile and home office expenses.

How to calculate and claim your GST/HST rebate

The rebate you are entitled to is calculated on form GST370 "Employee and Partner GST/HST Rebate Application."

The title of form GST370 includes "partner" because the form is used by a partner to calculate the GST rebate on expenses he or she incurs to earn income that is not reimbursed by the partnership. The partnership is the GST registrant — not the individual partners. Common partnerships in Canada are law and accounting firms. Many health care practitioners (doctors, dentists) operate in partnerships as well, but their activities are GST-exempt, so they are not eligible for the GST/HST rebate. Partners do not complete form T777 because this form is specifically for employees. Refer to Chapter 9 for a discussion on reporting partnership income and expenses.

Form GST370 provides a work chart to separate your expenses among the following:

- ✔ Expenses on which you paid 7-percent GST

- ✔ Expenses on which you paid 15-percent HST

- ✔ Expenses eligible for the GST/HST rebate

- ✔ Expenses not eligible for the GST/HST rebate

In this chapter we saw that Fiona was able to deduct the following employment expenses:

Office supplies	$5,350
Salary to Katy, Fiona's assistant	$4,000
Automobile expenses (under the scenario where her car was leased)	$6,094
Home office expenses	$465
Total employment expenses	$15,909

Fiona would use form GST370 to calculate her 2003 GST/HST rebate. As Fiona incurred GST only (no HST), she will only use the GST portion of form GST370.

GST rebate on eligible expenses

Total employment expenses per T777		$15,909
Less non-eligible expenses (expenses on which no GST was paid)		
Salary to Katy		$4,000
Employment-use portion claimed of:	Car insurance $1,000 × 75-percent business usage	$750
Car licence and registration	$125 × 75-percent business usage	$94
Water	$100 × 10-percent business usage	$10
House insurance	$300 × 10-percent business usage	$30
Property tax	$2,000 × 10-percent business usage	$200
Total expenses eligible for the GST rebate		$10,825
Multiply by factor to "back out" 7% from total		7/107
GST employee rebate (to line 457 on tax return)		$708

Fiona will put the $708 on line 457 of her tax return. It will serve to reduce the total tax owing on her tax return or increase the refund owing to her.

Now you say, *HOLD IT!* You've just realized that Fiona received two benefits:

- ✔ She got a tax saving from being able to deduct the GST component of her employment expenses.
- ✔ She received back the GST she paid.

Isn't this double-dipping on a tax/GST break? Congratulations on being so observant. Fiona has indeed received a double benefit. In fact, the government purposely designed the system this way! (Who else could?) However, when Fiona does her 2004 tax return, the double benefit will be taken away.

In Chapter 4, we discuss the employment income inclusions under line 104 of your return. One of the inclusions is the prior year GST/HST rebate. The prior year GST/HST rebate relates to the GST/HST included in employment expenses deducted on the previous year's tax return. So, effectively, the GST/HST portion of employment expenses deducted on a tax return in one year are added back to income in the immediately subsequent year's tax return. In year one you have the benefit of deducting the GST/HST portion of the employment expenses. In year two the amount is added back to income. Therefore, the benefit of the deduction in year one is nullified by the income inclusion in year two. That's okay, because don't forget you actually received a refund of the GST/HST you paid on your employment expenses through the GST/HST rebate mechanism.

So, if we get back to Fiona's situation we will see that she'll include the $708 on line 104 of her 2004 tax return. It will be fully subject to tax in 2004. After two years and two tax returns, the only double-dipping Fiona will do is at Dairy Queen.

Provincial and territorial sales taxes

There is no rebate for provincial and territorial sales taxes. They simply remain part of the costs you incurred in carrying out your employment responsibilities.

Chapter 11

Tips for Deductions to Calculate Taxable Income

*N*et income, which we discuss in Chapter 10, is basically a snapshot of your current year's income. This snapshot is then used to calculate your entitlement to certain tax credits, such as the GST/HST credit and the Child Tax Benefit, among others. Net income also provides a basis for certain non-refundable tax credits, such as the spousal credit amount and the medical expense credit. Taxable income, the subject of this chapter, has a different focus altogether. It is the figure used to calculate your income tax liability for the year. The types of deductions allowed under the taxable income category are not necessarily related to current-year activities. For instance, the calculation of taxable income includes deductions for prior year losses. In fact, some of the deductions are permissive in nature, essentially allowing for tax deductions based on your personal situation. For example, there are deductions for employee stock options, for residence in northern areas of Canada, and for certain non-taxable payments received in the year.

On many returns, net income and taxable income will be the same amount; therefore, you won't have to worry about these deductions at all. However, if you do have additional deductions, it's important to keep in mind that there is a difference between net income and taxable income — be sure to use the right figures in the right places!

Ordering of Deductions in Computing Taxable Income

Sometimes you will have so many deductions to claim, you won't need them all to reduce your taxable income to the point where no taxes are owing. If this is the case, ordering of your deductions is key. In fact, the *Income Tax Act* dictates which deductions must be taken before others! The order is as follows:

1. Deductions for employee stock options, employee home relocation loans, non-taxable receipts such as social assistance, workers' compensation, Old Age Security (OAS) supplements, treaty-exempt income, and vow of perpetual poverty claims. There are also deductions for prospectors' and grubstakers' shares and the disposition of deferred profit-sharing plan shares (there is a one-half deduction allowed so that the disposition of these shares matches the treatment of other types of shares).

2. Loss claims, including non-capital losses, net capital losses, farm losses, and limited partnership losses.

3. Capital gains exemption.

4. Northern residents deductions.

 If you have more deductions than you need in the year, you must claim deductions in the order specified above. That means you can't claim your northern residents deductions before you deduct loss carryovers (from prior years) in calculating taxable income.

 Always reduce your taxable income to equal your total tax credits for the year. If you reduce your taxable income to zero, you won't owe any taxes, but you might be wasting some deductions. For example, most taxpayers are allowed to claim the basic personal credit amount of $7,756 — this means the first $7,756 of taxable income is fully offset by this tax credit. Take a look at your non-refundable tax credits and other federal tax credits you have on schedule 1 of your tax return (such as the dividend tax credit, overseas employment tax credit, and alternative minimum tax carryover) to minimize your taxes, and maximize the deductions you can use in future years.

Some deductions can be carried forward to use in future years, while some cannot. So, when given the choice, always try to reduce your "discretionary" deductions, to use up all the deductions and credits that can't be carried forward. Discretionary deductions include some items used to calculate your "net income," such as RRSP deductions and moving expenses. Losses from prior years can also be carried forward (although keep in mind the ordering provisions above), so try to use up other deductions before you dip into these!

Line 248: Employee Home Relocation Loan Deductions

This is one deduction that you'll know you're entitled to claim. Why? Because it shows up right on the T4 slip you'll receive from your employer. If you have an amount shown in box 37 of your T4 slip, you can claim a deduction for your employee home relocation loan.

Generally, almost any benefit your employer gives you (including those that pertain to you as a shareholder) is taxable in your hands. This includes all employment perks, unless our tax laws specifically exempt the perks from tax. Lucky for you, an employee home relocation loan is one of these exemptions — albeit a partial exemption.

So what qualifies as a home relocation loan? Unfortunately, a loan to allow you to move down the street because you want a view of the lake does not. A home relocation loan is a loan your employer gives you, usually at a zero or low interest rate, to help you move for business reasons. Generally, this means you are changing jobs and your new employer is helping you out with a loan, or your current employer is transferring you to a new location.

To qualify for the employee home relocation loan deduction, some criteria must be met. All of the following must apply:

- The loan must be received by an employee (or the employee's spouse).
- You must be moving at least 40 kilometres.
- You must commence work in a new location in Canada.
- The loan must be used to acquire a new residence.

When you receive a home relocation loan, the amount received is not included in your T4 slip. However, an amount representing the "interest benefit" you have enjoyed (by not paying the interest!) is included in your T4 slip. Your employer has to report the interest benefit on all loans given to you, if the interest rate you are paying (if any) is less than the CCRA's prescribed interest rate.

The CCRA's prescribed interest rates are posted each quarter of the year. They can be found on the CCRA's Web site at www.ccra-adrc.gc.ca. The rate that should be used to calculate your taxable benefit is the rate in effect when your employee loan was granted. However, if the rate subsequently drops, you can start using this new lower rate. If the rate increases, you can continue to use the rate at the time the loan was received. In other words, you are protected from rate increases above the rate at the time you received the loan but you benefit from lower rates. This protection lasts for five years as a new loan is considered to be granted every five years.

If you are required to pay at least the CCRA prescribed interest rate on your employee loan, no taxable benefit needs to be calculated.

Now for the good part: the deduction! When an imputed interest benefit is included in your income for an employee home relocation loan, and you meet the criteria above, you can claim a full or partial deduction from your income.

Your deduction is the lesser of the following:

✔ The interest benefit included in your income

✔ The amount of interest benefit that would have been computed if the home relocation loan had been $25,000

In friendlier terms, if you've received a $20,000 interest-free loan from your employer, the prescribed interest rate is 3 percent, and this loan meets the definition of a home relocation loan, your deduction will be the lesser of $600 and $750 ($25,000 × 3 percent). In this case, your entire taxable benefit of $600 will be offset by the deduction. Just to keep it interesting, there is another rule surrounding employee home relocation loans. You see, the deduction does not last forever. It is only applicable for a maximum of five years from the day the loan was originally granted, or until the loan is actually paid off, whichever is shorter.

In negotiating your compensation for a new job that will require moving at least 40 kilometres, ask for a $25,000 home relocation loan. Due to the deduction for the interest benefit on the first $25,000 of a home relocation loan, you effectively receive the loan tax-free for five years.

Line 249: Stock Option and Shares Deductions

Stock options are one of the most popular forms of non-monetary compensation offered by employers. But make no mistake about it, they are a taxable benefit. The taxable benefit you receive in the year should be included in your total employment income reported on box 14 of your T4 slip. Here's a brief synopsis of the rules.

Public company shares

Normally in the year you exercise your stock options, you are considered to have received a taxable benefit equal to the difference between the market value of the shares on that day, and your actual cost. Thanks to fairly recent legislation in the *Income Tax Act*, this is no longer the case in all instances. In fact, you may now be able to postpone the taxation of qualifying employee stock options to when the shares are sold, instead of when the option is exercised.

Don't think you're off the hook for taxes on your stock options simply because you didn't sell your shares this year. The maximum benefit that can be deferred is $100,000 per vesting year. This $100,000 is based on the value of the underlying shares when the option was granted to you. The option price doesn't matter — it is the value of the underlying shares that is used to calculate the $100,000 limit. For example, say you were granted the option to purchase 100,000 shares of your employer corporation, at a price of $2 per share in 1998. (Assume the shares were trading at $2 at the time the option was granted to you.) At the time you exercise your option, the shares are trading at $5. (If you're quick at math you realized you had a $3 benefit per share, so for 100,000 shares the benefit is $300,000.) If you exercise all your options this year, you will only receive a partial deferral of tax. At the time the options were granted to you, they were worth $200,000 (100,000 × $2). This means that you will manage to defer taxes on only one-half of your options ($200,000 less $100,000 divided by $2 per share = 50,000 options). Your taxable benefit this year will be $150,000 ($5 less $2 × 50,000 options), and the other $150,000 will be taxed only when you sell the shares ($150,000 taxed now, $150,000 taxed later, $300,000 taxed in total — as expected).

If you wish to take advantage of this deferral for shares acquired in 2003 you must make an "election" with your employer before January 15, 2004. The election is simply a letter to your employer that must contain the following:

✔ A request for the deferral to apply

✔ The amount of the stock option benefit being deferred

✔ Confirmation that you were resident in Canada when you purchased the shares

✔ Confirmation that you have not exceeded the $100,000 annual limit

Your employer needs to be informed so that your T4 is prepared correctly.

Canadian-controlled private corporations

If your employer is a Canadian-Controlled Private Corporation (CCPC), you're in luck. When you exercise your stock options, you can defer all of your taxable benefit until you actually sell the shares. The taxable benefit for CCPCs is calculated the same way as that for public companies. That is, the market value of the shares on the date you exercise your option less your cost. By the way, your cost includes your exercise price (the amount you must pay for the shares under your option agreement) and any amounts you paid to acquire the option itself (if any).

The CCPC rules for stock options will apply to you so long as your employer was a CCPC at the time the option was granted to you (not when the option is exercised). So, if your company goes public in the future, you can still benefit from the more favourable CCPC stock option rules.

Stock option deductions

Now to the part you really want to know about — the stock option deduction. This deduction is available because the taxable benefit you'll be charged when you exercise your stock options (either this year or in a future year when you sell the stock) is taxed as employment income. In other words, 100 percent of the benefit is taxable in your hands. To many people this seems unfair, since the benefit is from a stock, which is normally treated as a capital item. If you recall from Chapter 7, capital gains are only one-half taxable, so you are taxed a full one-half more by exercising an employee stock option rather than purchasing the share yourself on the open market and then selling it for a profit.

But don't fret. Our tax laws understand this difference and allow a deduction, known as the stock option and shares deduction. The deduction is equal to one-half of the taxable benefit you must report. This means that your stock option benefit will effectively be taxed in the same way as a capital gain would be.

An additional stock option deduction of 25 percent is available if you exercise a stock option, then donate the stock to a registered charity. Yep, that's right. You'll get a tax deduction for 75 percent of your taxable benefit. And in addition, you'll get a donation receipt for the full market value of your donation. To take advantage of this incentive, you must have acquired the stock after 2000. In addition, the shares must be donated to the charity within the year and within 30 days of the option being exercised. When you donate such stocks to a registered charity, you report the disposition on form T1170 — "Capital gains on gifts of certain capital property" — and not on schedule 3 of your tax return as you would normally.

Shares qualifying for the deduction

Like most good things, the stock option and share deduction is not available in every case. In order to qualify, some criteria must be met (you didn't think a tax law would exist without qualifications, did you!).

The stock option deduction is available if all of the following conditions are met:

- Your employer corporation, or a corporation that does not deal at arm's length to the employer (a related company), is the seller or issuer of the shares.

- The shares must be common shares of the corporation.

- The exercise price of the option (that is, the amount you must pay to receive the share of your employer corporation — it's sometimes called the strike price) must be at least equal to the market value of the share at the time the option was granted to you. If you've paid an amount to acquire the option itself, this amount can be added to the exercise price of the option. For example, if you've paid $2 to acquire the option to purchase a share of your employer, and subsequently pay $5 to exercise the option, you will be eligible for the stock option deduction (assuming all other criteria are met) as long as the market value of the employer's shares on the date the option was granted to you was at least $7 ($2 plus $5).

- You must be dealing at arm's length with your employer. This means that if you control the corporation (that is, you own the majority of the voting shares), or are related to a person who controls the corporation, you will not be eligible for this deduction.

Regulation 6204 of the *Income Tax Act* covers the entire list of criteria (good reading for anyone with insomnia).

If the option was granted to you while the corporation was a CCPC, you don't necessarily have to worry about the above rules. You see, if you hold the shares you've acquired under your stock option agreement for at least two years, you'll automatically qualify for the stock option deduction. However, if you don't hold the shares for two years, but meet the above criteria, you'll still qualify. (CCPC options are more flexible than public company options in terms of the respective tax rules.)

Although these rules might sound fairly complex, it will not be up to you to determine whether or not you are eligible for the deduction. Your employer should make this determination, and your T4 slip for the year will indicate that your taxable employment benefit is in fact eligible for the "110(1)(d) or 110(1)(d.1) deduction." (Yes, you are correct, the references are to the *Income Tax Act*.) The amount eligible for the deduction is reported in either box 39 or 41 of your T4 slip. If an amount shows up in these boxes, report it on line 249 of your tax return.

Line 250: Other Payments Deductions

Did you report amounts on line 147 of your tax return? If so, you're likely entitled to a deduction for the full amount reported. You see, the types of payments reported on line 147 are not taxable amounts. And although they must be reported as part of your "net income," they are not intended to be part of your "taxable income." Hence the deduction. (Yes — slightly confusing, but these sources of income are received tax-free!)

The types of payments reported on line 147, and then deducted on line 250, are the following:

✔ Workers' compensation (form T5007)

✔ Social assistance payments (form T5007)

✔ Supplements to your Old Age Security pension payments (T4AOAS)

Lines 251 to 253: Loss Carryovers

Filing a tax return is one time that being a loser is to your advantage. You see, if you've incurred losses (including limited partnership losses, non-capital losses, and net capital losses) in prior years, and were unable to use those losses on your prior years' tax returns, you are allowed to carry those losses forward to offset some of your current income.

 If you've had losses in the past, you may be able to use those losses on your 2003 tax return to offset your taxable income, and reduce your 2003 tax bill! If you're unsure what your unclaimed loss balance is, give the CCRA a call. Their computer system tracks unused losses, and they will assist you in claiming the correct amount on your current year's tax return. However, it's up to you to claim the correct loss carryover amount on your tax return. If you forget to claim an amount, the CCRA will not apply your unused losses to your current income because these are optional deductions.

Depending on the type of loss you've incurred, there may be limitations on the amount of loss you can carryforward, and the number of years it can be carried forward.

 It's generally most beneficial to apply a prior year's loss to income taxed at a high rate. For example, if your income is low this year, but is expected to increase in future years, you may want to forgo claiming the loss carried forward this year. Instead, you can save the loss for a future year when you know you'll be subject to a higher tax rate. Of course, since certain types of losses have a limited carryforward period, you'll want to be absolutely certain you'll be able to use the loss in future years. If there's any doubt, claim the loss this year — use it, don't lose it — even if you're in a low tax bracket.

 Never claim losses to bring your taxable income to zero. Although you'll have no tax to pay with taxable income of zero, you'd also have no tax to pay if you report income equal to your non-refundable tax credits. As the 2003 basic personal credit amount is $7,756 (meaning your first $7,756 of taxable income can be received tax-free), you do not want your income to be less than $7,756.

Limited partnership losses

Limited partnerships are most commonly purchased as tax shelters. A limited partner, as opposed to a general partner, has limited liability with respect to the partnership's liabilities. The main reason (and perhaps not the best reason) for investing in a limited partnership is often the up-front tax losses allocated to partners.

Although some of these partnerships eventually make a profit, there are often huge losses in the first years. These losses are passed on to investors (the partners), to be deducted on their personal tax returns. This means that limited partnerships are most popular with taxpayers subject to the highest rates of tax. You see, the huge losses generated by these partnerships can actually push investors into a lower tax bracket! The tax authorities are not fans of limited partnerships in general, and the tax laws limit the amount of losses that you can claim. Specifically, investors can only deduct cumulative losses up to the investor's at-risk amount.

If you've received form T5013 "Statement of Partnership Income" from your limited partnership in the year, your at-risk amount should be reported in box 45. If not, contact the partnership and ask them for details of this amount — this is something the partnership should track.

Your at-risk amount is the amount you paid to purchase the limited partnership, plus any further capital contributions you made to the partnership (in other words, your tax cost of the limited partnership investment). Put more succinctly, you can only deduct losses on your tax return up to the amount that you paid for your partnership interest. This differs from other types of losses, where you are generally entitled to deduct the full amount of the losses, whether they are more or less than your tax cost of the investment.

If your cumulative limited partnership losses exceed your at-risk amount, you can carry the remaining losses forward for possible use in the future. You can deduct the additional losses in the future to offset any income produced by the partnership or to offset any additional capital you contributed to the partnership. Limited partnership losses can be carried forward indefinitely. There is no expiry.

Your limited partnership losses available for carryover will be reported in box 31 of your T5013 slip. This is the amount that can't be deducted on your current year's tax return, but can be carried forward to offset limited partnership income in the future.

If you have a limited partnership loss in 2003, this loss can be used to offset income from any source in this year. In fact, the loss must be used this year if it can be. If not, it becomes part of your non-capital loss balance and can be carried back for up to three years to offset a prior year's taxable income or carried forward for seven years. But don't forget, if any portion of the loss couldn't be used because of the at-risk rules, it can only be carried forward to offset against limited partnership income in the future, unless you increase the at-risk amount of your limited partnership investment.

Non-capital losses

In general, any business, employment, or property transaction is considered non-capital (see Chapter 7 for details on capital versus non-capital losses). So, if you have your own business and it generates a loss, this is considered to be a non-capital loss. In addition, if you've incurred an allowable business investment loss, otherwise known as an ABIL (see Chapter 10, lines 217 and 226 for more details), this is also considered to be a non-capital loss.

The amount of non-capital loss that is generated in a particular tax year is calculated on form T1A "Request for Loss Carryback." This is also the form that allows you to carryback any current-year losses to prior tax years, and reports the amount of the loss that can be carried forward to future years.

Form T1A is important because not all items on your tax return are figured into the calculation of your non-capital loss. Therefore, if you have a negative net income or taxable income amount (which is actually reported as a zero balance on lines 236 and 260 of your tax return), you should fill out form T1A so you know how much of the losses can be carried over to other tax years.

Once the CCRA receives and processes your form T1A it will reassess the year to which you carried the loss back . . . *and send you a tax refund cheque!*

The items included in the calculation of non-capital losses are as follows:

- ✔ **Employment income/loss:** This includes lines 101 and 104 of your tax return less any amounts reported on lines 207, 212, 229, and 231.

- ✔ **Investment income/loss:** Add together lines 120 and 121 of your tax return and deduct any amount reported on line 221.

- ✔ **Partnership income/loss:** This includes any amounts reported on line 122 of your return. Note that only the allowable loss (not the restricted portion of the limited partnership loss) is included on this line.

- ✔ **Rental income/loss:** This is reported on line 126 of your tax return.

- ✔ **Business, professional, or commission income or losses:** These are reported on lines 135, 137, and 139 of your return.

- ✔ **Farming or fishing income or losses:** These are reported on lines 141 and 143 of your return. The amount of farming losses you can claim may be restricted if farming is not your chief source of income for the year (see Chapter 9 for more information). Farming and fishing losses are included in the calculation of non-capital losses; however, they are subject to their own carryover rules. These losses can be carried forward for ten years (rather than the normal seven) and back for three years. So, once the calculation of total non-capital losses is complete, the amount relating to fishing and farming is removed from the non-capital loss carryforward balance, and put in its own "farming loss" pool to help keep track of the carryforward period.

✔ **Taxable capital gains:** This is reported on line 127 of your tax return.

✔ **Non-taxable income:** This is reported on line 147 of your tax return.

✔ **Net capital losses of other years:** This is reported on line 253 of your return.

✔ **Certain other deductions:** These include the capital gains deduction, deduction for business investment losses, employee home relocation loan deduction, stock option and shares deductions, other payments deduction, and income exempt under a tax treaty. Amounts are reported on lines 254, 217, 248, 249, and 250 of your tax return.

Form T1A requires you to separate the income and loss items on your tax return. For example, any deductions claimed would be placed in the "loss" column. You must then total all the income and loss items separately.

If you've claimed any amounts on lines 208, 209, 214, 215, 219, 220, 232, or 235 of your tax return, these amounts are deducted from your total income. It's possible that these deductions will cause you to have negative income; however, these amounts do not result in a non-capital loss. If the deductions claimed on these lines result in negative income (before taking into account allowable deductions in the loss column), your total income is deemed to be nil. You then take your total income, less the total amount reported in the loss column, to calculate the net loss for the year. You must then deduct any farming or fishing losses incurred in the year to come up with your total non-capital loss available for carryover. It is this amount that can be carried back to offset taxable income in any of the previous three taxation years, or carried forward.

Calculation of non-capital losses

Pam had more tax deductions than income in the 2002 tax year. She would like to know if she can take advantage of her losses on her 2003 tax return. Here is a summary of items claimed on her 2002 tax return:

Interest income	$1,200
Business income (loss)	($9,000)
RRSP deduction	$2,000

Pam's 2002 non-capital loss is calculated as follows. Note that "personal" streams of income and dedutions are handled separately from the business loss.

	Current Year Income ("A")	Current Year Loss ("B")	2002 Non-capital Loss ("A–B")
Interest income	$1,200		
Business loss		$9,000	
Subtotal	$1,200	$9,000	
Subtract: RRSP	($2,000)	n/a	
Subtotal (if negative = 0)	0	$9,000	$9,000

The 2002 $9,000 non-capital loss can be carried forward to 2003 to reduce Pam's 2003 taxable income.

Non-capital losses can only be carried forward for seven years. Due to the limited carryforward period, you should consider carrying your losses back (up to three years back), if possible, to guarantee that you will receive a tax benefit from the loss.

Like other non-capital losses, an ABIL can be carried forward seven years to reduce other types of income. If, at the end of the seven years, the ABIL is still unused, it becomes a capital loss and can be carried forward indefinitely to reduce capital gains.

If you are certain you will have taxable income in the future, you may want to forgo a loss carryback and instead carry the losses forward to offset your future income. You see, it is always most beneficial to claim the losses against income taxed at the highest marginal tax rate. So, if you're expecting to generate significant income in the future that will be taxed at a higher marginal tax rate than you're subject to this year, you may want to keep the losses intact until you're in that higher tax bracket.

Net capital losses

Capital losses for the current year are calculated on schedule 3 of your tax return. Capital losses will arise whenever you sell capital property (such as shares, mutual fund units, or real estate) for proceeds of disposition that are less than the tax cost of the property.

You may have both capital gains and capital losses this year. Your capital losses must first be used to offset any capital gains this year. However, if your losses exceed your total gains, you will have a net capital loss for the year. It is this net loss that can be carried back to offset capital gains taxed in any of the previous three taxation years, or forward to offset any capital gains in the future.

Net capital losses can only be used to offset taxable capital gains of other years. They cannot be used to offset any other types of income. Net capital losses can be carried forward indefinitely to offset future capital gains.

Net capital losses are also known as *allowable capital losses*. Only one-half of capital gains incurred in 2003 are taxable (as discussed in Chapter 7). Likewise, only one-half of any capital losses incurred in 2003 are deductible. It is the taxable, or deductible, portion of the gains and losses that are known as *taxable capital gains,* or net (or allowable) capital losses.

If you've incurred capital losses in prior years, you can deduct these losses on your 2003 tax return against any taxable capital gains reported on line 127 this year. Claim these losses on line 253 of your tax return.

Your Notice of Assessment will normally inform you if you have net capital losses carried forward from prior years. If you haven't kept track of your losses, call your local CCRA office and they will give you your net capital loss carryforward balance.

The allowable portion of capital losses (and the taxable portion of capital gains) has been changing over the years. Therefore, when you're claiming net capital losses of other years on your current year's tax return, it's important to note the year in which the loss arose, and the capital gains inclusion rate in place during that year. The term *inclusion rate* means the portion of the capital gain that was taxable in that year, and the portion of the capital loss that was deductible. Table 11-1 lists the capital gains inclusion rates over the years.

Table 11-1	Capital Gains Inclusion Rates
Year	**Inclusion**
1971 and earlier	0% (Those were the days!)
1972 to 1987	50%
1988 and 1989	66.67%
1989 to February 27, 2000	75%
February 28, 2000 to October 17, 2000	66.67%
October 18, 2000 and later	50%

If you've incurred capital losses in prior years, and want to apply them to the current year, you'll have to adjust your net capital loss for that year (that is, the loss after the above inclusion rates have been applied). Basically, the amount of the loss is adjusted to match the inclusion rate in effect for the year in which the loss is being applied. These are the steps to take:

1. Determine the year when your net capital loss occurred.

2. Divide your net capital loss for that year by the inclusion rate in effect during that year. For example, if you have a net capital loss of $50,000 carried forward from the 1988 tax year, you will divide that loss by 66.67 percent. This gives you a total or gross capital loss from 1988 of $75,000.

3. Multiply the total capital loss ($75,000) that you want to apply to your current-year capital gains, by the current-year inclusion rate. If you want to apply the loss to gains incurred in 2003, multiply the total loss by 50 percent. Therefore, you can claim up to $37,500 of net capital losses on line 253 of your tax return this year (assuming you have taxable capital gains on line 127 of at least this amount).

Likewise, if you have incurred capital losses this year (which given the state of the market may apply to more of us than we'd like!) and you want to carry them back to a prior year, you will need to adjust your net capital loss for this year. Just follow these steps:

1. Divide your net capital loss by this year's inclusion rate to get your total capital loss. For example, a net capital loss of $25,000 incurred in 2003 should be divided by 50 percent. This gives you a total or gross capital loss of $50,000.

2. Multiply the total capital loss by the inclusion rate for the year you want to carry the loss back to. If you realized $90,000 of net capital gains in 2001 that you wish to apply your losses against, you would multiply your total capital loss for 2003 by 50 percent (the inclusion rate for 2001). This means you would have $25,000 ($50,000 multiplied by 50 percent) of net capital losses to apply against your 2001 capital gain.

3. Complete form T1A "Request for Loss Carryback" Area III to advise the CCRA of the capital loss amount you wish to carryback.

Remember, you can only carry back capital losses for three taxation years to offset capital gains so . . . in 2003, 2000 will be the farthest back you can go.

As the capital gain inclusion rate was higher in 2000 (a combination of 75 percent, 66.67 percent, and 50 percent) than it is now (50 percent) it is preferential to carryback your capital losses to this year as the tax refund can be greater than if the losses are used in a future year.

Line 254: Capital Gains Deduction

If you've claimed a taxable capital gain on line 127 of your tax return, it's possible that you are eligible for an additional deduction in computing taxable income. In fact, if you've disposed of qualifying property for a gain, up to $500,000 may be exempt from tax. Of course, not all sales of capital property are eligible for the capital gains deduction. It only applies to disposition of qualified small business corporation shares (QSBC shares) or qualified farm property.

The $500,000 capital gains deduction available is a lifetime limit. In other words, you can't double dip — that is, claim the deduction more than once. Once you've claimed $500,000 in total deductions throughout your lifetime, you're cut off from future deductions.

Between 1985 and 1994, there were two capital gains exemptions available. One was the $500,000 capital gains exemption that is still in effect. The other was a $100,000 exemption available on the sale of any capital property. Now that the $100,000 deduction is gone, the only time you can claim a capital gains exemption is if you sell qualifying property — that is, QSBC shares or qualifying farm property.

If you've claimed any part of the $100,000 capital gains exemption in the past, the amounts claimed will reduce your $500,000 capital gains exemption available on qualifying property. For example, if you claimed the maximum $100,000 prior to 1994, you'll only have $400,000 of the $500,000 exemption to claim in 2003 and future years.

Qualified small business corporation (QSBC) shares

If you've disposed of QSBC shares in the year, you may qualify for the capital gains exemption, as long as you are a Canadian resident and you haven't used your entire capital gains exemption in the past.

Not just any share of a Canadian corporation will qualify under the QSBC rules. In fact, these rules are quite stringent. If you own shares in a small Canadian corporation, you should visit a tax professional to ensure that you can claim the capital gains exemption in the future. Even if your corporation does not currently qualify for the exemption, there are steps you can take to ensure the exemption can be claimed (known as "purifying" the corporation).

To review what criteria must be met for a company to qualify as a "small business corporation" see Chapter 7.

If you hold shares in a Canadian-controlled small business corporation (for example, a family business), visit a tax professional. There are steps that can be taken to ensure you are eligible for the capital gains exemption, even if your shares do not currently qualify. And even if you're not currently planning on selling your business, remember that should you meet an untimely death, you will be deemed to have disposed of all your assets, including these shares, at their market value at that time (unless you leave them to your spouse). Some current tax planning could save your family from a significant tax bill on your death!

If you own shares in a QSBC that will be going public in the future, ensure you elect to dispose of these shares on your tax return before they become public company shares. You will have to include the taxable portion of any deemed gains on your tax return, but these will be offset by the capital gains deduction. You can then add the deduction claimed to the tax cost of your new shares, effectively sheltering some, or all, of a future tax bill on the sale of the public company shares.

Qualified farm property

To provide an incentive for Canadians to invest in certain types of farm property, the $500,000 capital gains exemption is available to offset gains on the disposition of certain farm properties as well.

To qualify for the exemption, there are a number of criteria that must be met. These criteria are outlined in Chapter 7.

The definition of qualified farm property is technical and complex. In fact, since there are so many factors to consider, and the potential tax savings are so high, this is one area where a visit to a tax pro is necessary!

The CNIL problem

With a name that sounds like a horrid disease, it's no surprise that a CNIL spells bad news when you're trying to claim a capital gains exemption. The CNIL's full name is a Cumulative Net Investment Loss. It is basically a cumulation of all your investment expenses, less investment income, claimed after 1987. If you've claimed significant investment expenses or losses in the past, you may have a problem if you plan to claim a capital gains deduction on your tax return. However, if you've claimed minimal expenses and losses, and mostly income, you probably have nothing to worry about. A CNIL is a problem because your capital gains deduction will be reduced to the extent of your CNIL. So, if you have a CNIL of, say, $10,000, and your taxable capital gain on the disposition of QSBC shares or qualified farm property is $200,000, you'll only be allowed to claim a capital gains deduction of $190,000.

 If you're planning on claiming a capital gains deduction, you need to know your CNIL balance. Call your local Tax Services Office — they keep track of your CNIL balance and will let you know where you stand.

 The CNIL balance is calculated on form T936 "Calculation of Cumulative Net Investment Loss" of your tax return. It's a good idea to fill out this form each year to ensure that you keep an up-to-date running total of your CNIL.

 If you expect you will never have a capital gain on QSBC shares or qualifying farm property, you can forget about the CNIL rules! Sleep easy.

Line 255: Northern Residents Deductions

Rainy Hollow, B.C.; Belcher, Manitoba; Flin Flon, Saskatchewan; Pickle Crow, Ontario. What do these places have in common (other than intriguing names)? Well, their residents can claim a northern residents deduction. In recognition of additional costs of living incurred by those living in remote areas of Canada, the CCRA allows special tax deductions to help with the extra burden. Living in a remote area does not mean the nearest McDonald's is an hour away. In fact, the CCRA has a very detailed (and very long) list of specific areas of Canada where you have to live to claim the deduction.

The actual deductions you can claim depend on where you live. There are two different "zones" set out by the CCRA. If you live in a "northern zone," you are allowed the full northern residents deduction. If you live in an intermediate zone, you can deduct half the potential amount.

If you think you may live in a northern zone or an intermediate zone, check out the CCRA's publication T4039 "Northern Residents Deductions — Places in Prescribed Zones." (You can find it on CCRA's Web site at www.ccra-ardc.gc.ca.) All places in Yukon, Northwest Territories, Nunavut, and Labrador are prescribed northern zones, as are some locations in British Columbia, Alberta, Saskatchewan, Manitoba, Ontario, and Quebec. Prescribed intermediate zones include some places in British Columbia, Alberta, Saskatchewan, Manitoba, Ontario, Quebec, and all of Sable Island, Nova Scotia.

There are two types of northern residents deductions available:

- ✔ Residency deductions
- ✔ Travel deductions

If you qualify for the northern residents deduction, you must fill out form T2222 "Northern Residents Deduction" and file it with your personal tax return. Keep any supporting receipts, in case the CCRA asks to see them.

Residency deduction

To claim the residency deduction you need only live in one of the prescribed zones. Stopping by for a visit won't do. In fact, to qualify, you must have lived, on a permanent basis, in one of the zones for at least six consecutive months beginning or ending in 2003.

Even if you live in a prescribed zone on December 31 of the year, you won't automatically get the residency deduction. The deduction only kicks in after you've lived in the northern location for six consecutive months. However, once the six months are complete, you can file an adjustment to your tax return to request the deduction. For example, Walter moved to Gods Lake, Manitoba (in a northern zone), on December 1, 2003. When he filed his 2003 tax return on April 30, 2004, he had only lived in the prescribed area for five months, so he couldn't claim the residency deduction. However, once his six months are up (June 1, 2004, to be exact), he can file form "T1 Adjustment Request" to ask that his 2003 tax return be amended to claim the deduction. This is because he moved to a "zone" during 2003.

If you're preparing the tax return for someone who died in the year, the deceased can still claim the residency deduction so long as this person lived in a northern or intermediate zone for at least six months before the date of death.

Two types of residency deductions

There are two separate types of residency deductions you may be able to claim:

- **Basic residency amount.** This is a credit for simply living in a zone. The credit is $7.50 per day for living in a northern zone, and one-half of this, or $3.75, for living in an intermediate zone.

- **Additional residency amount.** This is an additional credit of $7.50/$3.75 per day that you can claim if the following situations apply:

    - You maintained and lived in a dwelling during your time up north (generally a house or apartment — sorry, a hotel room or bunkhouse won't qualify).

    - You are the only person claiming the basic residency amount for living in that dwelling for that time.

You are considered to have maintained and lived in a dwelling even if your employer or another person paid for your accommodations and other costs relating to the dwelling.

If more than one taxpayer lived in the same dwelling at the same time during the year, either each taxpayer can claim the basic residency amount deduction ($7.50 or $3.75 per day), or one taxpayer can claim both the basic residency amount deduction and the additional residency deduction. As soon as one person claims the additional residency deduction, no other person living in the dwelling during the same period can claim a basic residency amount. Since you're given a choice, you should consider the income and marginal tax rates of all members of a household before deciding how to allocate the residency amounts.

Board and lodging benefits

If you received a non-taxable benefit for board and lodging at a special work site in a northern or intermediate zone you may have some or all of your residency deductions taken back. Normally, when your employer pays your room and lodging, you would receive a taxable benefit. However, when you work in a "special work site," no taxable benefit is charged if your principal place of residence was not at this special site. For example, if you normally live in New Brunswick, but your employer sent you to Labrador for work (and paid for your room and board there), while your family remained at home in New Brunswick, you would not be charged a taxable benefit for the room and board paid on your behalf.

So what is a "special work site"? It is a place where you were required to work temporarily, and which was too far away from your ordinary residence to commute to daily, and you were required to be away from your ordinary residence, or at this special location, for at least 36 hours.

If you are considered to receive a non-taxable benefit for board and lodging at a special work site in a northern or intermediate zone, the non-taxable benefit (as reported on your T4 or T4A slip) is to be deducted in calculating your residency deduction. Keep in mind that these rules only apply if you normally reside outside the special work site area (that is, you have a home somewhere else).

If you received non-taxable board and lodging benefits but the special work site is more than 30 kilometres away from an urban area having a population of at least 40,000, you do not have to reduce your residency deduction.

Travel deductions

The second type of northern residents deduction you may be eligible to claim is the travel deduction. Generally, whenever your employer pays for something on your behalf, you are considered to have received a taxable benefit. This means that some travel benefits that your employer offers to you and your family may be taxable. When you live in a remote northern area, the fact that your employer will pay for some trips for you and your family could be a popular employment perk. Unfortunately, this could also lead to a tax bill. In recognition of the costs involved in traveling in remote areas, there is some relief from the taxable benefit rules. You can claim an additional northern residents tax deduction under these conditions:

✔ You qualify to claim a northern residents deduction (although you don't have to claim it to meet this criteria — *qualify* is the key word).

✔ You were an employee.

✔ You received taxable travel benefits in connection with your employment in a northern and/or intermediate zone.

✔ The travel benefits have been included in your employment income.

Box 32 of your T4 slip, or box 28 of your T4A slip, will report the taxable travel benefits you received in the year. If you received non-taxable benefits, such benefits will not show up on your slips, and you are not eligible to claim the travel benefits deduction.

Designated cities

The designated cities in Canada for purposes of the travel deduction are as follows:

✔ Vancouver, British Columbia

✔ Edmonton, Alberta

✔ Calgary, Alberta

✔ Saskatoon, Saskatchewan

✔ Winnipeg, Manitoba

✔ North Bay, Ontario

✔ Toronto, Ontario

✔ Ottawa, Ontario

✔ Montreal, Quebec

✔ Quebec City, Quebec

✔ Moncton, New Brunswick

✔ Halifax, Nova Scotia

✔ St. John's, Newfoundland

You must claim the travel benefits deduction in the same year that you report the taxable benefit received from your employer. For example, if you leave for a trip in December 2003 and return in January 2004, you should claim the deduction in the 2003 tax year *if* your taxable benefit shows up on your 2003 T4 (or T4A) slip. If the taxable benefit is not charged until 2004, the deduction can likewise only be claimed in the 2004 tax year.

Types of travel qualifying for deduction

There are different rules depending on your reasons for traveling. If you are traveling for medical services that are not available where you live, there is no limit on the number of trips you can make in the year. However, if you are traveling for any other reason, you can only claim a deduction for two trips a year for each member of your household. Trips for medical or other reasons can be taken by the employee paying tax on the benefit or by any member of the employee's household.

If you are claiming a travel deduction for trips made for medical reasons, no one can claim the expenditures as medical expenses as well.

If you are travelling for medical reasons, ensure that your employer notes this fact on your T4 or T4A slip. You should report taxable benefits for medical trips in box 33 of the T4 slip or in the footnotes to your T4A. If this isn't reported properly, have your employer reissue your slip to ensure your deduction will be accepted by the CCRA.

Amount of deduction available

Can you take a first-class, whirlwind trip, and hope to deduct it as a travel deduction? Let's not be greedy. As with many of our tax rules, there are maximum amounts that can be claimed. Here are the rules. The maximum deduction that can be claimed for each eligible trip in the year is the lowest of the following:

- ✔ The taxable employment benefit considered received for the trip

- ✔ The total travel expenses for the trip. These travel expenses include such items as:

  - Air, train, and bus fares

  - Meals. Actual cost (keep your receipts) or claim a flat rate of $11 per meal to a maximum of $33 per day per person

  - Motor vehicle expenses. You can claim motor vehicle expenses based on actual costs incurred, or on a fixed per-kilometre amount. The per-kilometre amounts are published in a CCRA Fact Sheet titled "Travel Expenses For

Northern Residents Deductions, Medical Expenses and Moving Expenses." It can be found on the CCRA Web site at www.ccra.adrc.gc.ca/tax/individuals/topics/ fs_northern_residents-e.html

- Hotel and motel accommodations

- Other incidental expenses, such as taxis, road tolls, ferry costs

✔ The cost of the lowest return airfare available at the time for the trip between the airport closest to your residence and the nearest designated city. This airfare amount is part of the calculation, whether or not you travelled by air, or to that city.

So, if you are travelling from a northern or intermediate zone to Cape Breton, Nova Scotia, you will have to determine the airfare from the closest airport to your remote location, to Halifax, Nova Scotia (the closest designated city to Cape Breton), even if you didn't fly between these two locations, and even though you're not planning on visiting Halifax!

If you don't know the actual cost of the trip taken (for example, when you're given free airline tickets), include the market value of a similar trip as the actual cost.

If you're travelling for medical reasons and cannot travel alone, you can claim a deduction for your travel expenses, as well as those of another member of your household who will act as your attendant (assuming the other conditions for the deduction are met).

Line 256: Additional Deductions

Additional deductions — who doesn't like the sound of that! But don't get too excited. Not any old deduction you think you should be entitled to can be written off on your tax return. In fact, the rules for additional deductions are pretty specific. We'll discuss some of them here. And trust us, they're actually not all that common.

Income exempt under a tax treaty

Canada has a number of tax treaties with many countries around the globe. These tax treaties outline, among other issues, how each country will treat certain types of income earned within its borders. Sometimes tax treaties state that certain types of income you earn from a foreign country will not be taxable in Canada. It could be that the income is taxed in the foreign country, or is altogether exempt from tax. Whatever the case, when you've received income that is exempt under a tax treaty, it is included in your "net" income but not your "taxable" income. This is why you receive an additional deduction. Income exempt under a tax treaty includes the following items:

- ✓ **United States social security payments.** These payments are only 85-percent taxable in Canada; therefore, you should deduct 15 percent of the total amounts received, on line 256.

- ✓ **Other foreign pensions.** Some pensions received from certain treaty countries, including certain French, German, Italian, and Spanish pensions, are exempt from tax in Canada. If you are unsure whether your pension is exempt from Canadian tax, contact your local Tax Services Office.

- ✓ **Child support payments received from residents of the United States.**

If you receive income from a foreign source, and you are unsure how it should be taxed in Canada, check with the CCRA. Under the terms of a tax treaty Canada has with the foreign country, you may be able to claim tax relief.

Vow of perpetual poverty

Living in a dingy basement apartment in downtown Toronto may make you feel as if you've taken a vow of perpetual poverty. However, this tax deduction doesn't apply to you. If you are a member of a religious order, have taken a vow of perpetual poverty, and have turned over your entire earned income and superannuation and pension benefits in the year to your religious order, you're in for some tax relief. In fact, you can deduct the entire amount of this income on line 256 of your personal tax return.

Earned income includes any salaries, wages, bursaries, scholarships, or research grants. It doesn't include any investment income such as dividends or interest. Even if you pay any investment income earned to your order, you are not entitled to a deduction on line 256.

To claim a deduction for a vow of perpetual poverty, you should include with your tax return a letter from your religious order. This letter should state that you are, in fact, a member of the order, have taken a vow of perpetual poverty, and have given your entire superannuation or pension benefits, and your entire earned income for the year, to that order.

If the above criteria apply to you, and you earn employment income in the year, you should provide evidence to your employer to this effect. The employer can then forgo the income tax and Canada Pension Plan contributions that normally have to be deducted from your pay.

Want more info? Take a look at the CCRA's Interpretation Bulletin #IT86R "Vow of Perpetual Poverty."

Employment with a prescribed international organization

If you earn employment income from certain international organizations, you can claim a deduction for your net employment income in the year. The international organizations to which this deduction applies include the United Nations and its specialized agencies. If this deduction applies to you, you must include your employment income and any related employment expenses in your "net" income, then deduct the income, net of related employment expenses, on line 256.

Tuition assistance payments

The December 10, 2001 Federal Budget provided for a deduction for amounts included in a taxpayer's income representing certain tuition assistance payments received from the Employment Insurance Commission (EIC) or Human Resource Development Canada (HRDC). The deduction should be taken on line 256 of the personal tax return.

Chapter 12

Tips for Non-Refundable Tax Credits

* *

In This Chapter

▶ Understanding how non-refundable tax credits work

▶ Claiming personal amounts

▶ Knowing when to claim the spouse or common-law partner amount

▶ Special credits for disabled persons

▶ Making the most of student loan interest, tuition, and education amounts

▶ Claiming your medical expenses

* *

*N*on-refundable tax credits directly reduce the amount of income tax you owe. In this way they differ from exemptions or deductions, which are subtracted from income subject to tax. The deduction allowable against federal taxes is 16 percent (except for charitable donations) of the total non-refundable tax credits for which you are eligible. Federal non-refundable tax credits are reported in schedule 1 of your tax return. Each province also calculates its own non-refundable tax credits to help offset provincial taxes. These provincial credits are reported on your provincial tax forms.

If the total of your non-refundable tax credits is more than the amount of tax you owe, you will *not* get a refund for the difference. The unused portion of the credits will be lost permanently, with a few exceptions to be discussed later in the chapter. Now you see why they're called non-refundable tax credits?

Line 300: Your Basic Personal Credit

For the year 2003, you are eligible to claim $7,756 as a personal amount credit for yourself on line 300 of schedule 1. In other words, the first $7,756 you earn this year is not subject to tax!

If you immigrated to or emigrated from Canada in 2003, you have to reduce your claim for the basic personal amount (among certain other credits). These amounts should be pro-rated for the number of days you were resident in Canada over the total number of days in the year.

Line 301: Age Amount

You qualify for an age amount of $3,787 if you were 65 years or older by December 31 of the year for which you want to claim this credit.

The amount you are able to claim is reduced by 15 percent of your net income (from line 236 of your return) in excess of $28,193, so that the age amount is reduced as income exceeds this level. For example, suppose Alice turned 65 in 2003, and she is wondering if she is entitled to claim the age credit. Her income for the year as reported on line 236 is $35,000. Her age credit is reduced by $1,021 ([$35,000 less $28,193] × 15%). This means that she can claim $2,766 on line 301 of her tax return.

You won't be entitled to any age credit if your net income exceeds $53,440.

Line 303: Spouse or Common-law Partner Amount

You may claim a credit of $6,586 if you were married or had a common-law partner at any time in the year, and if you supported that spouse at any time while you were married.

Just being married isn't enough to allow you to claim this credit — you must also have supported your spouse or common-law partner. What does this mean? Well, it doesn't mean you have to pay for everything, but it does mean you must pay for a reasonable proportion of the expenses for your spouse. These expenses may include items such as food, utilities, taxes, insurance, repairs, and clothing.

If your spouse had income for the year, the $6,586 amount is reduced by the amount of your spouse's income over $659. Therefore, if your spouse's income was greater than $7,254, the credit available to you is reduced to nil.

Your spouse's net income is the amount reported on line 236 of your spouse's tax return. If you separated in the year and were not back together by December 31, reduce your claim by your spouse's net income before the separation only. If you cannot claim the spousal amount, or you have to reduce your claim because of a spouse's dividend income from taxable Canadian corporations, you may be able to reduce your tax if you report all of your spouse's dividends on your return.

Who is your spouse? Well, it includes the person you are legally married to, and your common-law partner. Common-law partners are defined to be two persons, regardless of sex, who cohabit in a conjugal relationship for at least 12 months. Common-law partners can jointly elect to be treated as spouses for taxation years commencing from 1998.

Line 305: Amount for Eligible Dependant

This credit of $6,586 is available to you if you have a dependant and you were single, divorced, separated, or widowed at any time during the year. Not just any dependant will qualify for this credit, so unfortunately you can't claim a credit for your 28-year-old son who still lives in your basement, even if he does eat all your food. Your dependant must be the following:

✔ Under 18, your parent or grandparent, or mentally or physically infirm

✔ Related to you by blood, marriage, or adoption

✔ Living with you in a home that you maintain

✔ Wholly dependent on you for support

This claim is usually made by a single parent for a child, although claims by children for a parent and by one sibling for another are fairly common as well.

Like the spousal amount, the amount for eligible dependant of $6,586 is reduced by the dependant's income over $659.

You cannot claim this amount if you are claiming a spousal amount, or if someone else in your household is claiming this amount for the same dependant.

You can claim this credit for a dependant who lives away from home while attending school, if that dependant ordinarily lives with you when not in school.

Line 306: Amount for Infirm Dependants

You may be able to claim a deduction of up to $3,663 for each relative dependent on you or your spouse who is 18 years or older and was dependent on you during the year by reason of physical or mental infirmity. The credit is reduced by the dependant's income in excess of $5,197. The credit is completely eliminated once the dependant's income reaches $8,860.

A dependent relative may include either your or your spouse's father, stepfather, mother, stepmother, grandfather, grandmother, brother, sister, uncle, aunt, niece, or nephew.

To claim this amount the dependant must meet the following criteria:

- Eighteen years of age or older at the end of the year for which the tax return is filed
- A resident of Canada at some time during the year, if claim is made for a dependant other than a child or grandchild
- Dependent on you by reason of mental or physical infirmity
- Dependent on you for support at some time during the year

You may be able to claim a personal amount for children or grand-children even if they live outside Canada, provided they depended on you for support. You must provide proof of support paid. Dependants other than your children or grandchildren must have been resident in Canada at some time during the year. You cannot claim an amount for any other relatives who lived outside Canada for all of 2003.

You cannot claim this credit if someone other than you is claiming the equivalent-to-spouse credit for the same dependant. However, if you are claiming the equivalent-to-spouse credit on line 305, you may also claim the amount for infirm dependants on line 306.

Generally an individual is dependent on you for support if the individual does not have income in excess of the basic personal amount and you have contributed to the maintenance of that person — that is, paid for food, clothing, and other bills.

Lines 308 to 310: Canada Pension Plan/Quebec Pension Plan Premiums

Enter the total of the amounts shown in boxes 16 and 17 of your T4 slips. Do not enter more than $1,801.80. If you contributed more than $1,801.80, enter the excess amount on line 448 of your return. This often occurs when you've worked for more than one employer in the year. If you've paid more than you should, don't worry. The CCRA will refund this overpayment to you, or use it to reduce your balance owing. If you lived in Quebec on December 31, 2003, and contributed more than the max, claim the overpayment on your Quebec provincial return.

If you would like to calculate your CPP overpayment yourself, use form T2204 "Employee Overpayment of 2003 Canada Pension Plan Contributions and 2002 Employment Insurance Premiums." Otherwise, the CCRA will calculate the overpayment for you and will adjust your T1 return for the difference.

Canada or Quebec Pension Plan contributions payable on self-employment and other earnings

If you are self-employed you are required to pay both the employer and employee portion of CPP/QPP contributions to a maximum of $3,603.60. If you have both employment and self-employment earnings, the amount of CPP or QPP contributions that you have to make on your self-employment earnings will depend on how much you have already contributed to the CPP or QPP as an employee. schedule 8 will help you with these calculations.

You cannot use self-employment losses to reduce the CPP or QPP contributions that you paid on your employment earnings.

Self-employed individuals can claim a deduction on line 222 for the portion of CPP/QPP contributions that represents the employer's share (that is, one-half of the premiums paid). Only the portion of the contributions that represent the employee's portion will now qualify as a non-refundable tax credit.

Line 312: Employment Insurance Premiums

Enter the total of the amounts shown in box 18 of all your T4 and T4F slips. Do not enter more than $819.

If you contributed more than $819, enter the excess amount on line 450 of your return. The CCRA will refund this overpayment to you, or, if applicable, will use it to reduce your balance owing.

In some cases, you may have an overpayment even if you contributed less than $819. If so, the CCRA will calculate your overpayment and show it on your Notice of Assessment.

If you would like to calculate your overpayment, use form T2204 "Employee Overpayment of 2002 Canada Pension Plan Contributions and 2003 Employment Insurance Premiums."

If the total of the Employment Insurance (EI) insurable earnings shown in box 24 of all your T4 slips (or box 14, if box 24 is blank) and box 16 of your T4F slips is $2,000 or less, the taxman will refund your total EI premiums to you or will use the amount to reduce your balance owing. In this situation, do not enter your total EI premiums on line 312. Instead, enter the amount on line 450.

If your total EI insurable earnings are more than $2,000 and less than $2,042, the CCRA will refund a part of your EI premiums to you or use the amount to reduce your balance owing. In this situation, enter your total EI premiums on line 312. The CCRA will calculate your refund and show it on your Notice of Assessment.

If you would like to calculate your refund yourself, use form T2204.

Line 314: Pension Income Amount

You can claim up to $1,000 if you reported pension or annuity income on line 115 or line 129 of your return. But watch out. Only pension or annuity income you report on line 115 or 129 qualifies for the pension income amount.

Amounts such as Old Age Security benefits, Canada Pension Plan benefits, Quebec Pension Plan benefits, Saskatchewan Pension Plan payments, death benefits, and retiring allowances do not qualify for the pension income amount.

If you are aged 65 or over, but do not have sufficient pension income to qualify for the full credit (that is, your pension income is less than $1,000), you can create pension income by converting all or part of your RRSP to an RRIF or a life annuity. Or you can purchase a life annuity with other available funds.

If you are under 65 the credit is only available for payments out of a superannuation or pension plan (provided they are life annuity and not lump sum payments), annuity payments arising by virtue of the death of your spouse under an RRSP, RRIF, or DPSP, and the income portion of any annuity payment arising by virtue of the death of your spouse.

Line 315: Caregiver Amount

If, at any time in 2003, you maintained a dwelling where you and a dependant lived, you may be able to claim this $3,663 credit.

Your dependant must have been one of the following:

- ✔ Your child or grandchild
- ✔ Your brother, sister, niece, or nephew, parent, or grandparent (including in-laws) who was resident in Canada
- ✔ Your aunt or uncle who was resident in Canada

In addition, the dependant must meet all of the following conditions:

- ✔ Been 18 or over at the time he or she lived with you
- ✔ Had a net income of less than $16,172
- ✔ Been dependent on you due to mental or physical infirmity, or, if he or she is your parent or grandparent (including in-laws), born in 1938 or earlier

This credit of $3,663 is reduced dollar for dollar by your dependant's income in excess of $12,509. Once your dependant's income reaches $16,172, the credit is completely eliminated.

This claim is different from the infirm dependant amount claimed on line 306. To claim the caregiver amount, the dependant must have lived with you at some time during the year. This was not a requirement to claim the infirm dependant credit. Since this credit will always be greater than or equal to the infirm dependant credit, you should claim this credit if the dependant has lived with you. You cannot claim both credits. However, you can claim both the equivalent-to-spouse amount plus the caregiver amount in the same year.

Claims made by more than one person

If you and another person support the same dependant, you can split the claim for that dependant. However, the total of your claim and the other person's claim cannot be more than the maximum amount allowed for that dependant.

You cannot claim this amount for a dependant if anyone claims an amount on line 306 for that dependant or anyone other than you claims an amount on line 305 for that dependant.

You may have noticed by now that if you have a dependant who is infirm or disabled, there are many potential credits you can claim. The rules surrounding infirm and disabled persons are some of the most confusing in our tax laws. At times, the permutations and combinations of credits you can claim seem impossible to figure out. The CCRA has a guide entitled "Information Concerning People with Disabilities" that you should read. This guide discusses all the potential credits and who can claim them. It's a good start to help ensure you don't miss out on any potential tax savings!

Line 316: Disability Amount for Yourself

You may be able to claim a disability amount of $6,279 if a qualified person certifies both of the following:

✔ You had a severe mental or physical impai...
which caused you to be markedly restricted an,
of the time in any of the basic activities of daily livin...

✔ Your impairment was prolonged, which means it has laste...
is expected to last, for a continuous period of at least 12 months.

The only people who are qualified to certify that your impairment was severe and prolonged are medical doctors, optometrists, psychologists, occupational therapists, audiologists, and speech language pathologists.

You may be markedly restricted in a basic activity of daily living if you are blind or are unable to feed or dress yourself, control bowel and bladder functions, walk, speak, hear, or perceive, think, and remember. This includes certain individuals who undergo therapy to sustain their vital functions, such as dialysis and cystic fibrosis patients.

You may also be markedly restricted if it takes you an extremely long time to perform any of these activities, even with therapy and the use of appropriate aids and medication.

There have been many court cases in the past few years dealing with taxpayers attempting to claim the disability tax credit where the CCRA disagreed with the eligibility for the credit. The 2003 Federal Budget attempted to clarify the eligibility criteria to ensure that the credit will benefit those who need it most. These are the three areas of clarification:

✔ Individuals markedly restricted in either feeding or dressing themselves will continue to qualify for the credit.

✔ "Feeding oneself" does not include any of the activities of identifying, finding, shopping for or otherwise procuring food, or preparing food.

✔ "Dressing oneself" does not include the activities of finding, shopping for, and otherwise procuring clothes.

If you are making an application for this amount for the first time, you have to submit a completed and certified form T2201 "Disability Tax Credit Certificate." The CCRA will review your claim before it assesses your return to determine if you qualify. Once your claim is approved, you will be able to claim this amount for future years, as long as your circumstances do not change.

Line 318: Disability Amount Transferred from a Dependant Other than Your Spouse

You may be able to claim all or part of any disability amount on line 316 for which your dependant qualifies. You can claim the unused portion if he or she lived in Canada at any time in 2003, and was dependent on you because of mental or physical infirmity.

In addition, one of the following must apply:

✔ You claimed an equivalent-to-spouse amount on line 305 for that dependant, or you could have if you did not have a spouse and if the dependant did not have any income.

✔ The dependant was your or your spouse's child, grandchild, parent, or grandparent, and you made a claim on line 306 or 315 for that dependant, or you could have made a claim if he or she had no income and was 18 years of age or older in 2003.

✔ The dependant was your or your spouse's brother, sister, aunt, uncle, niece, or nephew.

If you are required to make child support payments for your child, you cannot claim a disability amount for that child.

In the first year you claim this credit, you must attach to your paper return a properly completed and certified form T2201 "Disability Tax Credit Certificate" for each dependant.

If you are splitting this claim for a dependant with another supporting person, attach a note to your tax return including the name and social insurance number of the other person making this claim. The total claimed for one dependant cannot be more than $6,279.

You can claim this credit only if the spouse of the person with a disability is not already claiming the disability tax credit or any other non-refundable tax credit (other than medical expenses) for the person with a disability, and you supported that person.

If you can claim this amount, you also may be able to claim an amount on line 315 for the same dependant.

If you have a child with a severe and prolonged impairment, there is a new Child Disability Benefit (CDB) that you may qualify for. The CDB is a tax-free supplement to the Canada Child Tax Benefit and Children's Special Allowance that provides up to 133.33 per month per eligible child. Ensure the CCRA has a T2201 on file for your child and that you file your tax return so that the government can assess your eligibility for this credit.

Line 319: Student Loan Interest

You can claim the amount of the interest you, or a person related to you, paid on loans made to you for post-secondary education under the *Canada Student Loans Act*, the *Canada Student Financial Assistance Act*, or similar provincial or territorial government laws.

Interest on personal or family loans will not qualify for this credit. Likewise, loans obtained through a bank that are not official government student loans do not qualify.

If you do not wish to claim these amounts on the return for the year they are paid, you can carry them forward and apply them on any one of the next five years' returns. Receipts should be attached to your paper return for the amounts you claim.

Line 323: Tuition and Education Amounts for Yourself

You can claim a 16-percent federal tax credit for any eligible tuition and education amounts incurred in 2003, and any unused amounts carried forward from previous years that are shown on your 2002 Notice of Assessment or line 323. You may also qualify for provincial credits on your provincial tax form.

Tuition amount

You can claim only the tuition paid for courses you took in 2003. Qualifying courses include most at the post-secondary level or those that develop or improve skills in an occupation.

You must have paid more than $100 during the year to each educational institution whose fees you claim.

You cannot claim other expenses related to pursuing your education, such as books, or board and lodging. Credit for these amounts is allowed for in the education amount (see below). To claim tuition fees paid to an educational institution in Canada, you must obtain from your educational institution an official tax receipt or a completed form T2202A "Tuition and Education Amounts Certificate."

To claim tuition fees paid to an educational institution outside Canada, you must receive from your institution a completed form TL11A "Tuition Fees Certificate — University Outside Canada," which you can obtain from any Tax Services Office. In order to qualify, you must attend a university outside Canada, and must be enrolled full-time in a course that lasts at least 13 weeks and leads to a degree.

Education amount

You can claim this amount for each whole or part month in 2003 in which you were enrolled in a qualifying educational program. Your educational institution has to complete and give you form T2202 "Education Amount Certificate," or form T2202A "Tuition and Education Amounts Certificate" to confirm the period in which you were enrolled in a qualifying program.

The following amounts apply:

- ✔ You can claim $400 for each month in which you were enrolled as a full-time student.
- ✔ You can claim $120 for each month in which you were enrolled in a qualifying part-time program.

You cannot claim more than one education amount for a particular month.

A full-time program is a program at the post-secondary level that lasts at least three weeks, and requires at least ten hours per week on courses or work in the program. A part-time program must also last at least three weeks, but it does not have a ten-hour per week course or workload requirement.

You can claim $400 a month if you attended your educational institution only part-time because of a mental or physical impairment. In this case, you have to complete form T2202 "Education Amount Certificate" to make your claim.

Transferring and carrying forward amounts

In many cases, students simply do not have the cash flow to pay for their own education. However, for tax purposes, the student — not the person who paid the fees — gets first crack at tuition and education credits. It is only if you do not need all the credits to reduce your tax bill to zero that you may transfer the credits to another person.

First, you can transfer to your spouse the part of your tuition and education amounts that you do not need to use to reduce your federal income tax to zero. Your spouse would then claim the unused portion of your tuition and education amounts on line 326 of his or her return.

 You must use all the credits necessary to reduce your taxes to nil before you can transfer the credits to another person. If you do not transfer your unused amount to your spouse, you can transfer it to your or your spouse's parent or grandparent, who would claim it on line 324 of his or her return. Complete the back of form T2202 or form T2202A, as well as schedule 11 on your tax return, to calculate and designate this transfer. The maximum amount you may transfer to a spouse, parent, or grandparent is $5,000 less whatever credits you needed to reduce your taxes payable to zero.

You can carryforward and claim in a future year the part of your tuition and education amounts that you did not need to use and did not transfer for the year in which they were incurred. However, if you carryforward an amount, you will not be able to transfer it to anyone else in the future. You must claim your carryforward amount in the earliest year possible. In other words, you can't pick and choose the tax years to claim the credits. The carryforward amount should be calculated on schedule 11 of your tax return.

If you are transferring a tuition or education amount to another person, do not transfer more than the person needs to reduce his or her federal income tax to zero. That way, you maximize the benefit of the credit and can carryforward the unused amount to a future year to offset your future tax bill.

Line 324: Tuition and Education Amounts Transferred from a Child

A student who does not need all of his or her 2003 tuition and education amounts to reduce federal income tax to zero may be able to transfer the unused portion to you if you are a parent or grandparent of the student or of the student's spouse. The maximum amount that each student can transfer is $5,000 minus the amount the student needs, even if there is still an unused amount. To make the claim, the student has to complete form T2202 "Education Amount Certificate" or form T2202A "Tuition and Education Amounts Certificate" to calculate the transfer amount and to designate you as the parent or grandparent who can claim the amount.

If a student's spouse claims amounts on line 303 or 326 for the student, a parent or grandparent cannot claim the tuition and education amounts transfer.

Line 326: Amounts Transferred from Your Spouse

Your spouse can transfer to you any part of certain amounts that he or she qualifies for but does not need to reduce federal income tax to zero.

The credits that may be transferred from one spouse to another are the age credit, the disability credit, the pension credit, and tuition and education credits. For additional details and to calculate your allowable claim, see schedule 2 of your tax return. In the identification area on page 1 of your return, be sure to report your marital status and your spouse's name and social insurance number so your claim is not rejected.

Lines 330 and 331: Medical Expenses

You can claim medical expenses you or your spouse paid for any of the following persons:

- ✔ Yourself

- ✔ Your spouse

- ✔ Your or your spouse's child or grandchild, who depended on you for support

- ✔ Your or your spouse's parent, grandparent, brother, sister, uncle, aunt, niece, or nephew, who lived in Canada at any time in the year and depended on you for support

You can claim medical expenses paid in any 12-month period ending in 2003 and not claimed in 2002. Generally, you can claim all amounts paid, even if they were not paid in Canada. Your total expenses have to be more than either $1,755 or 3 percent of your net income (line 236), whichever is less. This makes it more beneficial, in most cases, to claim the medical expenses on the tax return of the spouse with the lowest net income.

Checklist of allowable medical expenses

- ✔ **Fees for professional medical services:** These include the services of doctors, dentists, surgeons, chiropractors, acupuncturists, registered or practical nurses, physiotherapists, speech therapists, naturopathists, professional tutors that a medical practitioner certifies as necessary because of a person's learning disability or mental impairment, and so on.

- ✔ **Payments for apparatus and materials, and repairs thereto:** Eligible apparatus and materials might include artificial limbs, wheelchairs, crutches, hearing aids, prescription eyeglasses or contact lenses, dentures, pacemakers, iron lungs, orthopedic shoes, reasonable expenses relating to renovations or alterations to a dwelling of an impaired person, reasonable moving expenses if incurred by an impaired person moving to a more accessible dwelling, and so on.

- ✔ **Medicines:** These might include costs of prescriptions, insulin or substitutes, oxygen, and so on.

✔ **Fees for medical treatments:** These treatments might include blood transfusions, injections, pre- and post-natal treatments, psychotherapy, speech pathology or audiology, and so on.

✔ **Fees for laboratory examinations and tests:** These include blood tests, cardiographs, X-ray examinations, urine and stool analyses, and so on.

✔ **Fees for hospital services:** These include hospital bills, use of the operating room, anesthetist, X-ray technician, and so on.

✔ **Amounts paid for attendant care, or care in an establishment:** Seniors who are eligible to claim the disability amount and who live in a retirement home can claim full or part-time attendant care expenses as medical expenses. The claim is the portion of salaries and wages of attendants that can reasonably apply to the senior, limited to $10,000 per year, or $20,000 in the year of death.

✔ **Ambulance charges**

✔ **Expenses for guide and hearing-ear animals**

✔ **Premiums paid to private health services plans** (other than those paid by an employer) and premiums paid under the Quebec Medical Insurance Plan, including travel medical insurance.

✔ **Group home:** If you paid fees to a group home in Canada for individuals who qualify for the disability amount (line 316), the portion of those fees paid to someone to care for or supervise such an individual, if nobody has claimed it as an attendant or institutional care medical expense on line 330, a child care expense on line 214, or an attendant care expense on line 215 for that person.

✔ **Travel expenses, if medical treatment is not available locally.**

As proposed in the 2003 Federal Budget, the list of eligible medical expenses also now includes:

✔ The cost of real-time captioning, paid to persons engaged in the business of providing such services, on behalf of individuals with a speech or hearing impairment;

✔ The cost of note-taking services used by individuals with mental or physical impairments and paid to persons engaged in the business of providing such services, and the cost of voice recognition software used by individuals with a physical impairment (the need for these items must be certified by a medical practitioner); and

✔ The incremental cost associated with the purchase of gluten-free food products for those with celiac disease.

Individuals who have a severe or prolonged mobility impairment may be eligible to claim as medical expenses the renovation costs incurred to make their homes more accessible. The list of eligible medical expenses is extended to include expenses relating to the construction of a principal residence if the expenses enable the individual to gain access to or be mobile or functional within the home.

Items you cannot claim as medical expenses

Things you cannot claim as medical expenses include the following: toothpaste, maternity clothes, athletic club memberships, funeral, cremation or burial expenses, illegal operations, treatments or illegally procured drugs, and so on. In addition, you cannot claim the part of an expense for which you have been or can be reimbursed. However, you can claim all of the expense if the reimbursement is included in your income — such as a benefit shown on a T4 slip — and you did not deduct the reimbursement anywhere else on your return.

Attach your receipts and other documents (other than your health services plan premium receipts) to your paper return. Receipts for attendant care or therapy paid to an individual should show the individual's name and social insurance number.

The medical expense adjustment

If you claimed medical expenses for a dependant, other than your spouse, whose net income was more than $7,756, you have to reduce your medical expenses by making the following adjustment:

✔ Subtract $7,756 from the dependant's net income (line 236 of his or her return) or the amount that it would be if he or she filed a return.

✔ Multiply the result by 4.25.

✔ Complete this calculation for each such dependant.

✔ Enter on line 331 of your return the total of the amounts you calculated.

If the medical expenses adjustment you calculate for a dependant is more than the medical expenses you claimed for that dependant, it is not to your benefit to claim the medical expenses for that dependant.

Line 349: Donations and Gifts

You can claim donations made by either you or your spouse. Enter your claim from the calculation on schedule 9 and attach it to your return.

These donations and gifts do not include contributions to political parties. If you contributed to a federal or provincial political party, see Chapter 19 to find out about claiming a credit.

Allowable charitable donations and government gifts

Add up all of the donations made in 2003, plus any donations made in any of the previous five years that have not been claimed before. Don't forget any donations you made through payroll deductions — these donations will be shown on your T4 slip. Generally, you can claim all or part of your total donations, up to the limit of 75 percent of your net income reported on line 236.

For the year a person dies and the year before that, this limit is 100 percent of the person's net income.

It is generally most beneficial to claim donations made by both spouses together on one tax return. This is because the first $200 of donations is only eligible for a 16-percent tax credit while any additional donations attract a 29-percent tax credit. That's quite a difference! Combining your donations will ensure you are only subject to the 16-percent limit on the first $200 once — not twice.

You do not have to claim on your 2003 return the donations you made in 2003. It may be more beneficial for you not to claim them for 2003, but to carry them forward to claim them on your return for one of the next five years. This may be to your benefit, for example, if you already have sufficient non-refundable tax credits to completely eliminate your taxes payable.

You can claim only amounts you gave to Canadian registered charities and other qualified donees. A registered charity will show its charity registration number on the receipt. These receipts must be attached to paper-filed tax returns. The CCRA will not accept cancelled cheques, pledge forms, or the like as proof of payment.

Cultural and ecological gifts

Unlike other donations, your claim for these types of gifts is not limited to a percentage of net income. You can choose the portion you want to claim in 2003, and carryforward any unused portion for up to five years.

Donations of cultural property enjoy an exemption from capital gains tax plus an eligibility for the charitable donations tax credit for individuals. That's an added tax advantage! Normally when a capital asset is directly donated to charity, a disposition occurs for tax purposes and the difference between the market value and cost base of the asset is taxed as a capital gain. Elimination of the capital gains tax greatly enhances the desirability of donating cultural property!

Donations of publicly traded securities

Capital gains on shares of publicly traded companies that were donated to charities any time after February 19, 1997, will be included in income at 50 percent of the normal one-half inclusion rule for capital gains — that is, 25 percent for donations made in 2003. Rather than selling the security and donating the cash, you should instead consider donating the security. This way, you'll pay less tax and still get the same donation credit.

Donations to U.S. charities

Generally, donations to foreign charities are not eligible for a credit on your Canadian tax return. However, you can claim donations to U.S. charities, subject to a limitation of 75 percent of your U.S. source income, as long as the charitable organization is recognized as such by U.S. law and would have qualified in Canada if it had been a Canadian organization.

If you make a donation to a qualifying foreign university, the donation can be treated as if it were a Canadian donation; that is, you do not have to have U.S. source income in order to benefit from the donation. A qualified university is one where the student body normally includes students from Canada. A listing of these universities can be found in schedule 8 of the Income Tax Regulations. Most large U.S. universities are found on the list.

Donations of RRSPs, RRIFs, and life insurance

Changes in the tax legislation in 2001 now make it possible to name a registered charity as the beneficiary of an RRSP, RRIF, or insurance policy and to obtain a donation tax credit for the donation in the year of death. When gifts of life insurance are made, it may also be possible in some circumstances to claim the insurance premiums as donation credits.

Chapter 13

Figuring Out Your Federal Tax

● ●

In This Chapter

▶ Calculating federal tax credits

▶ Calculating social benefits repayment

▶ Calculating the Goods and Services Tax rebate

● ●

T o help you calculate the total federal tax you get to pay we have provided tips for other tax credits and items in this chapter. We hope they help. . . may the force be with you.

Line 425: Federal Dividend Tax Credit

In Chapter 6 we talk about the fact that dividends you receive from Canadian corporations has to be multiplied by 1.25 (or 125 percent). Tax techies call this the dividend gross-up (perhaps gross-out would be a better term). This is one rule that's hard to forget because the amount of dividends reported on line 120 of your tax return is actually 25 percent higher than the amount you received this year. What's the catch? Where is the logic?

Due to some heavy-duty corporate and personal tax rules that we won't bore you with here, the dividend gross-up actually works in your favour. You see, you are now entitled to a dividend tax credit. So, if you reported dividends on line 120, enter on line 425 of schedule 1 the total of the dividend tax credits from taxable Canadian corporations shown on your tax information slips. These credits normally show up on T5, T3, T5013, and T4PS slips. If you did not receive dividend information slips, don't fret. You can actually calculate this amount yourself. It is simply 13.33 percent of the taxable amount of dividends you received from Canadian corporations. (For the mathematically inclined, that's 16.667 percent of the actual amount of dividends received.)

Foreign dividends do not qualify for this credit. So, remember that foreign dividends should not be grossed up on your tax return and should not be reported on line 120, and you should not claim a dividend tax credit. (Foreign dividends are included on line 121 of your return.)

Line 426: Overseas Employment Tax Credit

The overseas employment tax credit is available to you if you were a Canadian resident but were working abroad for six months or longer in connection with a resource, construction, installation, agricultural, or engineering project. To claim the credit, form T626 "Overseas Employment Tax Credit," needs to be completed and signed by your employer.

The credit amount is calculated on form T626 and then carried to line 426 of schedule 1.

If you have severed your ties with Canada and have become a non-resident, you will not be eligible for the credit because your income as a non-resident will generally not be taxable in Canada.

Line 427: Alternative Minimum Tax (AMT) Carryover

If you paid AMT on any of your 1996 to 2002 returns, but you do not have to pay AMT for 2003, you may be able to claim a credit against your 2003 taxes for all or part of the AMT you paid in those years. To calculate your claim, complete parts 1, 2, and 8 of form T691. The carried-over amount to be applied against regular tax in 2003 is entered on line 427 of schedule 1.

Lines 431 and 433: Federal Foreign Tax Credit

If you've received income from foreign sources this year, you may have already paid tax to foreign tax authorities. But as we've learned throughout this book, Canadians are taxed on their worldwide income, which means that this same income is being taxed in Canada. Does this mean you're being double taxed? Probably no. Lucky for you, Canada lets you claim a credit for the foreign taxes you've paid.

The federal foreign tax credit is for foreign income taxes you paid on income you received from outside Canada and reported on your Canadian return. You may have paid foreign tax on foreign *non-business* income (that is, foreign investment income) and/or on foreign *business* income. (You normally can tell if you've received non-business or business income from a foreign source because these are separately reported on your information slips.)

Claiming this credit can take a bit of work. If you paid tax to more than one foreign country, and the total non-business income tax you paid to the foreign countries is more than $200, you have to do a separate calculation for each country for which you claim a foreign tax credit. In addition, a separate calculation is required for business income for each country.

Generally, the foreign tax credit you can claim for each foreign country is the lowest of the following:

> ✔ The foreign income tax you actually paid
>
> ✔ The tax due to Canada on your net income from that country

Use form T2209 "Federal Foreign Tax Credits" to calculate the amount of your foreign tax credit. Once you've calculated the amount of foreign tax credits you're entitled to, enter the total on line 24 of schedule 1.

If you paid tax on income from foreign investments (that is, foreign non-business income), your foreign tax credit cannot be more than 15 percent of your income from that investment. However, you may be able to deduct the excess amount on your return at line 232.

If you can't use all your foreign business income taxes in 2003, you can carry unclaimed foreign business income taxes back three years and forward seven years.

If your federal foreign tax credit on non-business income is less than the tax you paid to a foreign country, you may be able to claim a provincial or territorial foreign tax credit. You should complete form T2036 "Provincial Foreign Tax Credit" to determine the amount, if any, of the credit available.

How to claim the federal foreign tax credit

First, ensure you complete the federal foreign tax credit area on schedule 1 and attach form T2209 to your return. Also attach the following:

✔ A note showing your calculations. Show all amounts in *Canadian* dollars.

✔ Proof, such as an official receipt, showing the foreign taxes you paid. For example, if you paid taxes in the U.S., attach your W-2 information slip, U.S. 1040 tax return, and any other supporting documents. Foreign taxes paid may also be noted on your T3 and T5 slips.

Lines 409 and 410: Federal Political Tax Credit

If you contributed to a federal political party or a candidate in a federal election, enter the total amount of your contribution directly on line 409 on page 4 of your tax return.

You may deduct from your federal tax payable a *portion* of the political contributions you made. The amount of the credit deductible depends on the amount contributed.

The credit is calculated as the total of the following:

75 percent of the first $200 contributed	+	50 percent of the next $350 contributed	+	33 percent of the next $525 contributed

Therefore the *maximum* credit you will be able to claim in a year is $825, and that's when $1,075 has been contributed. Credit is not available for contributed amounts over $1,075.

Enter the amount of the credit calculated on line 410.

Attach your official receipts to your return. (By the way, if you are paper-filing your tax return, all your tax slips are to be attached to the top of page 3 of your return. Now you know!) You do not have to attach receipts for amounts shown in box 36 of your T5013 slips, or on financial statements showing the amount of federal political donations allocated to you by a partnership.

Since the amount of the available credit diminishes with the size of the contribution, consider spreading political contributions over two tax years. Two annual contributions of $750 will result in a larger credit amount than a contribution of $1,500 all in one year ($780 versus $500). Before making your contributions, consider how to maximize the available credit.

The federal political contributions tax credit only applies to federal political contributions. If you've made provincial political contributions, you're likely eligible for credit against your provincial taxes owing. (Take a look at Chapter 14.) Contributions to candidates in municipal elections do not qualify for a credit on your tax return.

Line 412: Investment Tax Credit (ITC)

You may be eligible for this credit if any of the following apply:

✔ You bought certain new buildings, machinery, or equipment, and they were used in certain areas of Canada in qualifying activities such as farming, fishing, logging, or manufacturing

✔ There's an amount shown in box 13 of your T101 or T102 slip

✔ There's an amount shown in box 41 of your T3 slip

✔ There's an amount shown in box 38 of your T5013 slip

✔ There's an ITC amount allocated to you on a financial statement of a partnership

The ITCs once available have been cut back to the point where the only expenditures eligible for an ITC are:

✔ Scientific research and development expenditures (R&D)

✔ Expenditures for equipment used in a variety of activities carried on in the Atlantic provinces or the Gaspé Peninsula of Quebec

To claim an ITC for an eligible expenditure, you need to complete form T2038 "Investment Tax Credit" (IND) and send it as part of your tax return.

If you have not used ITCs generated in earlier years (perhaps because the ITCs exceeded your tax liability), you can carryover these amounts to offset 2003 or future year taxes.

Lines 413 and 414: Labour-Sponsored Funds Tax Credit

A *labour-sponsored venture capital corporation* (LSVCC) is a venture capital fund established under specific federal or provincial legislation and managed by labour unions or employee groups. You can claim the labour-sponsored fund tax credit if you purchased an approved share of the capital stock of an LSVCC from January 1, 2003 to February 28, 2004. If you bought a share between January 1, 2004 and February 28, 2004, you can claim a credit for that share either on your 2003 return or on your 2004 return, but not both.

Technically, you are purchasing a share of an LSVCC. However, most people refer to it as a purchase of labour-sponsored funds.

Enter the cost of purchasing your labour-sponsored fund on line 413 of page 4 of your tax return. Enter the amount of the credit on line 414. The allowable credit is 15 percent of the cost, to a maximum of $750.

Labour-sponsored funds can be contributed to your RRSP. If you choose to do so, don't forget to claim an RRSP deduction as well as the federal (and perhaps provincial) tax credit for your investment!

If a spousal RRSP became the first registered holder of the labour-sponsored fund units, either the RRSP contributor or the RRSP annuitant (the spouse) may claim the credit for the investment.

Attach to your return either a T5006 slip "Statement of Registered Labour-Sponsored Venture Capital Corporation Class A Shares," or an official provincial or territorial slip documenting your investment. If the labour-sponsored funds went into your RRSP, an official RRSP receipt needs to be attached to your return as well.

Line 418: Additional Tax on RESP Accumulated Income Payments

Many Canadians are purchasing registered education savings plans (RESPs) to help fund their children's education. But when the moment of truth arrives, and your child decides to forgo post-secondary school, who do you think may be stuck paying the tax on the RESP growth? You guessed it — you!

Don't get us wrong, *we* think RESPs are a great tax deferral and income splitting tool. We're just warning you of one of the repercussions. You see, if you received an accumulated income payment from an RESP in 2003, you may have to pay regular tax plus an additional tax of 20 percent on all or part of the amount received. It is reported in box 40 of your T4A slip.

 You are liable for additional tax when you have contributed to an RESP that has been running for at least ten years, and the beneficiary of the plan does not pursue a post-secondary education by 21 years of age. You are then entitled to the accumulated investment income in the plan.

 There are some ways you can use this accumulated income to avoid the additional tax. For example, you are able to transfer the income to your RRSP or that of your spouse, subject to your contribution limit and an overall total of $50,000. However, any surplus amount will be subject to the additional 20 percent tax.

 You can withdraw the capital you contributed to the RESP at any time without paying additional tax because you have already paid tax on these funds.

Line 421: Canada Pension Plan Contributions on Self-Employment Earnings

 If you are self-employed, you must fill out schedule 8 to see if you owe any CPP on your self-employment earnings.

Enter the Canada Pension Plan contributions you have to pay, from schedule 8 of your return. If you were a resident of Quebec, this line does not apply to you; enter on your Quebec tax return the Quebec Pension Plan contributions you have to pay.

 If you pay CPP or QPP contributions on your self-employment income, you can claim a deduction for half of your contributions on line 222 of your tax return. You can also claim the other half as a non-refundable tax credit on schedule 1.

Line 422: Social Benefits Repayment

Did you receive social benefits such as the Old Age Security (OAS) pension or Employment Insurance benefits this year? Well, you could be in for a surprise. You see, you can't always have your cake and eat it too. Some taxpayers will actually have to repay the benefits they received in the year. If this applies to you, you must enter the amount of social benefits you have to repay, from line 235 of your return, on line 422. More details can be found at the end of Chapter 10.

Employment Insurance (EI) clawback

Your EI payments may be subject to a "clawback" (that is, repayment) to the extent that your net income is greater than 125 percent of maximum insurable earnings, being $39,000. The government claws back payments at a 30-percent rate to the extent they exceed 125 percent of $39,000, which is $48,750.

 If you received maternity, parental, or sickness benefits in any year since 2000, you do not have to repay those benefits even if your income exceeds this threshold. This ensures that parents who stay home with their newborn children or employees who are too sick to work are not penalized because of the income earned prior to the change in circumstances.

Old Age Security (OAS) clawback

 Your Old Age Security benefits will be taxed back at a 15-percent rate if your income is greater than $57,879. If your income exceeds $94,148, 100 percent of your Old Age Security benefits will be clawed back.

The $57,879 threshold for OAS is indexed to the Consumer Price Index.

Line 448: CPP Overpayment

Finally, a breath of fresh air! After pages of pay this, pay that, here is one area where you can recoup some of the money you've paid in the year. As you probably know, your employer has to take CPP premiums off your pay. However, it's possible that you paid too much! This most commonly happens when you held more than one job in the year. You see, since each employer is obligated to withhold CPP without regard to your other employers, you may have maxed out your payments for the year. However, it is also possible that your employer messed up and took too much CPP off your pay. Either way, relief is on its way — you're entitled to a refund of your CPP overpayment.

If you were not a resident of Quebec and you contributed more than you were required to, as explained in Chapter 12, enter the difference on line 448. The CCRA will refund the excess contributions to you, or will apply them to reduce your balance owing. If you were a resident of Quebec, this line does not apply to you; claim the excess amount on your Quebec provincial tax return.

Don't worry if you do not realize that you made a CPP overpayment. The CCRA will catch it on assessing your return!

Line 450: EI Overpayment

As with the CPP overpayment, you may have had too much EI deducted from your pay in the year. If you contributed more than you had to, enter the difference on line 450. Refer to Chapter 12 if you need help calculating the correct amount. The CCRA will refund the excess amount to you or use it to reduce your balance owing.

If you repaid some of the Employment Insurance benefits you received, do not claim the repayment on this line. If you were required to repay any of your 2002 or previous year EI received, the repayment is entered on line 232. If the repayment was in connection with EI received in 2003, you need to include the amount on line 235. Refer to Chapter 10 for a discussion on lines 232 and 235.

Again, if you fail to calculate that you have overpaid EI premiums, the CCRA will catch it on assessing your return.

Line 452: Refundable Medical Expense Supplement

You can claim a credit of up to $544 if you have an amount at line 332 (the medical expense credit) and both of the following apply:

- ✔ You were resident in Canada throughout 2003
- ✔ You were 18 or older at the end of 2003

In addition, the total of the following two amounts has to be equal to or greater than $2,676:

- ✔ Your employment income on lines 101 and 104 minus the amounts on lines 207, 212, 229, and 231 (but if the result is negative, use "0")
- ✔ Your net self-employment income (not including losses) from lines 135 to 143

To claim this credit, complete the calculations on the federal worksheet.

You can claim both the refundable medical expense supplement and a medical expense credit for the same expenses.

You cannot claim this credit if the total of your net income (line 236) and your spouse's net income is $20,296 or more. (At this income amount, the calculation results in a credit of zero.)

Line 457: Goods and Services Tax (GST)/Harmonized Sales Tax (HST) Rebate

If you were able to deduct expenses from your income as an employee or as a partner, you may be eligible for a rebate of the GST/HST you paid on those expenses. You see, if your employer (or partnership) paid for these expenses directly, the employer would have been able to claim an input tax credit for the GST/HST paid. Since you paid for the expense yourself, the GST/HST rebate works as if you are getting the input tax credit instead.

Generally, you can claim this rebate if either of the following applies:

- ✔ Your employer has a GST/HST registration number.
- ✔ You are a member of a GST/HST-registered partnership, and you have reported on your return your share of the income from that partnership.

If your employer is not registered for GST purposes (perhaps because your employer is a financial institution, health care provider or, non-profit organization that provides "GST exempt" services), you won't be able to take advantage of this rebate.

You can only claim a GST/HST rebate if you paid GST/HST on your expenditures. If you've paid for expenses that do not attract GST, such as insurance or interest, you're out of luck. To claim this rebate, complete form GST 370 "Employee and Partner GST/HST Rebate Application." Attach a completed copy of this form to your return, and enter on line 457 the rebate you are claiming.

You have to include in income any rebate you receive, in the year you receive it. For example, if you claim a rebate on your 2003 return and you receive your rebate in 2004, you have to report the rebate on your 2004 return.

Chapter 14

Provincial and Territorial Taxes and Credits

● ●

In This Chapter

▶ Taking a look at provincial and territorial tax rates

▶ Assessing the taxes for all provinces and territories

● ●

*I*n Canada, we pay taxes to both the federal government and a provincial or territorial government, although in every province but Quebec it may not seem this way since the Canada Customs and Revenue Agency (CCRA) administers income taxes on their behalf.

In this chapter we will discuss the tax rates that apply in your province or territory of residence, the method of taxation, and any special tax credits that may apply to you. And by the way, any time we refer to "provincial tax," we mean the territories too!

Provincial and Territorial Tax Rates

As we cover in Chapter 1, our federal government levies taxes based on the taxable income you earn in a year. The federal tax rates that apply in 2003 are as follows:

Taxable Income	Marginal Tax Rate
$0–$32,183	6%
$32,184–$64,368	22%
$64,369–$104,648	26%
Over $104,648	29%

Your basic federal tax is calculated by using the above rates, then deducting any federal tax credits such as non-refundable tax credits, dividend tax credits, foreign tax credits, and others. This basic federal tax calculation is done on schedule 1 of your personal tax return. Now that all the provinces and territories have adopted the tax-on-income system, in order to calculate your provincial/territorial tax, you must take your taxable income figure and multiply it by the provincial/territorial tax rates. You may then deduct tax credits available in that province to come up with your provincial tax payable. Table 14-1 shows the provincial tax rates as a percentage of taxable income.

Table 14-1	Provincial Tax Rates for 2003
Taxable Income	**Tax Rate as a Percentage of Taxable Income**
British Columbia Taxes	
$0–$31,653	6.05
$31,654–$63,308	9.15
$63,309–$72,685	11.70
$72,686–$88,260	13.70
Over $88,260	14.70
Alberta Taxes	
All levels of taxable income	10.00
Saskatchewan Taxes	
$0–$35,000	11.00
$35,001–$100,000	13.00
Over $100,000	15.00
Manitoba Taxes	
$0–$30,544	10.90

Taxable Income	Tax Rate as a Percentage of Taxable Income
$30,545–$65,000	14.90
Over $65,000	17.40

Ontario Taxes

$0–$32,435	6.05
$32,436–$64,871	9.15
Over $64,871	11.16

Quebec Taxes

$0–$27,095	16.00
$27,096–$54,195	20.00
Over $54,195	24.00

New Brunswick Taxes

$0–$32,183	9.68
$32,184–$64,368	14.82
$64,369–$104,648	16.52
Over $104,648	17.84

Nova Scotia Taxes

$0–$29,590	9.77
$29,591–$59,180	14.95
Over $59,180	16.67

PEI Taxes

$0–$30,754	9.80

(continued)

Table 14-1 *(continued)*

Taxable Income	Tax Rate as a Percentage of Taxable Income
$30,755–$61,509	13.80
Over $61,509	16.70

Newfoundland Taxes

$0–$29,590	10.57
$29,591–$59,180	16.16
Over $59,180	18.02

Northwest Territories Taxes

$0–$32,183	7.20
$32,184–$64,368	9.90
$64,369–$104,648	11.70
Over $104,648	13.05

Yukon Taxes

$0–$32,183	7.04
$32,184–$64,368	9.68
$64,369–$104,648	11.44
Over $104,648	12.76

Nunavut Taxes

$0–$32,183	4.00
$32,184–$64,368	7.00
$64,369–$104,648	9.00
Over $104,648	11.50

If you've lived in more than one place in 2003, you may be wondering which province or territory you should pay tax to. In the past, wherever you live on December 31, 2003, was your province of residence for the entire year. However, now the answer may not be as simple. The CCRA came out with a revised IT bulletin "Determination of an Individual's Residence." According to this, an individual is considered to be resident in the province where he/she has significant residential ties. So even if you reside in one province on December 31, you will be considered resident in the province where you have the most ties. Most often this will be the province where your house, spouse, or dependants are located.

If you are planning to move this year, time your move carefully to save taxes. Since each province and territory has different tax rates, if you're moving from a higher taxed place to a lower taxed place, you're better off moving during this taxation year. This means that all your income from the entire year, even when you lived in the higher taxed jurisdiction, will be subject to the lower tax rates in your new province or territory of residence. On the other hand, if you're moving to a higher taxed jurisdiction, consider postponing your move until next year.

Provincial and Territorial Tax Credits

Like the calculation of federal tax, each province has its own set of credits that may be available to you. Below we'll take a look at some of the more common credits available in each of the provinces and territories.

British Columbia

If you live in British Columbia, your first step in calculating your tax bill is to figure out your provincial tax owing. Subtract from this your provincial non-refundable tax credits in 2003. Some of the most common credits are shown below in Table 14-2. Other credits can be found on forms BC 428 and BC 429.

Table 14-2	B.C. Non-Refundable Tax Credits
Credit	*Amount*
Basic personal amount	$8,307
Spouse or common-law partner amount	$7,113
Amount for an eligible dependant	$7,113
Age amount	$3,725
Infirm dependant credit (over age 18)	$3,635
Caregiver amount	$3,634
Disability amount	$6,230
Additional credit for mental or physical impairment for child under age 18	$3,635
Education amount (per month) full time	$200
Education amount (per month) part time	$60

To determine the value of the credit, you must multiply the base amount by the lowest rate of B.C. tax (6.05 percent). If you've made charitable donations in the year, the low 6.05-percent rate only applies to the first $200 of donations. Any donations in excess of this will give rise to a 14.7-percent non-refundable tax credit.

The dividend tax credit is 5.1 percent of the grossed up amount of Canadian dividends.

Alberta

If you don't like paying high income taxes, Alberta is the place to be. And what is more, if you want your tax calculation to be simple (yes, we said simple), consider making a move to Alberta. You see, Alberta has made the headlines by being the first province ever to implement a flat tax: a single rate of provincial tax (10 percent) of taxable income, regardless of the amount of income you earn. And to top it off, there are no additional taxes or surtaxes. (We told you it was easy!)

Since Alberta calculates its tax based on taxable income, it has its own set of non-refundable tax credits. In order to determine the amount of the credit, the base amount should be multiplied by the flat rate of 10 percent. Table 14-3 shows the base amount for some of the most common non-refundable credits available in Alberta. Other credits can be found on form AB 428.

Table 14-3   Alberta Non-Refundable Tax Credits

Credit	Amount
Basic personal amount	$13,525
Spouse or common law partner amount	$13,525
Amount for an eligible dependant	$13,525
Age amount	$3,794
Infirm dependant credit (over age 18)	$3,669
Caregiver amount	$3,670
Disability amount	$6,291
Education amount (per month) full time	$419
Education amount (per month) part time	$126

If you have made donations during the year, you'll receive a credit equal to 10 percent on the first $200, and 12.75 percent on any excess over $200.

The dividend tax credit for Alberta is 6.4 percent of the grossed up amount of Canadian dividends.

Saskatchewan

As it did last year, Saskatchewan calculates its tax based on net income. So to determine the amount of tax you'll have to pay in 2003, start off first by applying the tax rates found in Table 14-1 to your various income levels.

After applying the various tax rates to taxable income, you can deduct any provincial non-refundable tax credits that you are entitled to. Table 14-4 provides you the base amounts for the various non-refundable credits available. Additional credits can be found on form SK 428.

Table 14-4 Saskatchewan Non-Refundable Tax Credits

Credit	Amount
Basic personal amount	$8,000
Spouse or common law partner amount	$8,000
Amount for an eligible dependant	$8,000
Dependant child amount	$2,500
Senior supplementary amount	$1,000
Age amount	$3,787
Infirm dependant credit (over age 18)	$3,663
Caregiver amount	$3,663
Disability amount	$6,279
Education amount (per month) full time	$400
Education amount (per month) part time	$120

In its 2003 budget, the government proposed to begin indexing tax brackets starting January 1, 2004. Once you know what credits you're entitled to, add them all up and multiply the total by 11 percent. This is the amount that you can use to reduce your Saskatchewan tax liability.

The dividend tax credit for Saskatchewan is 8 percent of the grossed up amount of Canadian dividends.

The provincial donation tax credit is calculated as 11 percent of the first $200 of donations, and 15 percent on all amounts in excess of $200.

Manitoba

Manitobans will find themselves paying a little less tax in 2003, thanks to a reduction of the tax rate on the middle tax bracket from 15.4 percent to 14.9 percent. In addition, the maximum education property tax credit for seniors was increased from $775 to $800 in 2003. To calculate your tax bill this year, start by using Table 14-1.

Once you've calculated your Manitoba tax based on your taxable income, you're entitled to claim non-refundable tax credits. See Table 14-5 for the most common non-refundable tax credits that will apply in Manitoba. Other credits can be found on forms MB 428 and MB 479.

Table 14-5 Manitoba Non-Refundable Tax Credits

Credit	Amount
Basic personal amount	$7,634
Spouse or common law partner amount	$6,482
Amount for an eligible dependant	$6,482
Age amount	$3,728
Infirm dependant credit (over age 18)	$3,605
Caregiver amount	$3,605
Disability amount	$6,180
Education amount (per month) full time	$400
Education amount (per month) part time	$120

To determine the value of the credit you must multiply the total credits by the lowest Manitoba tax rate of 10.9 percent. The first $200 of donations will receive a 10.9-percent non-refundable tax credit in Manitoba, while any further donations will receive a 17.4-percent credit.

The dividend tax credit for Manitoba is 5 percent of the grossed up amount of Canadian dividends.

Once you take your taxable income, multiply it by the appropriate tax rates, and deduct your non-refundable tax credits, you will have your adjusted Manitoba tax.

Ontario

Although there were a few personal tax changes announced this year, the top marginal tax rate for combined Ontario/federal tax remain unchanged. Some other changes include a property tax relief for seniors who own or rent their homes, as well as a new schedule for the implementation of the Ontario Equity in Education Tax Credit. Last year, the government announced a delay to the original timetable for the credit, and this year they are back to the original schedule. Confused? This credit is available for taxpayers whose children attend private school. The credit will apply to the first $7,000 of fees paid, and for 2003, taxpayers will receive a refund of up to 20 percent. The rate is currently scheduled to increase by 10 percent per year until it reaches 50 percent in 2006.

To calculate your Ontario tax bill, multiply the rates shown in Table 14-1 by your taxable income at the various levels.

Table 14-6 illustrates some of the more common non-refundable tax credits. Additional credit can be found on forms ONT 428 and ONT 479.

Table 14-6	Ontario Non-Refundable Tax Credits
Credit	**Amount**
Basic personal amount	$7,817
Spouse or common law partner amount	$6,637
Amount for an eligible dependant	$6,637
Age amount	$3,817
Infirm dependant credit (over age 18)	$6,637
Caregiver amount	$6,637
Disability amount	$6,637
Disability supplement for children	$6,637
Education amount (per month) full time	$421
Education amount (per month) part time	$126

Once you've calculated your Ontario taxes owing, you can reduce this number by applying non-refundable tax credits and certain Ontario tax credits. Non-refundable tax credits will be calculated by taking the total credits, and multiplying them by the lowest Ontario tax rate (6.05 percent). The table above summarizes the more common non-refundable tax credits available in Ontario for 2003.

If you made a donation during the year in addition to the federal credit, you'll also be entitled to a provincial donation tax credit. The first $200 of donations will receive a credit calculated at the lowest Ontario tax rate of 6.05 percent, and any donations above this level will receive a credit at Ontario's highest tax rate of 11.16 percent.

The dividend tax credit for Ontario is 5.13 percent of the grossed up amount of Canadian dividends.

Ontario surtax

In addition to basic Ontario tax, there is also surtax to calculate. As a result of indexing, the surtaxes for the 2003 taxation year are calculated as follows:

20 percent of Ontario income tax in excess of $3,747, plus

36 percent of Ontario income tax in excess of $4,727.

For example, if you have taxable income of $60,000 in 2003, your basic Ontario tax before applying non-refundable tax credits would be $4,485 ($32,435 × 6.05% plus $60,000 less $32,435 × 9.15%). Assuming you will claim the basic personal credit of $473 ($7,817 × 6.05%), your basic Ontario tax will be $4,012. This means that you will have surtax to pay. Your surtax will be as follows:

$4,012 less $3,747 × 20% = $53, plus

$4,012 less $4,727 × 36% = $0

For a grand total of $53.

Quebec

As a resident of Quebec, you have your work cut out for you. Not only does Quebec have its own system of taxation, you also have to file a whole separate tax return each year to calculate your provincial taxes. Yes, this is in addition to your federal tax return.

If you are a resident of Quebec, you must file two tax returns this year. Your federal return will be sent to the Canada Customs and Revenue Agency (CCRA), while your Quebec return must be sent to the Ministère du Revenu. Your Quebec return is due on the same day as your federal return.

Preparing your Quebec tax return is, for the most part, the same as preparing your federal tax return. The types of income you must report and many of the deductions are identical, although they may be reported on different slips. For example, for Quebec taxation purposes, a T4 slip is called the RL-1. In addition, many of the forms that apply to your federal return also apply to your provincial return — the only difference is the names. For example, if you've moved in the year, you should fill out form T1M "Moving Expenses" with your federal return, and form TP-347-V "Moving Expenses" with your Quebec return. Therefore, you can safely use the tips in the rest of this book to calculate your Quebec income.

If you are a resident in Quebec, you must report your income from all sources on your Quebec tax return. Even if you worked outside Quebec during the year, you must still report this income on your return.

Like the other provinces, to calculate Quebec tax owing, you must first start with Table 14-1. From there, there are other credits and deductions that you may be entitled to. Here are some of the more common ones.

Table 14-7   Quebec Non-Refundable Tax Credits

Credit	Amount
Basic personal amount	$6,150
Amount with respect to age	$2,200
Amount for a person living alone	$1,095
Amount respecting dependent children:	
For first child	$2,710
For additional children	$2,500
Child attends post secondary studies	$1,720
Amount for a single parent	$1,355
Amount respecting a severe and prolonged mental or physical impairment	$2,200
Amount for a dependent with infirmity	$3,650
Flat amount	$2,820

Here are some important points to note about these and other credits:

- ✔ The amount with respect to age, for a person living alone, and for retirement income are reduced for net family income in excess of $27,095.

- ✔ Under the simplified system many of the tax credits and deductions (QPP contributions, EI premiums, union or professional dues, and medical expenses) are replaced by a flat amount of $2,820.

- ✔ Medical expenses are reduced by 3 percent of family income.

- ✔ If you make a donation, the first $2,000 of donations will entitle you to a non-refundable credit of 20 percent, while any further donations will receive a 24 percent credit.

- ✔ The dividend tax credit for Quebec is 10.83 percent of the grossed up amount of Canadian dividends.

There may be other deductions and credits you may be entitled to. Be sure to refer to your guide (TP-1.G-V) for more information.

Newfoundland

Not too much new to report in Newfoundland this year. Although there were no dramatic tax cuts, some changes include an increase in the low-income seniors benefit to $350 per senior or $700 per couple who qualify, the introduction of a new Student Loan Credit program, an increase in the disability amount, and the introduction of a new a new non-refundable disability tax credit supplement for mentally and physically infirm children under the age of 18.

Use Table 14-1 to calculate your taxes owing for 2003. (By the way, you'll find the rates and brackets are the exact same as last year.)

After calculating Newfoundland tax payable, you'll be entitled to claim non-refundable tax credits. Some of the more common credits are shown in Table 14.8 below. Additional credits can be found on Form NL 428. The base amount for the credits has still been set at the 1999 levels (don't ask us why!). The total credit you can use to offset any provincial tax payable is calculated by multiplying the base amount by 10.57 percent.

Table 14-8 Newfoundland Non-Refundable Tax Credits

Credit	Amount
Basic personal amount	$7,410
Spouse or common law partner amount	$6,055
Amount for an eligible dependant	$6,055
Age amount	$3,482
Infirm dependant credit (over age 18)	$2,353
Caregiver amount	$2,353
Disability amount	$5,000
Disability amount supplement under age 18	$2,353
Education amount (per month) full time	$200
Education amount (per month) part time	$60

If you make a donation, the first $200 of donations will entitle you to a non-refundable credit of 10.57 percent, while any further donations will receive a 17.4 percent credit.

The dividend tax credit for Newfoundland is 5 percent of the grossed up amount of Canadian dividends.

The bad news for Newfoundlanders is that the surtax has not been reduced this year. For 2003, there is still a 9 percent surtax on provincial tax payable in excess of $7,032.

New Brunswick

Not a lot to report to those of you in New Brunswick (which isn't necessarily all that bad). The only real change you'll see in your tax return this year is that the values for the tax brackets and personal tax credits have once again changed due to inflation. The good news is that for 2003, the provincial system continues to mirror the federal system; therefore, you can offset your New Brunswick taxes owing by the same tax credits that are used to offset your federal taxes, except that you will use provincial tax rates for this calculation (that is, you multiply the credits by 9.68 percent). Table 14.9 shows some of the more common tax credits available. Additional credits can be found on Form NB 428.

Table 14-9 New Brunswick Non-Refundable Tax Credits

Credit	Amount
Basic personal amount	$7,756
Spouse or common law partner amount	$6,586
Amount for an eligible dependant	$6,586
Age amount	$3,787
Infirm dependant credit (over age 18)	$3,663
Caregiver amount	$3,663
Disability amount	$6,279
Education amount (per month) full time	$400
Education amount (per month) part time	$120

If you make a donation in New Brunswick, the first $200 of donations will entitle you to a non-refundable credit of 9.86 percent, while any further donations will receive a 17.84 percent credit.

The dividend tax credit for New Brunswick is 3.7 percent of the grossed up amount of Canadian dividends.

Nova Scotia

There were no significant tax changes announced this year in Canada's Ocean Playground, so preparing your tax return shouldn't bring on any unwanted surprises. Table 14-10 shows the base amounts for the more commonly used credits to help reduce your provincial taxes. Additional credits can be found on forms NS 428 and NS 479. To determine the amount that can be used to offset your provincial tax, you simply have to multiply the credits by the lowest Nova Scotia marginal tax rate of 9.77 percent to come up with the amount that can be used to reduce your Nova Scotia taxes in the year.

Table 14-10 Nova Scotia Non-Refundable Tax Credits

Credit	Amount
Basic personal amount	$7,231
Spouse or common law partner amount	$6,140
Amount for an eligible dependant	$6,140
Age amount	$3,531
Infirm dependant credit (over age 18)	$2,386
Caregiver amount	$4,176
Disability amount	$4,293
Education amount (per month) full time	$200
Education amount (per month) part time	$60

If you make a donation in Nova Scotia, the first $200 of donations will entitle you to a non-refundable credit of 9.77 percent, while any further donations will receive a 16.67 percent credit.

The dividend tax credit for Nova Scotia is 7.7 percent of the grossed up amount of Canadian dividends.

After calculating your basic Nova Scotia tax, a surtax is added on equal to 10 percent of basic Nova Scotia tax in excess of $10,000

Prince Edward Island

The home of Anne of Green Gables didn't announce any major tax changes in 2003. So, to calculate your 2003 PEI tax liability, apply the rates found in Table 14-1 to your taxable income this year. After that, you'll be able to deduct the provincial non-refundable tax credits, shown in Table 14-11 below. Additional credits can be found on Form PE 428.

Table 14-11	PEI Non-Refundable Tax Credits
Credit	**Amount**
Basic personal amount	$7,412
Spouse or common law partner amount	$6,294
Amount for an eligible dependant	$6,294
Age amount	$3,619
Infirm dependant credit (over age 18)	$2,446
Caregiver amount	$2,446
Disability amount	$5,400
Education amount (per month) full time	$200
Education amount (per month) part time	$60

To determine the amount of the credit, take the credit amounts and multiply them by 9.8 percent.

If you make a donation in PEI, the first $200 of donations will entitle you to a non-refundable credit of 9.8 percent, while any further donations will receive a 16.7 percent credit.

The dividend tax credit for PEI is 7.7 percent of the grossed up amount of Canadian dividends.

Oh, and after all these credits, don't forget to add on the PEI surtax of 10 percent on tax bills over $5,200 (couldn't let you forget about that!).

Yukon

Unfortunately, Yukon's history of tax changes has finally come to an end. This year's budget didn't announce anything too exciting when it comes to tax measures.

To make things simple, Yukon uses the same tax brackets and non-refundable credit amounts as the federal system. Table 14-12 below illustrates some of the more common credits. Additional credits can be found on forms YT 428 and YT 479.

Table 14-12   Yukon Non-Refundable Tax Credits

Credit	Amount
Basic personal amount	$7,756
Spouse or common law partner amount	$6,586
Amount for an eligible dependant	$6,586
Age amount	$3,787
Infirm dependant credit (over age 18)	$3,663
Caregiver amount	$3,663
Disability amount	$6,279
Education amount (per month) full time	$400
Education amount (per month) part time	$120

If you make a donation in Yukon, the first $200 of donations will entitle you to a non-refundable credit of 7.04 percent, while any further donations will receive a 12.76 percent credit.

The dividend tax credit for Yukon is 5.87 percent of the grossed up amount of Canadian dividends.

In addition to the basic Yukon tax, don't forget the additional 5-percent surtax for those of you whose Yukon tax exceeds $6,000.

Northwest Territories

For those of you who like your April to be plain and simple, then the Northwest Territories is the place to be. Similar to last year, the Northwest Territories indexes its tax brackets based on inflation, making them identical to the federal brackets.

Once you've calculated your tax liability using the rates found on Table 14-1, you may be eligible to certain tax deductions and credits. Table 14-13 illustrates some of the more common credits available. Additional credits can be found on forms NT 428 and NT 479.

Table 14-13   NWT Non-Refundable Tax Credits

Credit	Amount
Basic personal amount	$11,050
Spouse or common law partner amount	$11,050
Amount for an eligible dependant	$11,050
Age amount	$5,405
Infirm dependant credit (over age 18)	$3,663
Caregiver amount	$3,663
Disability amount	$8,961
Education amount (per month) full time	$400
Education amount (per month) part time	$120

If you make a donation in the Northwest Territories, the first $200 of donations will entitle you to a non-refundable credit of 7.2 percent, while any further donations will receive a 13.05 percent credit.

The dividend tax credit for the Northwest Territories is 6 percent of the grossed up amount of Canadian dividends.

Nunavut

Unlike last year, Nunavut announced no new tax changes for 2003 (which is good if you hate change, we guess). To calculate your Nunavut tax liability start with the rates found in Table 14-1. Then you may be eligible for some deductions. The more common non-refundable credits are illustrated in table 14-14 below. Other credits can be found on forms NU 428 and NU 429.

Table 14-14   Nunavut Non-Refundable Tax Credits

Credit	Amount
Basic personal amount	$10,160
Spouse or common law partner amount	$10,160
Amount for an eligible dependant	$10,160
Age amount	$7,620
Infirm dependant credit (over age 18)	$3,663
Caregiver amount	$3,663
Disability amount	$10,160
Education amount (per month) full time	$400
Education amount (per month) part time	$120

If you make a donation in Nunavut, the first $200 of donations will entitle you to a non-refundable credit of 4 percent, while any further donations will receive a 11.5 percent credit.

The dividend tax credit for Nunavut is 4 percent of the grossed up amount of Canadian dividends.

Part IV
After You've Filed Your Tax Return

SO-HOW'D YOUR AUDIT GO?

In this part...

So you've filed your return, now what? Well, you sit and wait for a thank-you card in the mail from the CCRA called a Notice of Assessment. Does getting this hot little item in your hands mean you're free and clear? Unfortunately, not always. You see, the CCRA likes to perform random checks on people — think of it as a lottery you don't want to win. Sometimes they are requests for little pieces of information, while sometimes they are larger requests for all your information. These larger requests are simply a nice term for "audit."

So, even the nice, law-abiding folks out there will sometimes find themselves hassled by the tax police. For those of you in that boat, all we can say is, we're sorry, and you'll live. But don't panic. This part will tell you everything you need to know about dealing with the CCRA.

"The best measure of a man's honesty isn't his income tax return. It's the zero adjust on his bathroom scale."

— Arthur C. Clarke

Chapter 15

CCRA Administration

In This Chapter

▶ Understanding your Notice of Assessment

▶ Responding to requests for information

▶ Fixing mistakes

▶ Avoiding penalties and interest

Congratulations! You have completed your tax return and sent it in. One day (two to three weeks later if you have NETFILED or EFILED your return, or four to six weeks later if you mailed it), you will receive a Notice of Assessment. What does this mean? Has the Canada Customs and Revenue Agency (CCRA) audited your return and given it final approval? Unfortunately, the answer is no.

What you have is an acknowledgement that your return has been received and usually a confirmation that a basic review of your return has produced no *obvious* errors or omissions. "Obvious" means things like arithmetically the return adds up, you have not claimed a northern residents deduction (see Chapter 11) from your home in Windsor, and you have filed your return in the correct province of residence. You can interpret your receipt of the notice to mean that the CCRA accepts your return as filed and does not require any more information at this time. In the majority of cases, you will never need to concern yourself with this return again.

Understanding Your Notice of Assessment

The typical Notice of Assessment (form T451) contains a date, your social insurance number, the tax year being assessed, the Tax Centre where the return was assessed, a summary of your return by line number, the amount you owe or are owed, plus an explanation of any changes.

The explanation of changes area typically states that the return was assessed as filed, or that some changes were made due to calculation errors or omissions. The notice will go on to say that no additional interest will be charged on amounts owed if the debt is paid within 20 days, and it gives you a telephone number to call if you have any questions. At the bottom of the notice is your RRSP deduction limit statement that tells you how your RRSP limit was calculated and how much RRSP deduction room you have for the next year. This figure would include all your unused RRSP deduction room from 1991 and on.

If you have made RRSP contributions but did not deduct them in completing your returns, the amount of your "unused RRSP contributions available" for deduction in future years is noted. (This amount has not been considered in calculating your RRSP deduction limit. Therefore, be careful to "net" the two figures to ensure you do not overcontribute to your RRSP.

Your Notice of Assessment also contains some useful information for future years, including loss carryforward and alternative minimum tax carryforwards amounts. Keep this notice to help you in preparing your tax return for next year.

The date on your Notice of Assessment is of particular importance — it represents the day the assessment was mailed to you and is referred to as the "assessment date." This date is important because if you don't agree with any changes made by the CCRA, you have until the later of 90 days from the assessment date and one year from the original due date (usually April 30, or June 15 if you or your spouse is self-employed) of your tax return to object to the changes.

If you don't agree with any change made by the CCRA on your Notice of Assessment, don't wait too long to follow up! There is a time limit to file an objection, and if you miss this deadline you may be out of luck. (The CCRA does have the power to grant time extensions, but it's not something you should rely on getting.)

If your Notice of Assessment contains incorrect information, it is your responsibility to contact the CCRA and correct the error. Errors most commonly found include incorrect carryforward amounts and incorrect RRSP deduction limits. If you know that these amounts are wrong and you still use them to your advantage, the CCRA will view this as an intentional misstatement and penalize you accordingly. Examples of misused information include individuals who over-contribute to their RRSP because the contribution limit is incorrect or other individuals who stop paying tax because the notice has incorrectly declared them dead. (Hmm. . .)

Requests for More Information

During the initial tax assessment, or as a result of a re-review of your return, the CCRA may have additional questions. To obtain information to answer these questions, the CCRA will send you a letter called a "Request for Additional Information." This letter will usually ask for specific information and will include an address where this information is to be sent, a CCRA reference number, the name and phone number of the person requesting the information, and a date the information must be received by (usually 30 days from the date of the request).

Is this letter the beginning of a full audit of your return? Should you seek professional advice? Should you run screaming into the hills? The answer is no.

The first thing to remember is that a request for information is not an unusual thing. It is a normal part of the CCRA's verification process. Second, a request for information does not automatically mean you will owe more tax.

In fact, there are many reasons why a request might be sent to you. One of the most common is that a particular receipt or slip of paper was not included in your paper-filed return. Examples of this are charitable donation receipts or RRSP receipts. Perhaps the information you supplied was unclear or incomplete, or the CCRA is doing random compliance checks to test the accuracy of returns. For example, if you are claiming carrying charges or child care expenses, the CCRA may ask to see proof of these deductions, since you were not required to submit these receipts with your return.

This later request is usually the result of a desk audit. Such audits are done at the Tax Services Office and are primarily directed at testing a large number of returns and identifying potential problems that will be forwarded for a full audit. As long as the information you've reported on your tax return is truthful, supportable, and within the tax laws, you should have nothing to worry about.

If you did not send receipts to the CCRA because you NETFILED or EFILED (electronically filed) your return, a request for information is very common. You see, when you NETFILE or EFILE, no receipts are sent to the CCRA. By asking you to send in receipts, the CCRA is trying to maintain the integrity of the system by testing the accuracy of your return. With this in mind, it's best to read the letter carefully and respond with the correct information within the time limit set out.

If you cannot get the information within the time limit, call the number on the request and ask for an extension. In most cases, a further 30-day extension will be granted. This extension is usually a one-shot deal, however, and will not be granted a second time.

Record the name and phone number of the person on the letter. Most Tax Services Offices have hundreds of people with hundreds of phone numbers, and it's unlikely that you'll be able to locate this person if you lose the name and contact number.

If you ever have contact with someone at the CCRA and find them to be helpful, keep a record of their name and number and call them if you have a question in the future. A knowledgeable person inside a huge bureaucracy can be worth his or her weight in gold.

The worst thing to do if you receive a request for additional information is to ignore it. Ignoring the CCRA will not make your problems magically disappear. You see, if you don't provide the information in the time allowed, or if you do not make suitable arrangements for an extension, the auditor will simply conclude that the information does not exist and reassess you accordingly. This type of reassessment usually includes penalties and interest. As well, once this reassessment is complete, the CCRA is under no compulsion to accept supporting information at a later date, and can legally refuse to accept it.

For more serious situations where a substantial amount of money is involved or potential criminal activities are suspected, the CCRA can invoke a requirement or a judicial authorization forcing you to provide information. The *Income Tax Act* gives them authority to do so.

Fixing Your Mistakes on a Return You've Sent

If you think you have forgotten or omitted information on your already filed return, or if you discover new information that pertains to a previously filed and assessed return, will the CCRA allow you to submit this information late? The answer is yes!

As you can imagine, this is a common problem. But don't worry, there is a process to allow you to change or add information to both assessed and soon-to-be-assessed returns. The process is as follows:

- The CCRA asks that if you need to make a change to a return already sent in, you *do not file another return for the year*.

- Complete either form T1-ADJ "T1 Adjustment Request," available at all Tax Services Offices, (and on the CCRA Web site) or write a letter detailing the changes (including the years involved, the specific details, your address and social insurance number, your home and daytime phone numbers). This letter must be signed and dated by you.

- Provide *all* supporting documents for the requested changes.

- Send this adjustment request to the Tax Centre where you filed your return.

  If you follow this process, you will greatly assist the CCRA in making the correct changes in a timely manner. Upon review of the information, the CCRA will take one of three steps:

- Accept your changes and send you a Notice of Reassessment (or Notice of Assessment, if the return had not yet been assessed).

- Deny your request. A letter will explain the reasons.

- Request additional information.

The CCRA now accepts on-line requests for changes to your return. Go to "On-line Requests" on CCRA's Web site. Type in the requested information and click "submit." The CCRA will call you if they need to see anymore information. It is our experience that on-line requests are handled in "days," versus "months" when the mail is used.

What if I discover an error several years back that would have resulted in a refund had I filed correctly?

The CCRA will allow you to ask for a refund for years as far back as 1985 if it is satisfied that the request would have been accepted had it been made in the normal reassessment period and if all the relevant information is provided. The policy of allowing late refund requests is covered in the CCRA's Information Circular 92-3 "Guidelines for Refunds beyond the Normal Three-Year Period," available at Tax Services Offices or on the CCRA's Web site.

If the filing deadline is approaching (that is, April 30, or perhaps June 15) and you are missing slips or information, it is best to file your return on time to avoid the late filing penalties. Do your best to calculate your income and deductions, then follow the above adjustment process when the information is available. The CCRA suggests that you include any partial information you have, a description of the missing information, and an explanation as to what you are doing to obtain it.

Late-filed elections

The *Income Tax Act* contains various elections that allow you to adopt special treatment for particular tax issues. However, to take advantage of them, the elections must be filed within certain time frames, and the CCRA must be aware that the election is being made. Sometimes the election requires special tax forms to be filled out, while other times a note attached to your tax return is enough. If you don't take advantage of a favourable election on your tax return, you may not be totally out of luck. In certain circumstances, the CCRA will allow you to file an election late.

The CCRA has issued Information Circular 92-1 "Guidelines for Accepting Late, Amended or Revoked Elections," in which it outlines the circumstances under which it will allow you to late-file, revoke, or change elections. These situations generally involve honest mistakes or circumstances out of your control where you made a reasonable effort to do the right thing. If, on the other hand, it appears that you were simply negligent, careless, or trying to engage in retroactive tax planning, the CCRA will not permit a change to the election.

Voluntary Disclosures

If you have never filed a return, you sent a return that was incomplete or incorrect, or you stopped filing returns for two or more years, a voluntary disclosure could help you out of this situation. As you recall from the previous chapter, late returns and false or incomplete information can attract heavy penalties. To avoid these penalties, you can voluntarily come forward and provide all the missing information. Under these circumstances, the CCRA will always waive penalties if you tell them before they catch you, and you will only be responsible for paying the tax you owe plus interest. Here are the CCRA's only stipulations:

> ✔ You must provide full and complete information. If you intentionally provide incomplete information, the CCRA will not consider this a voluntary disclosure and will assess penalties.
>
> ✔ The CCRA must not have requested the information or started an action against you prior to the voluntary disclosure. If the CCRA has already requested the information, or if an audit has been initiated, yours is not considered a voluntary disclosure.

Refunds: Show Me the Money!

The rule is simple: To get a refund, you need to file a tax return. However, if you failed to file a return in the past, and you would have received a refund had you filed, you should still file a tax return for the missing years. The CCRA does not have to send you your refund if your return is more than three years late. However, the CCRA is prepared to accept returns requesting refunds back to 1985 if you provide *all* the pertinent information and the CCRA is satisfied that the refund would have been issued if the information had been supplied on time.

The CCRA doesn't have to accept your return if you file late. By filing outside the three-year limit, you are putting yourself at the mercy of the CCRA's discretion as to whether it will accept or reject your request. Information Circular 92-3 "Guidelines for Refunds beyond the Normal Three-Year Period," available at Tax Services Offices or on CCRA's Web site, provides details of this policy.

The real scoop on refunds

An important point to mention at this juncture is that refunds come from taxes you've already paid. Creating a big loss on a tax return will not get you a refund unless you have already paid tax (sorry to burst your bubble). The *Income Tax Act* requires the Minister of National Revenue (through the CCRA) to determine if an overpayment of tax has occurred and to pay a refund. Usually the refund arrives with your Notice of Assessment. If a refund is owed and you have not received it with your assessment, the CCRA is required to issue a refund upon receipt of your application in writing.

If you have any other tax liabilities outstanding (or even federal student loans in arrears!), the CCRA will use your refund to pay these taxes or loans instead of giving you the money directly.

Interest on refunds

The CCRA pays interest on refunds based on a "prescribed" interest rate that is set quarterly. The amount it pays on refunds is set at 2 percent below the interest it charges on balances owing. In 2003, the prescribed interest rate for the first and second quarters was 5 percent for refund interest and 7 percent for balances owing. The rates increased to 6 percent and 8 percent respectively in the third quarter. For the last quarter, the rates went back down to 5 percent and 7 percent respectively. (The CCRA publishes the prescribed interest rates on its Web site. Go to www.ccra-adrc.gc.ca/eservices/tipsonline/bis/pir-e-03.html. Look for "The 2003 Prescribed Interest Rates.")

Interest on refunds is compounded daily starting on the latest of the following three dates:

✔ The day after you overpaid your taxes

✔ 45 days after you filed your return

✔ 45 days after the balance due date for the year (June 15 if your return was due April 30, July 30 if your return was due June 15)

If a refund arose as a result of a loss carryback, no interest is payable for the period before you filed your tax return.

Direct deposit (DD)

Your refund can be automatically deposited into your bank account. If you paper file, complete form T1-DD "Direct Deposit Request" and send it with your tax return. For EFILING, complete part C on form T183 "Information Return for Electronic Filing of an Individual's Income Tax and Benefit Return." (The T183 form will be provided to you by the person or firm responsible for EFILING your return.)

Once you have asked for DD you do not need to request it again. It stays on the CCRA's computer records *forever*! If you close a bank account it is imperative you provide the CCRA with your new bank account information. Trust us, it takes weeks or months to trace a tax refund sent to a bank account that no longer exists. Avoid the hassle and avoid the delay in getting your refund!

Refund interest as income

Refund interest is income and must be included in your return in the year you received it. If you also paid interest on an underpayment of income tax, the income inclusion can be reduced by the amount of arrears interest accruing over the same period.

Balances Owing

The *Income Tax Act* requires that all tax for a year be paid by the balance due date. This date is April 30 of the year following the taxation year in question. For 2003, the balance due date is April 30, 2004.

Even if your tax return is not due until a later date (for example, if you or your spouse is self-employed, your tax return is not due until June 15), you must estimate your taxes payable and remit the amount to the CCRA by April 30.

Your tax bill is considered to be paid on the day that it was mailed to the CCRA, if it is sent by first-class mail or courier. If you're filing your tax return at the last minute, don't just drop it in any old mailbox. Ensure that your return is postmarked April 30 so it will not be considered late-filed. If the mail doesn't get picked up until the next day, you'll be stuck with a late-filed tax return! (Yes, there are penalties for late-filing!!)

If you are filing a tax return for a person who has died in the year, any balance owing on his or her terminal return is payable on April 30, following the year of death, except if death occurred in November or December. In this case, the final tax liability is due six months after death. If death occurs in January to April, payment for the prior year return is due six months following death. For example, if George died on February 1, 2004, his 2003 tax bill is not due until August 1, 2004. Any tax liability for 2004 would be payable by April 30, 2005.

Interest on balances due

If you have a balance owing for the current year, the CCRA charges compound daily interest starting May 1 on any unpaid taxes. As we discussed earlier, this also applies to reassessments. If you are reassessed for 2003, the interest calculation starts May 1, 2004 — one day after the tax should have been paid. If you incur any penalties, interest is also charged on the penalty starting the day after your return is due. The interest rate charged is a CCRA "prescribed" interest rate that is adjusted quarterly. You can find the interest rates on CCRA's Web site at www.ccra-adrc.gc.ca/eservices/tipsonline/bis/pir-e-03.html.

Pay your tax by April 30 to avoid significant interest charges. This also applies if you are filing your return late. Estimate your tax payable and send it in.

Instalments

If you are required to pay instalments in the year, be aware that late or deficient instalment payments also attract interest at the high prescribed interest rate.

If you are deficient or do not make an instalment payment, you can avoid interest by paying your next instalment early. The CCRA will give you credit for the overpayment interest (at the same rate as the late payment) and net the interest owed against the interest earned.

Non-deductible interest

Interest paid to the CCRA is non-deductible for tax purposes, although it can be used to offset refund interest, which is considered taxable income.

Penalties and Interest

Penalties are in addition to the interest payments made on late or deficient taxes. Penalties also attract the same interest as do unpaid balances. (So, you can have interest charged on outstanding taxes, interest charged on outstanding interest, and interest charged on outstanding penalties!)

Late-filing penalty

If you file your return late (after April 30, or perhaps June 15), a penalty of 5 percent of the tax owing will immediately be applied. A further penalty of 1 percent of the unpaid tax will also be added for each full month the return is late, up to a maximum of 12 months (additional 12 percent maximum penalty).

If you are late a second time within three years of the first late filing, the penalty is bumped up to 10 percent of the unpaid tax plus 2 percent per month, to a maximum of 20 months (additional 40 percent maximum penalty).

Even if you cannot pay your tax, make sure you file your return on time to avoid the late-filing penalties.

Repeated failure to report income

If you have failed to report income, and this has been reassessed by the CCRA, any subsequent failure to report income within the next three years will earn you a penalty of 10 percent of the unreported income.

Failure to provide complete information

If you fail to provide complete information, you'll face a fine of $100 per occurrence. Some examples include not providing a SIN on your return or omitting information that the CCRA requires to correctly assess your return. Don't be sloppy — complete all information asked for on your tax return.

If the information you need had to be obtained from a third party, and this person (or company) would not cooperate, the CCRA will waive your penalty. Attach a note to your tax return, outlining the steps you took to try to obtain the information.

Tax evasion, gross negligence, false statements, or false credit returns

For serious situations where the taxpayer has intentionally tried to misstate or misrepresent their return, a penalty of 50 percent of the tax avoided will be added to their tax liability. Cheating does not pay!

Criminal prosecutions

Tax evasion usually involves a criminal prosecution in addition to the above penalties. The courts can impose fines of up to 200 percent of the tax evaded and sentence you to five years in prison.

In one case, an individual was fined $36,000 after pleading guilty to two counts of tax evasion. The fine represented 120 percent of the amount of federal tax the individual was trying to evade. In addition to the fines, the individual was required to pay (obviously) the full amount of taxes owing, plus interest and penalties, for a total of $214,000! We can't say it enough — cheating does not pay!

Waiving of interest and penalties

As we discuss in the next chapter, the CCRA, through its Fairness Committees, can waive penalties and interest in certain circumstances, such as illness or natural disaster.

Chapter 16

Disagreeing with the Taxman

⦁⦁⦁

In This Chapter

▶ Filing a notice of objection

▶ Proceeding to tax court

▶ Making an application for fairness

⦁⦁⦁

*U*nfortunately, one of the realities of our tax system is that occasionally the CCRA will disagree with the way you have prepared your tax return. If the CCRA disagrees with you the first time it assesses your return you will receive a Notice of Assessment detailing the changes. Any adjustments after the original Notice of Assessment will be communicated to you by means of a *Notice of Reassessment*.

If you think the CCRA has made an error in assessing your return, this chapter details how to go about disagreeing with the taxman.

Objecting to Your Notice

A Notice of Objection is a formal document through which you notify the CCRA that you disagree with its assessment or reassessment and that you would like the return transferred to the independent Appeals Division for a review and judgment.

A *Notice of Objection* is filed by completing form T400A "Objection — Income Tax Act" or by writing a detailed letter outlining the reasons for your objection. You then send the form or letter to the Chief of Appeals at your local Tax Services Office or the Tax Centre where you filed your return.

An example of an objection letter is provided on the CCRA's Web site in the publication "Your Appeal Rights Under the Income Tax Act."

Use form T400A if you file an objection. Though not mandatory, it will act as a precise guide as to the information that the Appeals Division will need in order to deal quickly with your situation.

When can I file a Notice of Objection?

A Notice of Objection must be filed before the later of the following:

- 90 days from the mailing date of the Notice of Assessment or Notice of Reassessment (assessment or reassessment date)
- One year from the due date of the return

Let's say that the due date of your 2003 tax return is April 30, 2004. Assume your return's assessment date is July 1, 2004.

You will have until the later of 90 days after the date of mailing of the Notice of Assessment (assessment date), September 29, 2004, or one year after the return was due, April 30, 2005, to object to the assessment. In this case, you will have until April 30, 2005, to object to the assessment. In the case of a Notice of Reassessment, the rules are slightly different. Since a reassessment is usually well after the original Notice of Assessment, the date of one year after the return was due has usually passed. As a result, you must file your Notice of Objection within 90 days of the mailing date of the Notice of Reassessment (reassessment date).

The right to object to a reassessment is limited if a reassessment is the result of any of the following situations:

- A court decision on a previous appeal
- A late-filed election
- Losses carried back
- Denial of expenses related to a criminal activity
- Change due to a tax avoidance issue

The objection must be limited to the specific issues raised in the reassessment only. No new issues will be considered.

When your return is opened on a reassessment that does not involve any of the above circumstances, you can request adjustments of any issues in the return(s) in question.

When the CCRA goes back beyond the normal three-year limit to give you a refund, they will refuse to allow you to object to their assessment, unless a waiver was filed for that year. We discuss "waivers" later in this chapter.

Should I pay the disputed amount?

The answer is yes. This may seem strange, since the core of your argument is that you do *not* owe this money. The truth is that the CCRA will begin charging interest on the disputed amount if it is not paid within 20 days of your assessment or reassessment date. If you win the appeal, you will get your money back plus interest. If there's a chance you'll lose, why pay the extra interest?

Will collection actions start while my case is under appeal?

No. The CCRA will stop collection actions against you while your case is under appeal. Unfortunately, you will still continue to receive notices of outstanding amounts from the CCRA collections division throughout the period, but no action will be taken against you — yet. If you lose your appeal, however, watch out. The collections people at the CCRA mean business, and you should make every effort to cooperate with them.

Collections staff are specially selected for their easygoing approach to recovering money owed to the CCRA — NOT! (Remember, they are "bill collectors" with significant powers!)

When dealing with the CCRA it is always better to resolve issues before an assessment or reassessment is issued. Not only because of the time and trouble it takes to file a Notice of Objection, but because once you receive an assessment or reassessment, the onus is on you to prove the assessment or reassessment is wrong. The courts have accepted that the CCRA only needs to prove its case on a balance of probabilities and not beyond a reasonable doubt. This puts you at a distinct disadvantage once the assessments arrive. So much for the theory of innocent until proven guilty.

How long will the appeal take?

Generally speaking, appeals take many months to be resolved. It can take from six months to a year for a decision to be rendered.

What if I lose the appeal but still think I'm right?

Once your appeal has been rejected by the CCRA, Tax Court is your next stop.

We will look more closely at the court system in the next section, but for now you need to know that to be able to advance to Tax Court you must have filed a Notice of Objection within the time limit set out above. If you didn't follow the rules, the Tax Court will not hear your case.

As you can see, the Notice of Objection, filed correctly and within the required time limit, is a powerful tool for protecting your right to appeal.

If in doubt, file a Notice of Objection to protect your rights to appeal.

How long after I file my return can I be reassessed?

The general rule is that a return can be reassessed any time within three years from the mailing date of the original Notice of Assessment (the assessment date). After the three years has passed, the return becomes statute barred. When a return is statute barred, neither you nor the CCRA can go back and reopen the year for reassessment.

Let's say you mailed your 2003 return on April 30, 2004. A month later you receive your Notice of Assessment. The date on the notice is May 30, 2004. If the CCRA wants to reassess the 2003 tax return, it must do so before May 30, 2007. Even if your return is reassessed, the original Notice of Assessment date is the key date used to determine when the return goes statute barred. Subsequent Notices of Reassessment do not affect this original date.

Reassessment outside the three-year limit

The *Income Tax Act* does allow the CCRA the discretion under specific circumstances to reassess beyond the normal reassessment period of three years. Reasons for reassessment outside the three-year limit include the following:

✔ The taxpayer has made misrepresentations in his tax return due to fraud, neglect, carelessness, or willful default.

   If the CCRA can prove that you intentionally or unintentionally misrepresented information on your return because of fraud or carelessness, you can be reassessed at any time with no limitations.

✔ The taxpayer signs a waiver of the three-year limit. (We discuss this later.)

✔ The special six-year rules apply, which include the carryback of losses.

   Since the law allows you to carry losses back three years, any prior return within that carryback period stays open for six years from the original assessment date rather than the usual three.

   For example, say you have a non-capital loss in 2001 that you request to be carried back to 1998. The CCRA then reassesses your 2001 tax year, adjusting the loss previously claimed. This reassessment takes place in 2004 (which the CCRA can do because this is before the statute-barred date for the 2001 tax year). However, the CCRA has to be able to return to reassess the 1998 tax year as well, so that the loss you carried back can also be adjusted.

   If not for this rule, the 1998 year would be statute barred by the time the 2004 reassessment took place and the loss could not be adjusted.

✔ Transactions with related non-residents.

✔ Transactions involving the payment of tax to a foreign government.

✔ Consequential changes.

   Consequential changes are changes that occur in a year as a result of a court decision or a settlement with the CCRA, that affect other taxation years. In these cases the CCRA can reassess returns for otherwise statute-barred years.

In addition to the above rules, the CCRA was given special discretionary powers to reassess beyond the normal statue-barred period in the following circumstances:

✔ The CCRA receives a written reassessment request from the taxpayer, and

✔ The effect of the reassessment will be to reduce the tax originally assessed or give rise to a refund, and

✔ The CCRA is satisfied that the request for the adjustment would have been accepted if it had been made within the normal reassessment period.

For further information on these special rules, you can consult the CCRA Interpretation Bulletin IT-241 "Reassessment Made after the [Three-Year] Limit."

Waivers

Sometimes you won't want the regular three-year assessing period to apply to you because it is to your benefit to have the tax year remain open. In these cases, you should file a waiver with the CCRA. A waiver is a document that specifies the items reported on your personal income tax return that you don't want the regular three-year assessing period to apply to. You must file a waiver on form T2029 "Waiver in Respect of The Normal Reassessment Period," and it must be received by the CCRA within three years of the assessment date in question.

When signing a waiver, be very specific about which items you want to remain open. If you are too general, you are leaving the door open for the CCRA to reassess items you had not intended them to consider. The CCRA is limited to looking at only the items mentioned in the waiver. Since the CCRA is allowed to assess more tax, only include items that you expect will reduce your tax liability.

Why and when to sign a waiver

There are basically two situations in which waivers come into play:

✔ The CCRA asks you to sign a waiver on a particular issue because the three-year limit is approaching and the issue may not be resolved before the return goes statute barred. If you do not sign the waiver, the CCRA will assess the issue and force you to file a Notice of Objection and appeal its decision. This can be a long process, so you'll save a lot of time, effort, and money if you simply sign the waiver and hope the issue is resolved without additional tax being levied. The CCRA usually takes this approach if an issue is in dispute and it believes that additional tax is owed. By getting a waiver, the CCRA protects its right to enforce an assessment, while giving you more time to consider the issue and to help rectify the situation.

✔ You are asking the CCRA to reduce the tax you owe, and the three-year limit is approaching. By signing the waiver you can ensure that the issue will still be open for discussion, and you can avoid taking the entire return to appeal.

As mentioned earlier, the CCRA is given the discretion to reassess returns beyond the three-year limit if the effect is to reduce the tax originally assessed and the CCRA is satisfied that the adjustment would have been accepted if filed on time. By filing a waiver, you can avoid being victim to the CCRA's discretion and protect your right to appeal.

Can I revoke a signed waiver?

Yes, a waiver can be revoked on six months' notice by filing form T652 "Notice of Revocation of Waiver." After revocation, the waiver is permanently revoked and no reassessment can be made after this date.

 In some cases, it's a good idea to sign a waiver and file the revocation at the same time. For example, if the CCRA requests the waiver, your filing both forms at once gives them only six months to resolve the issue and does not leave your return open for years to come.

Here Comes the Judge

As we discussed in the previous section, the Appeals Division is the last level of recourse within the CCRA. If you continue to disagree with the decision, your next step is Tax Court. To proceed to Tax Court, you must have filed a Notice of Objection to your original assessment (see Chapter 22). If so, then your appeal to the Tax Court must be filed either:

✔ Within 90 days of the date of mailing of the confirmation of your assessment (or reassessment) to the Notice of Objection; or

✔ After 90 days have passed since you filed the Notice of Objection if you have not received a confirmation of assessment (or reassessment) from the CCRA appeals division.

The Tax Court has two procedures, informal and general. If the amount of federal tax in dispute is less than $12,000, you can have your case heard under the informal procedure. If the amount of federal tax is more than $12,000, you must follow the court's general procedure.

Informal procedure

Under the informal procedure, you do not need a lawyer to represent you. You may appear on your own or be assisted by a lawyer, accountant, or advisor. This court does not necessarily follow the "normal" rules of evidence and procedure, nor are decisions precedent-setting. The decisions of this court are quick and are usually delivered within a year of your appeal. (Yes, a year can be considered "quick" in court decisions!) If you want to appeal a decision, you are limited to issues of law or gross error, and must apply for a "judicial review" before the Federal Court of Appeal.

If you go to Tax Court using the informal procedures, it is advisable to seek the advice of an experienced tax professional (although you are not required to do so). The expert's advice can better prepare you for the proceedings and help you avoid costly errors that may jeopardize your case.

General procedure

The general procedure operates in a formal court atmosphere — and lawyers are required. These cases will involve all the usual aspects of a trial. As is the case in most formal court proceedings, the time involved can be several years from the initiation of the process until a decision is made. The amount of money involved is also substantial, with the added downside that you could end up paying the court costs if the decision goes against you. Beyond Tax Court, cases heard under the general procedure can be appealed to the Federal Court of Appeal and eventually to the Supreme Court of Canada — but only if the Supreme Court lets you appeal! If you are not given permission to appeal — tough, it dies.

Obtain form TLA7 "Appealing to the Tax Court" from your local Tax Services Office if you intend to appeal to the Tax Court. It will clearly explain your options and time constraints.

Making an Application for Fairness

Within each Tax Services Office there exists a committee responsible for reviewing taxpayers' requests to do the following:

- ✔ Waive penalties and interest on assessment
- ✔ Accept late, amended, or revoked income tax elections
- ✔ Allow refunds beyond the normal three-year period

Adjustments to returns are made for compelling reasons on compassionate or equitable grounds, or for circumstances beyond the control of the taxpayer. Examples would include serious illness or accident, incorrect information supplied to you by the CCRA in a written form, a natural disaster, strike, or civil disobedience. In the case of late-filed elections, the CCRA is also willing to accept honest mistakes as a legitimate reason for filing incorrectly.

Visit the CCRA's Web site at www.ccra-adrc.gc.ca to get a copy of the CCRA Information Circulars IC 92-1 "Guidelines for Accepting Late, Amended or Revoked Elections," IC 92-2 "Guidelines for Cancellation and Waiver of Interest and Penalties," and IC 92-3 "Guidelines for Refunds Beyond the Normal Three-Year Period." These guidelines will help you to better understand the situations where fairness may be applied. In addition to the above factors, the CCRA wants to see that the taxpayer has made every effort to minimize or correct the errors where possible.

Part V
The Part of Tens

The 5th Wave   By Rich Tennant

"It's a simple electronic collar with a homing device, Mr. Geller. The CCRA likes to know the whereabouts of those citizens it makes tax payment arrangements with."

In this part...

Well, you've made it to the end. These final few chapters are short tidbits of useful information you can read any time and any place. To be honest, these chapters are filled with information we thought you should know, but couldn't place anywhere else in the book. So here they are — on their own.

Read them over to find out the ten major tax changes that have taken place since 2002 that will have an impact on your return this year, the top ten ways to reduce your risk of an audit, and the top ten planning tips for families and investors. There are lots of great tips piled into these last few pages, so be sure not to miss them!

"The nation ought to have a tax system which looks like someone designed it on purpose."

— William E. Simon

Chapter 17

Top Ten Tax Changes for 2003

• •

*J*ust when you thought you understood all there was to know about tax! This chapter highlights the top ten tax changes for 2003.

Increased Maximum Limits for RRSP Contributions

The government finally announced increases to the maximum limit you can contribute to your RRSP. Maximum limits are increasing from the 2002 limit of $13,500 to:

2003	$14,500
2004	$15,500
2005	$16,500
2006	$18,000

Your maximum RRSP contribution continues to be restricted to 18 percent of your earned income for the prior year and your contribution amount can be decreased by your Pension Adjustment (PA) and increased by a Pension Adjustment Reversal (PAR).

Maximize your RRSP contribution — save tax immediately and maximize the growth of your retirement funds.

Deductibility of Legal Fees Incurred to Obtain Spousal Support/Increase Child Support

The CCRA has relaxed its stance on the tax deductibility of legal fees incurred to obtain *spousal* support. These legal fees are now tax deductible — previously they were not. A deduction for legal fees incurred to collect *child* support has been permitted in the past. The CCRA has now expanded the rules to permit a deduction for legal fees incurred in the process of *increasing* child support.

 Ensure your lawyer details the bill to highlight fees for services that are tax deductible.

"My Account" — A New Service from the CCRA

This is a new on-line service that lets you find out info about your personal tax situation (i.e., tax refund information) and benefits you may be entitled to (i.e., child tax benefit, GST/HST credit, and provincial and territorial credits).

Go to "My Account" (www.ccra-adrc.gc.ca/eservices/tax/ individuals/myaccount/menu-e.html) on the CCRA Web site and see what info the CCRA is storing on you. You need your social insurance number, date of birth, the amount reported on line 150 (total income) of your 2002 tax return and the eight-character access code from your 2002 Notice of Assessment.

Indexed Tax Brackets and Credits

Thanks to inflation, every year there are new thresholds for tax brackets and new amounts for most federal, provincial, and territorial tax credits. This is good news as it means you are not paying more taxes simply because of inflation.

Employees with Company Cars

When an employee is provided with a car that is owned or leased by the employer, the employee is considered to receive a taxable benefit referred to as a "standby charge." This is because the car is available for the employee for personal use as well as for employment duties.

The annual benefit included in an employee's income is equal to 24 percent of the cost of the car (no allowance for wear and tear) or two-thirds the lease payment. A reduction is provided if there is heavy employment use (90 percent or more) and little personal use kilometres (less than 12,000). The calculation rules have been changed to permit more employees to take advantage of the reduction. Now only 50 percent or more employment use is required, with less than 20,000 personal kilometres per year.

This is another reason to maintain an accurate log of the employment and personal kilometres you travel in a year for work.

RRSP/RRIF at Death

When a RRSP or RRIF holder dies, and the RRSP or RRIF is not passed on to a spouse, the value of the RRSP or RRIF is included in the deceased's personal tax return for the year of death. An exception to this is where the RRSP or RRIF is passed on to a child or grandchild of the deceased who was financially dependent on the deceased. If this is the case, then the RRSP or RRIF value is included in the income of the child or grandchild, rather than the deceased. If the child or grandchild is physically or mentally infirm, then the RRSP or RRIF proceeds can be transferred to an RRSP for the child or grandchild (or used to purchase a life annuity) — if so, no immediate tax is due.

Prior to a recent change, an infirm child or grandchild would be considered financially dependent if their income was below the amount of the basic tax credit amount — $7,756 for 2003. This was considered too low, so the amount to determine "financial dependency" of an infirm child or grandchild in 2003 was increased to $13,814. For 2004 and future years, the amount will increase as the cost of living rises. A child or grandchild that is not infirm will still be considered to be financially dependent only if income is below the basic personal amount.

Capital Gains Tax Deferral

An individual can defer the tax on the capital gain from the sale of shares of an eligible small business corporation where the proceeds on the sale are reinvested in another eligible small business corporation. The current rules provide for a complete deferral of tax if the sale proceeds are $2,000,000 or less and the maximum reinvestment of the proceeds is limited to $2,000,000. New rules eliminate these $2,000,000 restrictions and extend the time to reinvest to 120 days after the year in which the sale occurred.

Tax Shelters

Over the last few years the CCRA has been targeting tax shelter investments and schemes. Promoters of charity donation/loan schemes must now obtain a tax shelter number. The CCRA knows all about the shelter before it hits the market.

In purchasing a tax shelter investment or participating in a tax shelter scheme, be skeptical about the availability of the tax deduction or tax credits promised.

Ensure a tax shelter number has been obtained.

Stock Options and Capital Losses

When an employee exercises a stock option to purchase shares of his or her publicly traded employer corporation at a price less than the current trading price a taxable benefit is included in employment income. The income inclusion is equal to the value of the shares received in excess of the employee's stock option exercise price.

If the employee subsequently sells the shares at a value higher than what the share were worth on the day the option was exercised, the increase in value is taxed as a capital gain. We have no problem with this tax treatment.

If there is a subsequent loss in value the employee will have a capital loss. However, this capital loss does not offset the employment income inclusion in employment income. Capital losses can only be used to shelter capital gains from tax — not employment income.

The government said that it would look at this odd situation where an employee is taxed on a gain in a stock price that was never actually realized! Well, the government did look at this situation and it said "… tough luck…we are not going to change the rules."

Sell shares immediately after acquiring them under the stock option plan in order to eliminate the risk that these shares will be sold at a loss.

Medical Expense Credit Expanded

Taxpayer friendly changes to the definitions of medical expenses include:

- ✔ Real-time captioning services
- ✔ Note-taking services
- ✔ Voice recognition software
- ✔ Incremental cost of gluten free food products

Chapter 18

Ten Ways to Reduce the Risk of an Audit

● ●

*W*hat are the two most dreaded words in the English language? For some, they're "tax audit." Chances are, if you are reading this chapter you're just putting the finishing touches on your tax return and are looking for ways to reduce your risk of getting anything other than a thank you note — called a Notice of Assessment — from the CCRA.

Here are our pointers to help you avoid becoming the CCRA's target for an audit or review.

Audit Your Own Tax Return

Make sure you double-check your return before you send it in. Check first for mathematical accuracy. Make your life easy and use tax software or an on-line service to ensure your numbers add up properly. Also check that you've included all relevant information, including your name, address, and social insurance number. Avoiding these simple mistakes is the first step in keeping the CCRA from reviewing your return more closely.

Report All Your Income

Make sure that you've reported *all* income, including interest and dividends from all accounts. If you forget something, you can be sure the taxman will eventually find it. You see, the CCRA gets a copy of the same income slips you receive, and they cross-check them by computer to make sure everything is reported. One handy tip is to compare this year's return to last year's to ensure that you haven't missed anything.

Avoid Claiming Ongoing Losses

Be careful if you run your own business and are reporting a loss on this year's return. In order to claim these losses, you must be able to prove that your business is not a "personal" endeavour and is in fact a true commercial enterprise. If there are personal or hobby aspects to your business, your losses can be denied if your business does not have a reasonable expectation of profit. The tax collector generally only flags your return the first year you report business losses, but if you continue to report losses in the next two or three years, you could be a prime candidate for an audit.

Tax Planning 101: File a Return and File on Time!

Some people argue that the only way to ensure your return doesn't get audited is simply to not file a return at all. After all, the CCRA can't audit what isn't there. To these people we say, try again. In fact, every year, the CCRA sends out countless letters to individuals requesting them to file a tax return — proof that the taxman knows who these people are. Non-filers risk not only getting caught and getting hit with interest and penalties, but also going to jail. In addition, if the CCRA has to ask you to file a return, you can bet the chances are greater that they'll take a closer look. So make sure you file every year. And if you've been a non-filer in the past, remember, it's never too late to make things right.

Be Consistent with Your Expenses

Claims for expense deductions must be reasonable, and the expenses must be incurred to earn income. This means that claiming personal expenses is not only a bad idea, it's not allowed under our tax law. Also, if you own your own business, make sure your expenses are consistent from year to year. Of course, you still must be able to support all expenses claimed, but a significant jump in travel or entertainment costs may catch the taxman's eye.

If you are self-employed, make sure salaries paid to family members continue to be "reasonable" in view of the services provided.

Don't Cheat

Sounds simple enough, right? Well, those of you who are tempted to cheat should be aware that the taxman has ways to track you down. The CCRA has identified the industries that have, in the past, had a higher incidence of cheaters, including construction, subcontracting, carpet installation, unregistered vehicle sales, auto repair, independent courier businesses, and direct sales. If you're in one of these industries, don't be offended by our comments. You are probably aboveboard with your tax filings. But not everyone is. And so the list of industries the CCRA keeps its eye on grows longer each year.

Think Twice about Taking Cash Under the Table

Many people think that taking cash payments for services will get them out of paying tax. What the taxman doesn't know won't hurt him, right? Don't be so sure. There is no shortage of Canadians who are willing to quietly report you for offering services on a cash basis. In one instance we're aware of, a business owner offered a customer services at a discount if the customer was willing to pay cash. Turned out that the customer worked for the CCRA. *Oops!* The business owner's tax affairs were examined, and he was eventually reassessed for under reporting revenues.

Learn from Your Mistakes

If you're caught cheating, it's almost guaranteed that the CCRA will look at that particular item again the next year. Suppose, for example, that you receive a request to substantiate your child care expenses, and find that, whether by accident or design, you've overstated the amount claimed. You can be sure that the CCRA will ask you to submit your receipts next time around — perhaps for the next couple of years. The moral of the story? There's absolutely no excuse for getting caught making the same mistake twice.

Don't Give the Taxman Something to Audit

Some tax returns have very little worth auditing. An employee with one T4 slip has less chance of being audited than a self-employed person with significant expenses. The CCRA likes to flag the more risky items to get more bang, so to speak, for its time spent assessing. Items such as losses from tax shelters, significant interest deductions, rental or business losses, moving expense deductions, and clergy residence deductions (believe it or not) have an increased likelihood of being flagged for an audit. These deductions may be legitimate, but if you choose to complicate your tax affairs by reporting deductions that can be higher risk, be sure you have the information necessary to back up your claim — just in case the taxman comes knocking.

Keep Your Fingers Crossed

Even if you do everything right on your return, you may get selected for an audit or receive a request for information because of plain old bad luck. Every year, the CCRA selects taxpayers at random, and uses the results of these audits or requests to determine where people make the most mistakes, and in which areas people most often cheat. So even if you've crossed all your *t*s and dotted your *i*s, you may still receive an unwelcome letter in the mail on CCRA stationery. Don't assume you've done anything wrong — just be sure you can prove that you did it right!

Chapter 19

Top Ten Tax Planning Tips for Families

● ●

So what is income splitting? Income splitting involves shifting income from the hands of one individual who pays tax at a high rate to another who will pay tax at a lower rate. For example, if a husband gives money to his wife for investment purposes, and the wife is taxed at a lower rate than the husband (because she is in a lower tax bracket), income splitting can be achieved provided the investment income can be taxed in the wife's hands.

The key to income splitting is to ensure that the income will be taxed in the hands of the lower income family member — that's the hard part. To make income splitting all the more difficult, the CCRA introduced the attribution rules, which state that if you try to pass income-producing property (for example, property that earns interest, dividends, rents, and royalties) to your spouse, or to a minor child, grandchild, in-law, niece or nephew, *you* — not they — will be taxed on the income earned on this property.

The good news is, there are ways around the dreaded attribution rules so that you can make income splitting work for you and your family. Here are the top ten income splitting strategies.

Lend Money or Investments to a Family Member

You may loan money to a minor child or a spouse to be used for investment purposes — but as with everything, there's a catch. You see, interest-free loans or even low-interest loans won't cut it. To avoid the attribution rules, you must charge interest on the loan at the CCRA's prescribed rate, or the current commercial rate (you should choose whichever rate is lower). The interest must be paid to you by January 30 every year, and must be included in your income. Your family member can deduct this interest from the income he or she earns on the investment.

The CCRA announces the prescribed rates every quarter. The rates can be found on their Web site at www.ccra-adrc.gc.ca. At the time of writing, the prescribed rate on non–arm's length loans was 3 percent. By the way, you can lock in the rate that was in effect at the time the loan was made for the entire term of the loan, so you're not at risk should the interest rates go up in the future!

Consider Julie, who wants to transfer some income to her husband, Jim, because he is in a lower tax bracket. She knows that she can't give him money, so she decides to loan him $100,000 at 4-percent interest. Jim takes this money, invests it, and in the first year earns $8,000. If Jim pays Julie $3,000 in interest in January, he can report the $8,000 on his tax return — saving her from reporting it on hers. As well, he can deduct the $3,000 paid to Julie, so his total income is just $5,000. Julie must report the $3,000 interest in her income. If your head is spinning, here's the end result. Julie managed to transfer $5,000 of her income to Jim, who will pay tax at a lower rate.

You'll only manage to split income if your investments earn a rate of return higher than the prescribed rate set by the CCRA.

When a family member borrows money to invest, make sure that a higher-income family member doesn't guarantee the loan or give the borrower funds to make the repayment. The attribution rules will apply, causing any income earned on these borrowed funds to be taxed in the hands of the person guaranteeing the loan or providing the funds to make repayments.

Second-Generation Income

You now know that if you lend money to a spouse or minor child to invest, any income earned on the investments will generally be attributed back to you and taxed in your hands. The good news? Second-generation income — that is, income on the income — is not attributed back. It works like this: Lend or give money to your spouse or minor child, then transfer any income earned each year to a separate investment account in that person's name. Any future earnings in that second account are not subject to the attribution rules. Income splitting has been achieved!

Split Tax on CPP Payments

You know how it works when you're married: "What's mine is yours, and what's yours is mine." Well, the same holds true for CPP payments. You see, if both you and your spouse (or common-law partner) are over age 60, you're allowed to share up to 50 percent of your CPP payments. Since a portion of your payments will now be directed to your spouse, this means less income for you to report. If your spouse is in a lower tax bracket, it also means tax savings!

There's a formula to determine how much you can split. The amount that can be split is based on the length of time you and your spouse have been together as a percentage of your total contributory period, to a maximum of 50 percent. You can't just arbitrarily decide how much is to be taxed in your spouse's hands.

For further information about assigning pension benefits to your spouse, contact Human Resources Development Canada at 1-800-277-9914 or visit its Web site at www.hrdc-drhc.gc.ca.

Pay Salary or Wages to Family

If you have your own business, consider paying a salary or wage to members of your family. Of course, they must actually work in the business (and no, you won't get away with paying your four-year-old son to colour pictures you use for advertising). In addition, the salary you pay them must be reasonable for the work they do.

The advantage to this is that you can claim the amount paid as a deduction on your business statement, so your taxable income is reduced. On the flip side, the family member includes this amount in his or her income. You can pay a child that has no other source of income up to $7,756 in 2003 without generating a tax bill for that child. Assuming your marginal tax rate is 46 percent, that's a savings of over $3,500 in tax!

By paying your child or spouse a salary, you'll generate earned income in their hands. This gives rise to valuable RRSP contribution room, so even though these may be no tax owing, your child should still file a tax return each year.

Transfer Money for Business Purposes

You can either give or lend money to family members to be used in a business, and thereby avoid the dreaded attribution rules. Even if it's a loan, there's no need to charge interest. Since the funds will earn business income and not income from property, you'll avoid having the income come back to be taxed in your hands.

 If the business goes sour there are favourable tax rules that you may be able to take advantage of. The company you invest in must be a Canadian-controlled private corporation, and at least 90 percent of the assets must be used in active business that operates primarily in Canada. If the business takes a downturn and you won't recover your loan, you may be eligible to claim an allowable business investment loss on your tax return. See Chapter 10 for more details on allowable business investment losses.

Pay an Allowance to a Working Child

If you're paying your child an allowance for work around the house, don't stop paying once your child starts working. We know, you're probably thinking, "Why should I pay them, if they have their own spending money?" Here's why: Paying your child an allowance will free up their earnings for investment. When they invest their own income, the attribution rules won't apply and you effectively will have split income.

Another option is to lend money to your adult child, interest-free, to help pay for school. Suppose you have a daughter who attends university and earns $8,000 over the summer. In prior years she has used her income from the summer to help pay for school and books. Instead, consider lending her the $8,000 to help pay for school. She can then invest the money she made over the summer. Since the investment represents her own money, any income earned will not be attributed back to you, and will be taxed at her marginal rate (or not taxed at all, if her income is low enough). When she graduates, she can pay the loan off using the funds she's invested.

Get Higher-Income Spouse to Pay the Household Expenses

Another way to get more funds into the hands of the lower-income spouse is to have the higher-income spouse pay all the daily living expenses. This includes groceries, mortgage or rent payments, credit card bills, and so on. This frees up more cash in the hands of the lower-income spouse to earn income that is taxed at the low rate.

Similarly, another way to transfer funds is for you to pay the income tax liability and instalments of your spouse. Since the amount you pay is paid directly to the CCRA and is not invested by your spouse, the attribution rules won't apply. This means any funds your spouse would have used to pay the liability are now free to be used for investment purposes.

Invest Child Tax Benefits in the Child's Name

The government pays Child Tax Benefits monthly to qualifying families until their children reach 18 years of age. These benefit payments can be invested in your child's name and earn any type of income without the attribution rules kicking in.

 Make sure these funds are deposited directly into an investment account for your child. Keep them separate from other funds that you may have given your child previously, because the attribution rules still apply to these gifted funds.

Contribute to a Spousal RRSP

The optimum goal is for spouses to have equal incomes during retirement. This will accomplish perfect income splitting and keep the total family tax bill to a minimum. Spousal RRSP contributions work like this: You contribute to an RRSP under which your spouse is the annuitant. You claim the tax deduction for the amounts put into the plan and when money is withdrawn for retirement, your spouse is taxed on the withdrawal. Talk about shifting income from one spouse to the other!

Your spouse must keep the funds inside the RRSP for a minimum number of years, or else the withdrawal (up to the amount contributed during the three year period) is taxed in your hands. Don't take funds out if the contribution was made in that same year, or in either of the two previous years. Wait until the third calendar year after your last contribution, to withdraw the funds.

Make a spousal contribution on December 31. You'll then only have to wait two years plus one day to begin making withdrawals.

Contribute to an RESP

Registered education savings plans (RESPs) are used to help build an education fund for your child or grandchild. But did you realize that RESPs are a great way to income split with your family?

Although contributions made to an RESP are not tax deductible like contributions to an RRSP, they do grow tax-free. When the funds are taken out for educational purposes, you won't be the one to foot the tax bill. You see, the income earned in the plan is taxed in the child's hands, not yours. As a student, that child will probably have minimal income and will be eligible for the education and tuition credit, and therefore won't likely pay tax.

Chapter 20

Top Ten Tax Planning Tips for Investors

· ·

*A*t least once a week we hear people say "My taxes are too high. What can I do to reduce them?" Although we don't have the magical solution that will make your tax bill disappear altogether, there are some things you can do to reduce the amount you pay to the taxman, particularly if you are an investor. Keep in mind, however, that you should always weigh your investment *and* tax objectives before making any investment decision. Just because a particular investment suits you tax-wise, it may not fit your investment risk profile.

Invest Tax Efficiently

Investment returns are not created equal in the eyes of the taxman. In fact, the amount of tax you pay depends on the type of income your investment is earning. You'll find interest income is always the least tax efficient because it is taxed at your highest marginal tax rate. Investments that earn primarily interest income include money market investments, bonds, and fixed-income investments. Dividends generally sit in the middle of the tax-efficiency scale since they qualify for the dividend tax credit and are therefore taxed at a lower rate than interest. If you're looking to generate dividends income, you may want to invest in equities that pay dividends annually. Capital gains are often the most tax efficient, since they are only taxable when realized (that is, when your shares are sold, or, if you invest in mutual funds, when the securities in the fund are sold). Further, capital gains are just one-half taxable. If you're looking for potential capital gains, equities are your best bet.

Capital gains are not always taxed more efficiently than dividends — it depends on your tax bracket, province of residence, and other sources of income. However, you are generally better off earning capital gains if your income is greater than about $64,000 in Alberta, Saskatchewan, or the three territories, and about $32,000 in all the other provinces (except New Brunswick where the threshold is only about $12,500). In fact, assuming you have no other income, you can earn approximately $29,000 in dividends tax-free in most provinces!

Control Turnover of Your Investments

What if we told you that there is a type of return that you can earn that is not subject to current tax at all. You'd want more information, right? You may even think that there is some kind of scam involved. Well, this is possible, and we assure you it's no scam. The way to defer current tax is to earn unrealized capital gains. You see, when your investments rise in value, but are not sold (realized), and if the investment does not pay out distributions to you, this appreciation in value is not subject to current tax. In fact, the tax is deferred until you actually sell the investment (or capital gains distributions are made to you). This is known as controlling turnover.

Use Capital Losses to Your Advantage

With the market upheavals over the past several years, some of you may be faced with capital losses in your non-registered portfolios. Here are some tips to help trigger capital losses, and benefit tax-wise:

✔ Sell your losing investments only if you no longer like them or do not wish to repurchase them for at least 30 days after the sale. If you repurchase that same investment within 30 days of the sale (either before or after the sale), your loss will be denied for the time being under the "superficial loss rules." Because of these rules you should use the proceeds from the sale to purchase a different investment altogether, or something "similar" but not exactly the same. For example, if you are selling a mutual fund trust unit, you could repurchase a share of a mutual fund corporation without being offside these rules.

- ✔ Consider selling your loss investment and then contributing the proceeds to your RRSP. This will help trigger the loss for tax purposes while also providing you with cash to put into your RRSP for even more tax relief! Be careful, however, about directly transferring the investment into your RRSP — a loss in this case will be denied.

- ✔ If you triggered a loss in 2003, but do not have capital gains to use the loss against on this year's tax return, consider carrying the loss back to the 2000 tax year. Since the capital gains inclusion rate (the percentage of the capital gain that is taxable) was higher then, you'll get more bang for your buck versus applying the loss to any subsequent year.

Minimize Taxes on Capital Gains

Consider triggering capital gains periodically, especially in years where your income is particularly low. For taxpayers with no other sources of income (such as minors for whom you've set up in-trust-for accounts), you can trigger up to about $15,500 in capital gains ($7,750 of which is taxable) each and every year and not attract any tax. This is because each taxpayer has a basic personal tax credit ($7,756 in 2003) to help offset any taxes payable.

Borrow to Invest for Tax Savings

Leveraged investing, that is, taking out a loan and using the proceeds to invest, is becoming popular because you can use other people's money (usually the bank's) in order to make money for yourself! The advantage is that, over the long term, you can achieve higher effective rates of return on your investments and may even reach your financial goals faster than if you simply used your free cash flow to invest.

From a tax point of view, leveraged investing can help reduce the taxes you pay on any source of income you have. You see, so long as income from property (that is, interest or dividends) is a purpose of the borrowing; all of the interest on your loan is tax deductible. Even if your interest exceeds your investment income, you are still entitled to deduct the excess against other sources of income such as employment income or pension income!

Just because the initial purpose of your borrowing is to invest, this does not mean that you are guaranteed a tax deduction for the interest paid in the future. To ensure your interest remains tax deductible, avoid withdrawing any capital from your investment account (which includes both the growth and any reinvested distributions) for personal purposes. Doing so will result in you losing a portion of your interest deduction, unless you are simply withdrawing the funds to put into another investment.

Make Interest Tax Deductible

Many of us pay interest on personal borrowing, such as mortgage interest, car loans, lines of credit, and credit cards, but few of us can deduct that interest on our tax returns. There is a way, however, that some of us can convert that non-deductible interest into a tax deduction. This strategy is commonly known as debt-swapping.

Debt-swapping is possible if you have both non-deductible interest and non-RRSP investments such as shares, bonds, or mutual funds. The first step is to sell your investments, ideally choosing those that have not greatly appreciated in value since you've purchased them (since you will be responsible for paying tax on any capital gains you trigger on the sale). You will then use the proceeds from the sale to pay down your non-deductible debt. Finally, you will take out a new loan with the bank and use it to repurchase the investments you sold. At the end of the day you will have the same amount of debt, and the same amount of investments as before the sale (assuming you didn't have tax to pay on any capital gains), but because there is a direct trace between the borrowing and the investments, the interest you pay each year can be deducted on your tax return!

Consider Labour-Sponsored Funds

Both the federal and most provincial governments offer fairly generous tax credits to investors who invest in labour-sponsored venture capital corporations (or LSVCC, for short). You'll be entitled to a federal credit equal to 15 percent of your investment and a provincial credit equal to, in most provinces, another 15 percent. (Bad news for readers in Alberta, New Brunswick, and Newfoundland — you won't receive any provincial credits.) There is a cap of $1,500 on the total credits you'll be eligible for in a year so make sure you don't contribute more than $5,000 to a LSVCC in any one year.

If you bought a LSVCC after March 6, 1999, you'll have to keep these units invested, without selling them, for eight years from the date of purchase. If you cash them in early, you'll have to repay the tax credits you received!

Use Insurance for Investment Purposes

Life insurance is commonly used to cover tax liabilities on death and to help provide a source of income for heirs. However, if you purchase a "permanent" life insurance policy such as a *universal life policy* you can combine your insurance policy with a side investment fund. From a tax standpoint this side fund works very much like an RRSP in that the investments inside grow tax-free and you won't face a tax bill until the funds are withdrawn or the policy is surrendered (you don't get a tax deduction for amounts put into the fund though). Most universal life policies have a decent selection of investments to choose from which means that the investment component of the policy could grow at a respectable rate.

Before you go and put all your excess cash into a universal life policy so that the investment can grow tax-free, be aware of the limits. Unlimited tax-sheltered growth sounds too good to be true — and it is. Our tax law places a ceiling on the amount that can be in the investment account and there are penalties charged if too much investment ends up in your fund.

This type of strategy isn't for everyone. Since you will have to pay premiums for insurance, you must weigh these costs against the benefits of tax-free growth. Generally, it makes sense for individuals holding investments in excess of $500,000, who have already maxed-out their RRSP contributions.

Consider Specialty Investments

If its tax savings you're looking for, you may want to consider some specialty investments, including:

- **Flow-through shares.** These shares can benefit those who are expecting higher than normal income in a year that they do not want to see eroded by tax since they offer large tax deductions in the year the investment is made (probably about 90 percent of the investment) with the remainder of the deductions in the next year, or the year after. The cost base of flow-through shares is nil so whenever you decide to sell them, you will have a guaranteed capital gain. Flow-through shares, therefore, manage to reduce current taxes and defer them until the future when the shares are sold.

✔ **Real Estate Investment Trusts (REITs).** REITs, and their cousin, royalty trusts, may interest you if you require an income from your investments. These trusts will pay you an income, but due to some unique features, not all of this income will be taxable. The cost base of your investment is eroded as non-taxable payments are made to you, however, so you will generally have a capital gain to claim when you eventually sell your trust units.

Flow-through shares, REITs and royalty trusts may benefit you if you have unused capital losses, as you will have a high chance of generating a capital gain on these investments in the future.

Watch Out for Tax Shelters

In the past, some taxpayers bought into tax shelters where quantities of certain property (i.e., art, comic books, etc.) were purchased at a discount. The taxpayers then donated the property to charity and received a donation tax credit equal to the market value of the property donated. The net result was that the value of the donation tax credit exceeded the net cost of the property to the purchaser. The government was not impressed by these tax shelters and therefore wants to track them more closely. The 2003 Federal Budget proposed that tax shelters can no longer be sold without an identification number from the CCRA. If there is no number, there is no tax credit. And even then, if the CCRA is offended by any of the activities of the tax shelter, tax benefits will be disallowed. Buyer beware!

Index

●●

Official Rules

Open only to Canadian Residents, of majority age or older, except in the Province of Quebec. Void in the Province of Quebec. No Purchase Necessary.

1. **How to enter:** Complete an official entry form and mail the ballot to the address below. Limit of one 1 entry per person & only one 1 name may appear on an entry. All entries must be postmarked on or before May 31st, 2004. Neither Wiley Canada (Sponsor), participating retailers, affiliates, subsidiaries, advertising agencies, assume any responsibility for lost, late, misdirected or illegible entries.

    Dept. 44356
    Tax Tips Sweepstakes 2004
    PO Box 979
    Fonthill, ON L0S 1E0

2. **Drawing:** Subject to the conditions and projections set out in these rules, the winner will be selected by an independent agent in a random drawing to be held on/about June 4th, 2004 from among all entries received. Odds of winning depend on number of entries received. The selected entrant will be notified by mail by June 30th, 2004.

3. **Prize:** 1 Cash Prize of $5,000.00 CAD.

4. **Conditions and Prize Restrictions:** The selected entrant will be required to complete a time-limited mathematical skill-testing question which will be administered by phone as a condition to winning and receiving prize failing which, another winner will be selected. Winner may be required to sign an affidavit of eligibility/compliance with rules and a publicity/liability release, which must be retuned properly executed within 14 days of notification attempt or entrant may be disqualified & an alternate winner selected. Taxes, if any, are the responsibility of the individual winner. No transfer or substitution of prize. Winner agrees that Sponsor and its agents assume no responsibility or liability for damages losses or injuries of any kind resulting from participation in this sweepstakes or acceptance or use of any prize.

5. **Eligibility:** Sweepstakes open only to legal residents of majority age or older of Canada, except for the province of Quebec. Void in the province of Quebec or wherever prohibited or restricted by law. Employees of Sponsor, its affiliates, subsidiary & parent companies, participating retailers and the immediate family and household members of each, may not enter. Sweepstakes subject to all federal, provincial, and local laws.

6. **No purchase entry form available online at:**
    www.wiley.ca/WileyCDA/Section/id-102768.html

7. To request a list of winners, send a stamped, self-addressed envelope after June 15th, 2004 to: Dept 44357 **Tax Tips Sweepstakes 2004**, PO Box 979 Fonthill, ON L0S 1E0

Name:_____

Address: _____

City: _____

Province: _____   Postal Code:_____

Email Address*: _____

* If you do not wish to receive further correspondence from Sponsor with regards to products or promotions, leave blank.